Contents

The investment methods explained in the book are used in various quarters in the City, but are not exclusive to any specific firm. While these techniques have worked well for some in the past, no investment system is infallible. In addition, any specific investment featured in this book is purely for illustrative purposes, and should not in any way be construed as an investment recommendation. Any investment is ultimately your own choice – and at your own risk.

Acknowledgements

Thanks to friends, colleagues and interviewees in the City who have shared so much with me. I thank CD who will smile at this little book for reasons only she and I understand. A thank you to *Dealer 075* for helping to keep alive memories of that dealing floor of yesteryear that allowed – excuse the cliché – the most fun anybody could have with their clothes on. I thank Iain Martin for the lively discussions on economics.

Thanks to those folk in the timeshare industry who *yet again* went out of their way to help me. I also record my gratitude to professionals in the business opportunities market who allowed me insight into their trade.

Thanks particularly to my family and longstanding friends for understanding, not for the first time, that unsociability that is the unwelcome side effect of writing a book on top of doing a job.

Introduction

By investing in this book, you have taken your first step to being initiated into the many secrets of the City. The following pages will cultivate in you the vision and practical skills to seek out undervalued
investments and assets that may eventually soar in value. This is a
recognized technique of some professional investors and financial
advisers.

As you read this book – chapter by chapter – you will discover how
to develop the required outlook, and how to channel it into your
investing strategy. En route, you will learn how to *keep* your profits,
which requires getting the better of any sharks who try to rip you off.
Although these are in a minority, they often aim for small investors
and asset buyers.

As you become initiated into the methods described in this book,
you will come to grips with a secret system that, in various forms,
carries cachet in certain City circles. You will also be instructed in how
to buy investments from auction houses or discount dealers, and – a
little more on the wild side – how to trade shares from home.

Be warned that this book will *not* do all the work for you. However,
provided that you are prepared to make some effort, you will find in
these pages principles that you can apply in any area of investment
you choose. The principles are encapsulated in 115 golden rules,
summarized at the end of individual chapters. This is the only
summary of the Bargain Hunters' Investment FlexiSystem that has
ever been published.

The Internet has opened up hitherto unimaginable possibilities for
serious investors, and in this book I will show you how to capitalize
on this greatest of resources to increase your own profits, while at the
same time having more fun investing. I will show you how to find and
use an online dealer, and how to use the Internet's research facilities,

news services and message boards to best effect. Please note that the Internet is still in its early stages of mass availability. Some Web sites are more accessible than others, and Web addresses – valid at the time of writing – can change. In any such case, you may wish to use a good search engine to assist you researchers.

In addition, I will show you some proven methods for investing in Internet stocks, which, at the time of writing, is by far the most lucrative area of the stock market. This content alone should be worth to you many hundreds of times the cost of this book, *provided that you act on the advice given.*

You may at this point be querying how I am in a position to reveal all the investment secrets in this book. I have the highly unusual background of a City professional who also happens to be a financial journalist and book writer.

Walking this tightrope has given me first-hand experience of the securities industry, coupled with a financial journalist's willingness to enlighten and explain. At whatever level you operate as an investor, I believe that you will find this small volume unique and in your interest to study carefully.

To take in the book properly, you must read it carefully, and refer back to it when you start investing. This is, above all, a practical book, and you should keep a highlighter pen handy to underscore important points. Some parts of the programme may be of more interest to you than others, but they are all inter-linked. For this reason, you should cover the entire book before you start putting its principles into practice.

Two provisos: First, the ideas in this book are culled from a wide range of City sources, and *not* from anywhere specific that I have worked. Second, while the methods described in this book have worked well for some in the past, no investment system is infallible. If you follow this book's advice, it will be at your own risk.

I expect that you will enjoy reading this book as much as I have enjoyed writing it, so sit down and take a trip with me into the wonderland of stock market and other investments. I am going to tell you secrets of the professional investors which will make you gasp with amazement when you see how easy it is to put them into practice for your own benefit.

That is the introductory stuff out of the way. Let us enter the battlefield of dreams...

Alexander Davidson
London, 2000

1

Beat the professionals at their own game

If you are investing, or are thinking of doing so, on the stock market, you will harbour the secret dream of making a killing. You may have already done well in bull markets, but the upward momentum never seems to last long enough.

At worst, you can get caught high and dry as the market recedes, leaving you holding a portfolio of fast-fading stars. Up to this point, you may never have thought about any kind of value investing.

The plan to reveal the Bargain Hunters' Investment FlexiSystem, which has been used so profitably by some City professionals for their private investing, was conceived while I sat glued to the screens on the trading floor of one of Europe's leading investment banks. The bears were out that day and the FTSE 100 index was slipping almost by the minute. The Asian economy was in bad shape and the Russian rouble had almost collapsed. The issue of whether to sell, to stay put, or to invest more was preying on the mind of any responsible investor.

Most institutions had to keep trading on a short-term view. But for private investors who were lucky enough to be familiar with the Bargain Hunters' Investment FlexiSystem, some real longer-term buying opportunities had opened up.

Most private investors cower from buying shares when the stock market is depressed. This is exactly when you *should* be buying, as the Bargain Hunters' Investment FlexiSystem makes clear.

When the market is down, prices of individual stocks tend to fall substantially below the true value. This is because the market always overreacts to news, whether good or, as in this case, bad. Following a market correction, a 10–20 per cent fall in the share price is commonplace. After a full market crash, stocks could be trading at as little as half their true value, or much less.

Using the Bargain Hunters' Investment FlexiSystem, you will be picking out the best value stocks (as well as other investments and assets) in the depressed market and you will invest in them while your fellow investors are sitting tight. The system is rooted in the tradition of value investing that started more than 50 years ago with Benjamin Graham, who has been described as the 'father of investment analysis'.

The system has not, in the view of many who quietly practise it, been bettered. But it is still not for everybody. There are as many ways to pick stocks as there are ways to skin a cat. Traders, for instance, prefer to exploit short-term stock movements (a skill covered in Chapter 13) although, for their private medium- to long-term investing, the Bargain Hunters' Investment System is ideal.

Others invest in growth stocks, sometimes at a price far in excess of the company's net asset value. They hope to see the share price continue in its upward trend. If you join these speculators, make sure that you have a screen showing share price movements. You may only make profits if you can act quickly.

Your advantage over institutional investors

Many institutional investors take the plunge and move in and out of growth stocks rapidly, reacting to news flow. They tend all to select the same hot stock, giving a temporary boost to its price. Sometimes they get caught out.

Truth to tell, many institutions cannot afford the time investment required to invest only in undervalued stocks as the Bargain Hunters' Investment FlexiSystem dictates, which is a good reason for the difficulties most have in beating the market average. They must meet short-term profit targets and so fast-rising shares prove irresistible, even if the underlying companies have long overreached their fundamental value. An exception is to be found in some insurance companies that can afford a more long-term approach to investment.

In addition, some institutions are hampered by the need to hold a very broad range of companies in their portfolios, simply to achieve an adequate spread of risk. As a private investor, you are answerable only to yourself, and so have more flexibility than the institutions.

Your portfolio can be as small as you like and, while it is advisable to have a spread of investments in different sectors, every sector need not be included, as for major funds managed by institutional investors.

Assuming that you invest money that you can afford to tie up, you can stay invested until the share price rises – even if this should take years. Unlike pension fund managers, you are not burdened by quarterly targets.

In choosing the companies in which you invest, you similarly have freedom of choice. Fund managers have pressure on them to be cautious. If they invested in some small risky stock and it suddenly lost half its value, their corporate necks could be on the line. Not so if they invested in major blue chips, no matter how far the stocks might fall out of favour.

As a private investor, unlike your institutional counterparts, you will not be bombarded with investment research from major investment houses, giving diverse recommendations on the same major stocks. This can be a blessing.

Why you do not have to depend on investment research

Some decades ago, research produced by brokers was thin on the ground. Investment analysts were the back-room boys. Nowadays, star analysts run the show, issuing equity salespeople with their pitches, and selling stock personally to fund managers on the basis of their expertise.

Research literature is spewed out by the major broking houses in vast quantities every day, and fund managers receive more of it than they could ever read. Still, they have an insatiable appetite for this stuff. They find it comforting to know that there is a lot of hard work behind the recommendations they hear and act on daily, although they do not have time to read much of it in detail.

Institutional salespeople in Europe's leading investment houses smile to themselves when they hear this. They are glad that all the research sent out by their firms is not read too closely, as many of the recommendations turn out to have been wide of the mark.

Unsurprisingly, analysts will disagree amongst themselves in making stock forecasts. Owing to the frequent lack of information forthcoming from quoted companies, analysts may simply be making an educated guess in their forecasts. These guesses can be wildly misplaced. Even if analysts' earnings forecasts are broadly in line, their recommendations on whether to buy or sell may not be.

Analysts, even if they have spent years watching their sector, are outsiders looking in – even if, as in some cases, they once worked in the industry. When they speak to the company, they are often all fed the same information, at the same time.

Of course, individual analysts may sometimes stumble on better information. Unsurprisingly, the more interesting titbits passed to the firm's top clients are not committed to writing. In the firm's written research, there is often an unspoken policy to keep negative comments subdued or out.

To this end, outright sell recommendations are comparatively infrequent, with analysts more likely to use euphemisms. If they are too scathing about the company, they risk alienating themselves from its management, which they cannot afford. This is particularly so if the company is a corporate client of the broking firm.

Given their typically narrow focus within a single sector coupled with possible vested interests, analysts sometimes get too close to the companies that they follow, and become blind to the companies' mistakes. It is very difficult for an analyst to tell hordes of salespeople that he or she got it wrong, and that yesterday's buy recommendation has turned overnight into a sell.

For these reasons, you should not have complete faith in the objectivity of brokers' analysts. Most are, of course, directing their recommendations at institutional investors. The switch from one stock to another that they advise may be completely unsuitable for private investors.

Analysts have been criticized not just for bias but for incompetence at evaluating a company. Research has in the past suggested that only about a quarter of analysts are qualified or part-qualified accountants. This is disturbing since analysts should clearly be comfortable breaking down the numbers in a company's accounts.

Some analysts argue that a company's accounts throw most light on the past, whereas they are aiming to predict future earnings and prospects. It is true that items on the balance sheet can change quickly, and that the latest profits are yesterday's news. However, the accounts remain a crucial part of the developing picture.

Today, the trend is for analysts to look closely at the discounted rate of return, which is the estimated annual return on equity for the company reduced to its present-day value using a discount rate. They will project this for 5 or 10 years (or longer) into the future.

The analyst will compare the discounted rate of return with the weighted average cost of capital (WAAC), ie the company's cost of borrowing. If this return rate is consistently higher than WAAC, the analyst would see this as an indication of value in the stock. If the gap is increasing, or seen as likely to increase, the value signals are still more positive.

Comparisons are made with other stocks in the sector, and it will often be found that some have a discounted rate of return that is more than WAAC, while others cannot cover it. However, calculating discount rates is a subjective process, and there are other uncertainties. Hence this method is unreliable; we shall look at it critically at various points later in the book.

Part of the overall problem is that some analysts have an excellent knowledge of their sector, but simply cannot predict when the share price will go up. For example, one financial sector analyst working for a top-name investment bank is famous throughout the City for always 'getting it wrong'. The salespeople in his firm laugh at his recommendations.

This analyst is, however, a recognized expert on financials, far more so than some of his professional colleagues. He is an earnest and diligent researcher. So where does he go wrong?

The man simply has no feel for how the stock market works and he cannot predict price movements. There are other such analysts working for top investment banks. Some, nonetheless, win the industry's prestigious awards for quality of research and are on six-figure incomes. How do they survive and prosper in this way?

Major investment brokers can afford to employ analysts who produce prestigious research, even if their recommendations are misplaced. But most analysts, to keep their jobs, have to be often broadly right in their predictions about whether, when, and by how much the share price will go up.

Particularly in smaller firms, analysts are judged by the business they generate. The more ideas for buying and selling they come up with, the more valuable they are to the firm. If nothing much is happening in the industry, analysts will often create an area of focus. They will take a company in their sector and calculate its break-up value. If this is higher than the share price would represent it, they may suggest that the company is a takeover target.

A whisper to this effect from a well-regarded analyst will certainly be enough to set the rumour mill in motion. The share price may soar on such rumours and analysts have to be extremely careful as to what they say, and when and how they say it. They will be held responsible for this.

It is analysts at the top investment banks that wield the most influence. They are normally a gregarious bunch – quick-witted and ready to give an instant opinion. It is comparatively few in their midst who would on first appearance be more at home spending their days in the hushed ambience of a university library. In some of the lesser firms, the analysts are simply rewriting the work of others, or they are preparing simplistic sales pitches.

Be your own analyst

Given the uncertain value of analysts' output, despite their elevated status and salaries to match, you are certainly advised not to take their recommendations too seriously, but to do a little research yourself into the companies that interest you.

You must aim to pinpoint companies that are trading below their true value. This will involve looking at a few basic ratios, and for something new within the company that could send the share price soaring.

The good news is that, once you understand how ratios work, you need not calculate them yourself. There are regularly updated reference books and services to which you can subscribe that will do the calculations for you. These include *The Estimate Directory*, and, in particular, *REFS (Really Essential Financial Statistics)*. You can either subscribe to one of these or use a copy in your local reference library. *REFS* also has a useful online version. For further details of these directories, see Chapter 17, and see Appendix 7 for contact details.

If you have access to the Internet, you can find key ratios and price trend analysis, latest earnings and dividends and much more on 18,000 companies worldwide at Wright Research Center (http://www.profiles.wisi.com/). But in my view, for the best source of free information on a share, including a five-year summary profit and loss account with balance sheet, share price movements, major shareholders and similar, you should go to the Web site of Hemmington Scott, which publishes *REFS*, at www.hemscott.com/ EQUITIES/INDEX.HTM. However, checking out the ratios, important as it is, is not enough.

Keep your eye on City share recommendations

Although we have established that City analysts have an unreliable output, it is imperative you keep an eye on their recommendations and forecasts. The truth is, top City analysts have a powerful influence on the share price. It typically discounts their forecasts.

The easiest way to obtain analysts' forecasts is, again, through *REFS* or *The Estimate Directory*. The most important figure is the consensus forecast, although you will want to pay close attention to how wide is the deviation either side of it.

You can also obtain analysts' forecasts free on the Internet, from the relevant part of the *Financial Times* Web site at www.globalarchive. ft.com. Avoid the stock if analysts are forecasting a decline in earnings as the share price will normally then decline or prove sluggish.

Ideally, you will also want to get your hands on brokers' written research output, and this is sometimes possible via the World Wide Web. At the time of writing, investment banks Merrill Lynch and Salomon Smith Barney are making their research available free over the Internet on a free trial basis, while firms such as Durlacher offer research via their Web pages on an ongoing basis. But at this time, if you wish to access brokers' research via the Internet, you will often have to pay for it. There are Web sites referred to later in this book that specialize in providing such a service.

If you intend to approach a broker directly for its research, you may run into problems. Analysts may just make available to you a copy of their latest report if you telephone them at work and ask them directly. More often than not, they will not play ball. Institutions pay tens of thousands of pounds annually to broking houses to receive their research, so you cannot expect to receive it free without a struggle.

Analysts are more likely to give you their research if you make it easy for them. For instance, you could offer to collect the research from their office personally, rather than put them to the bother of sending it out to you. In some broking firms, analysts do not have assistants to do such administrative work, and are reluctant to take on more of it than they have to.

If you do ring up analysts to discuss a company with them, avoid doing so in the very early morning when they are at their busiest. Have your questions ready, and avoid making them too basic. An analyst will at most give you only a few minutes of his or her time.

If you go to analysts directly for their views in this way, you are tapping the main source of investment information provided to a good number of private client brokers.

These brokers often have no in-house research facilities (or very limited ones). They will often simply regurgitate to you the (already probably outdated) recommendations of other broking houses.

Your broker

This book releases you from total dependence on your broker's recommendations. Using the Bargain Hunters' Investment FlexiSystem, you will be able to select stocks for investment yourself, and so save money by using an execution-only broker. Such a broker is increasingly often offering an online service, which is not necessarily going to save you money, but may be very convenient for you.

If you wish to deal online, you must select your broker carefully, as you will need a broker with a reliable Web site that does not crash too often, and with an efficient backup telephone service for when it does. In Chapter 2, I will demonstrate to you what really matters when you select an online broker.

Alternatively, you can use the usual telephone-based advisory private client brokers, and familiarity with the system described in this book will enable you to question them more exactingly than before. By the way they deal with your questions, brokers will really show their mettle.

They may not agree with everything in this book, and that is healthy. Stock selection on value principles, as outlined in the Bargain Hunters' Investment FlexiSystem, is partly a science, as you will be applying methods of objective valuation, but it is also an art and there is room for disagreement on the investment principles that form its foundation.

What is indisputable is that, as a seeker of bargain stocks, you will be working on the premise that the market has overlooked value in some companies and that, by detecting the value yourself, you can beat the market.

Do not believe the efficient market theory

Do not fall for the argument, still put about by some US academics, that the stock market is 'efficient'. In its strongest form, the so-called efficient market theory stipulates that everything that is known or could be known about a company is reflected in the share price.

Superficially, the case is plausible and, if true, it makes all analysts redundant. If you open your *FT* at a page where stock prices are listed, close your eyes, and stick a pin on it at random, you are as likely to select a winner as somebody who chooses a stock on the basis of diligent research, so the argument goes.

The better investors know that this is not true, despite the power of the Internet, which is bringing stock market information faster to an increasing number of investors. Omaha-based Warren Buffett has become arguably the world's greatest living investor on the basis of his value-orientated stock selection methods. He knows that anomalies in value do exist on the stock market, and so should you.

By the time you have read this book, you will understand and be able to put into practice the Bargain Hunters' Investment FlexiSystem, which is based on the classic principles of great value investors, although with some variations to bring it up to date and make it simple to operate. For instance, you will be applying different rules to day trading, or to the purchase of Internet stocks, all of which will be explained thoroughly in this book.

But on value investing, here is a little warning for you. Buying investments for value is not always so exciting as buying those that are fashionable, although, in the long run, it is more profitable. It does require a little spadework and, in the beginning, you will need some patience. When investing in this way, you must consider whether you will be happier operating entirely on your own behalf or would prefer the security and companionship of doing so as part of an investment club.

The advantage of joining an investment club

Investment clubs, encouraged in the UK by the non-profit-making organization Proshare, are proving to be a major growth area, and are welcomed by some online brokers such as Charles Schwab. Armed with this book, you can make an outstanding contribution to stock selection at any club lucky enough to have you as a member.

Remember, however, that investment clubs vary in their emphasis.

Some go for wild and risky growth stocks, even if overpriced, while others specialize in controversial selection techniques, including technical analysis (see Chapter 9).

The views of such clubs can be in direct conflict with those in the Bargain Hunters' Investment FlexiSystem. Almost any investment club can, nonetheless, work well in a bull market. For your purposes, you need a club that will be happy to operate the system patiently. You will also need fellow members who are sufficiently cool-headed to treat investment as a business like any other, and who are willing to wait for their profits.

In a period when I was writing regularly for the money pages of *The Sunday Times*, I spent a long time searching for a club with high standards and I eventually found one. The International Investment Club, Hampstead, while not operating the Bargain Hunters' Investment FlexiSystem, based its investment decisions on analysis and facts rather than wild speculation.

This club had no use for stockbrokers who offer an advisory service. Over a 10-month period, it had made a 31 per cent gain on its share portfolio off its own bat. This was an extraordinary performance, despite its achievement in a bull market. The running of the club could not have been simpler. Each of the club's eight female members contributed £300 twice annually and had her say in how the pooled sum was invested.

Significantly, a high proportion of members of this investment club were ex-investment bankers or had links with such people. As you come to operate the Bargain Hunters' Investment FlexiSystem, you too will find that your approach has more in common with that of City professionals than that of the many small private investors who find the stock market a bit of a mystery.

If you cannot find an investment club prepared to implement or to take account of your system, you should consider setting up your own. This is easier than you think, and you can find details of many investment clubs on the World Wide Web.

How to set up your own investment club

To set up an investment club in the UK, your first step should be to buy the investment clubs' start-up manual from Proshare, the body that promotes wider share ownership (tel: 020 7394 5200). You will find the manual simple to follow, and in setting up a club you will be doing only what many others have done successfully before you.

To avoid conflict of interests, select as members of the club only those who are at least potentially in sympathy with the Bargain Hunters' Investment FlexiSystem. It is a good idea if they could all have read this book in advance.

As the Proshare manual explains, you will run your club most easily as a partnership with a legal maximum of 20 members. You will need a chairman, treasurer and secretary. Members will contribute an affordable regular membership subscription – perhaps £30 a month – to the club's fund for investing. By giving due notice, members may sell out – taking out their stake at its current value.

How can you maximize the chances of success for your club, given that some do not make it through their first year? As a journalist, I have discussed the problems faced by a start-up club with Derek Richards, chairman of Victoria Investment Club, Truro, who helped to write the Proshare manual.

In Richards's view, a club should hold monthly meetings on neutral ground – ideally in a pub or club. He advised against using members' homes since they can vary in status, causing potential embarrassment. All club members should be encouraged to become involved in their meeting. Most importantly, the treasurer should keep the club's finances in order and financial statements should be issued monthly to members.

Richards argued that a new club should not expect to make a profit in the first few months, although it may want to do so. The safest bet is a portfolio of blue chip companies only, with all dividends reinvested. But if the portfolio includes some companies capitalized at less than £100m, the return could be higher, he said.

You will find that you can put this advice into practice while adhering closely to the Bargain Hunters' Investment FlexiSystem, which makes our system ideal for investment clubs.

Anybody who becomes familiar with the system, whether as an individual investor or as part of a club, will quickly see how sensible it is. The few who currently know about the system have stuck by it through thick and thin.

If the truth be known, our system's underlying value principles are similar to those applied by any sensible business person in any walk of life. As millionaire stock market investor Robert Beckman once said, the secret of the stock market is that there is no secret.

Golden rules covered in this chapter

Rule 1   Buy after a market correction or crash, when share prices are depressed and bargains are there for the taking.

Rule 2   Keep your share portfolio as small as you like, but it is a good idea to diversify your investments where possible.

Rule 3   Obtain brokers' research directly from analysts or via the Internet and be sceptical. While the research can be useful, it is often biased. It may well be unsuitable for private investors.

Rule 4   Be your own analyst and pinpoint undervalued shares. Understand how ratios work, although you do not need to calculate them yourself.

Rule 5   Do not give credence to the efficient market theory.

Rule 6   Consider joining up or starting an investment club that sets a priority on value investing.

2

Select an ace broker and financial adviser

Before you even consider using a new broker or continuing with your old one, you should come to terms with certain eternal truths. It is a truism in City circles that brokers make money whether you, as their client, do or not. They are paid on turnover of business, not on performance of the stocks they select. It is no wonder that so many brokers are turning to online dealing, which leads to clients dealing more frequently.

In their defence, brokers insist that they must make you money in order to retain your custom. While this priority may be true if they are in the stockbroking business for the long haul – which cannot be assumed – it does not mean that brokers are efficient. Many brokers are inefficient, and extremely lazy to boot.

Of course, if your broker is efficient, he or she can obviously be useful to you. Even so, while carrying out the Bargain Hunters' Investment FlexiSystem, you should clearly not rely on your broker's wisdom and integrity in making investment decisions on your behalf.

You are particularly vulnerable if you have a discretionary portfolio, where you pay a broker to make investment decisions on your behalf – a strategy that by definition is not usually recommended under the Bargain Hunters' Investment FlexiSystem. The principle does make sense if you have a portfolio of say £100,000 or more and are too busy or uninterested to make your own stock selections, but only if you use a first-class firm.

To tempt you into giving them your business, many discretionary brokers offer free extra services, including help with capital gains tax and broader financial planning assistance. Do not be seduced this way into using a broker with a less than excellent track record.

Even if you have a discretionary broker, it will keep him or her on the ball if you ask about his or her stock selections periodically, and keep an eye on performance. It is dangerous to trust *anyone* blind with your money.

At the other extreme, execution-only brokers – operating by telephone or online – will carry out your orders but will not give you tailored investment recommendations. For this reason, their charges are comparatively low. To use such a broker makes sense if you prefer to select your own shares without any advice whatsoever. It also makes sense if you want to become a day trader or similar (see Chapter 13).

At this point, be warned that 'execution only' is not so standardized as the concept may suggest. The brokers in this category vary widely in charges, as well as in breadth and efficiency of service. They are often operating under extreme time pressure. For a list of brokers that have established execution-only services, including online, turn to Appendices 2 and 3 at the end of this book.

The ideal execution-only broker will provide statistics, news and views about companies over the telephone or via the Internet – everything except the dealing advice, which he or she is forbidden to give. For instance, Leeds-based broker Redmayne Bentley, which now has 18 branches throughout the UK, sometimes offers such a broad information service through its telephone-based execution-only service, and it has recently started Internet dealing.

On the negative side, you should avoid execution-only brokers with inadequate administration procedures, or – in the case of online brokers – Web sites that crash and inadequate backup telephone dealing services. Such problems affected more than one such broker in the past, and cheapest is not always best. In Chapter 14 of this book, I will illustrate the dangers of poor administration with an account of my horrendous experience with one execution-only telephone-based share dealing operation.

Beware also of stockbroking services built on newspaper deals with execution-only brokers. Some of these services hold your shares for a time, then deal in bulk for many investors. Some of the cheaper execution-only dealers that offer their services directly to the public operate, to a lesser extent, in the same way. The problem in such cases is that, before the group deal takes place, the share price may change significantly.

At the time of writing, the fastest-expanding area of broking is undoubtedly online investing. The first Internet share-dealing services were launched only in mid-1998. By 2002, the number of online dealing accounts in Britain will have reached a projected 1.9 million, from 100,000 at the end of 1999, according to US investment bank J P Morgan.

As in most areas of business, the US is ahead of Britain in online dealing and already boasts about 6.4 million online dealing accounts, with about 15 per cent of all stock trades being conducted on the Internet. Owing to the higher volumes of online trading, as well as payments made by market makers to brokers in the US, prices are more competitive than in the UK. But there are exceptions to the rule.

If you want to deal online, you will find a list of online brokers in Appendix 3. This list does not claim to be complete, as there is a continual stream of new entrants to the field. Electronic Share Information's Web site (www.esi.co.uk) gives you access to various online brokers. Financial news provider Datastream (www.datastream.com) has its own version of this service. What does dealing online involve?

The fast-expanding world of online broking

As competition increases, online dealing is becoming more sophisticated. Occasionally, online stockbrokers still offer clients a mere glorified facility for placing an order by e-mail, but an increasing number offer real-time prices, and a facility for executing your trade electronically on the spot. Facilities for dealing easily in international stocks are becoming more widespread, and as this book goes to press, margin trading – or buying shares partly on borrowed money – has become available in the UK through two online brokers.

But online dealing costs are not always lower than through execution-only telephone brokers, and the services offered still vary in range and quality. While most online stockbrokers will hold your shares in a nominee account, ie without paper certificates, there is the occasional exception.

Whichever way, online stockbroking is a young and, as yet, unperfected branch of the trade, where Web sites still sometimes crash due to level of demand, and the telephone lines offered as a backup in an emergency can be quickly congested. For precious long minutes – or much longer – it can be effectively impossible to contact your broker.

You should have an alternative broker or two to use at such times, but, even so, the hassle involved will still cost you time. In the world of share trading, a few minutes' or half an hour's delay could cost you hundreds – or thousands – of pounds, particularly if you are dealing in volatile Internet stocks.

As an investor told the 'Best online broker' thread on the *Silicon Investor* message board on the Internet, the cost of a trade is no longer important. He said that traders see how saving a little on commissions and costs for trading adds up to a tidy sum over the year, and 'Then something happens. And a missed trade or a stalled trade or a mixed-up trade costs some real money... and you begin to think about what is really important.' For more about the value of message boards, see Chapter 7.

The major costs from online investing clearly come when you are unable to buy or sell a volatile stock quickly. The risks are heightened for so-called fast stocks, which include many Internet companies. If you buy or sell fast shares through an online broker, the so-called real-time price on your screen is likely to differ from that at which the trade is executed.

The discrepancy would arise from delays as your order for a given stock joins a queue, and any orders ahead of yours will be executed first, a process that may lead to adjustments in the stock price. Charles Schwab, www.schwab-worldwide.com, the UK's leading online stock-broker, has issued warnings on its Web site about the potential rapid price changes when you deal in fast stocks.

As some online brokers stress, the risk of the price going against you in hot stocks can be minimized if you place a limit order by which you specify the highest price you will pay for a stock, or the lowest price that you will accept for selling it. Some online brokers will fill limit orders at any time during the day, while others operate only on a 'fill-or-kill' basis, executing the limit order only if they can do so immediately.

If you can find a broker that offers day limit orders, whose Web site does not crash too often from overuse, and that has an adequate backup phone line facility – prompt and well serviced – you are well on your way towards selecting a good dealing service. You also want a competitive dealing price. Amongst UK online brokers, Barclays Stockbrokers (www.barclays-stockbrokers.co.uk) can sometimes get you a better price than its rivals on the basis that it deals with several market-makers.

You will find that these factors are more important than saving a few pounds on the commission for every deal. Nonetheless, you do not need to pay high commissions or other costs when using an online broker, and, interestingly, the cheaper operators are not always inferior.

At the time of writing, Charles Schwab, like several other brokers, is offering an introductory free dealing facility designed to lure you into becoming a permanent client, at which point its dealing costs are by no means the cheapest. As a variation on the theme, broker Redmayne Bentley seeks to attract investors to its new online dealing facility REDM by offering registered individuals the chance to win £1,000 worth of free shares.

If you want to avoid special offers and simply go for the cheapest broker on a long-term basis, you should consider Cave & Sons Limited (www.caves.co.uk), which charges the incredibly low dealing commission of £5.00, plus 1 per cent on every deal, up to a maximum charge of £35.00. Another particularly cheap online broker is The Share Centre (www.share.co.uk), which both I and other users of the Bargain Hunters' Investment FlexiSystem have found reasonably efficient.

Some brokers offer cheaper trades to clients who deal frequently, perhaps introducing a lower rate after a specified number of trades. For example, at Stocktrade, a service of Brewin Dolphin Securities, which bills itself as the UK's first online broker, there are two commission levels. Regular traders pay 0.4 per cent commission on every deal, with a minimum of £14.50, while star traders – for which clients qualify after doing 50 deals – pay just 0.2 per cent, although with the same minimum payment.

If you pay a comparatively high charge for an online broker, take a long hard look at the frills that may cost you extra, and assess whether you want them. For example, you do not *need* the research available on the Web sites of online brokers, convenient as it may be. The reason is that similar or better research facilities are available free elsewhere on the Web, provided you know where to look.

If you check out the research actually on offer from the online dealers, you will find that its quality, its level of availability, its sources, and even its medium of communication to you vary considerably. Such research is likely to be a compendium of that produced by major brokers, and much of it may already be out of date. If the research is even a few days old, the institutional investors that move markets will probably already have acted on it, and the analysts may have already changed their recommendations in response to ensuing price movements or news flow.

Potentially more valuable is when the broker offers its *own* research to online clients, as broker Killik & Co does through its outlet 'The Research Centre' (www.killik.co.uk). Generally, a broker's research is only as good as the analysts who produced it and, a cynic would add, the clout of the corporate finance department and sales force of their firm.

But research is too lofty a word for the information facility on offer at some online brokers. Graphs of share prices over a period, ratios and statistics, as provided by some online brokers, are not always accompanied by interpretation or analysis, and are available elsewhere on the Web. Furthermore, the information at some online brokers' Web sites is harder to access than at others.

Quite useful, although again available elsewhere on the Web, are the market commentaries offered by online brokers. For example, The Share Centre offers a reasonable daily market comment on its *Morning Meeting Reports* page. Not to be ignored are the many articles about investment techniques available on the better of the online dealers' Web sites – usually without any requirement to be registered for access. Again, the material available can vary in quality.

Charles Schwab offers *Bull's Eye* online, which includes some interesting articles, of varying levels of sophistication, about investment strategies. As a twist on the theme, online broker E*Trade offers extracts from published books on how to invest. Some online brokers, at the time of writing, are toying with the idea of introducing message boards.

Of course, online dealers can offer services that are not delivered by the Internet. The Share Centre promotes via its Web site its pay-as-you-go telephone-based advisory service, which is particularly cost-effective for those who need advice or feedback on stock selection only on an occasional basis. Some may prefer traditional service on an ongoing basis to accompany their online dealing. Killik & Co would appear to be the only broker at present that offers its traditional telephone advice to online dealing clients.

Most online dealing sites offer you FAQs – frequently asked questions – which will let you know, for instance, how much money you need to put up before dealing, how quickly trades are executed, commission costs, settlement arrangements, interest paid on money kept on deposit, and so on.

Sometimes, the questions and answers are accessible by scrolling down the page, while at other times, the answer to each question is available one at a time by a click of the mouse, which can slow up the reading process considerably – at your expense.

For the sites of most online brokers, security is good, but you must use (and keep to yourself) your personal identity number (PIN), user name and password. PIN numbers are case-sensitive, so avoid the common mistake of inadvertently pressing the lock-on button on your computer keyboard. Fill in your order carefully as, once you have dealt, you cannot usually change it. Your online broker should provide facilities for tracing the status of your order, and the price at which it was dealt.

It is normal to be able to deal outside the London Stock Exchange's trading hours, in which case your order will be stored, and executed when the market opens. Portfolio analysis facilities are often available on the Web sites of online dealers, so you can build and view your portfolio online, complete with share price movements.

How to buy US shares online

If you want to buy US shares online, choose a broker that will deal for you at a low commission. Charles Schwab, for instance, has established a reasonably low-cost facility for UK clients to buy US shares. Since October 1999, DLJ Direct's UK dealing service has provided UK clients with access to US stocks at normal US dealing rates.

You can also use one of the US online brokers, provided that, in most cases, you deposit a significant sum of money up front in US dollars. US online broker Ameritrade, for instance, will allow UK clients to trade online at only $8.00 a time. To register with US online dealers, you will often find the registration forms online, but will need to print them off, fill them out, and send them to the broker by 'snail' (ordinary) mail, with funds in US currency.

As an investor in US shares, bear in mind that you will be taking a risk on the sterling/dollar exchange rate, as well as the performance of the shares. This can, of course, work *for* as well as *against* you. Meanwhile, you will pay no stamp duty, and the bid-offer spread is usually lower than in the UK.

In the eyes of the US tax authorities, you will be a non-resident alien, and so you must complete a W-8 form, which is a certificate of foreign status, and send it to your broker. You can download this form from the Web site of the US Internal Revenue Service.

Once you are involved in the US markets, you will find plenty of ways to follow the share prices and relevant news flow on the Internet.

In Appendix 8, you will find some Web sites listed that will give you specialist information about the US markets.

For specific guidance about investing in the US market, go to the Web site of Nasdaq (www.nasdaq.co.uk), the US market that bills itself in its UK television adverts as 'the stock market for the next 100 years'. As this book goes to press, Nasdaq has announced a joint venture to create an Internet-accessible pan-European stock market for IPOs, scheduled to start in the fourth quarter of 2000.

While online brokers represent the future of stockbroking, there is still plenty of demand for the traditional advisory broker.

Advisory brokers

Advisory broking services are sometimes more choosy than their online or other execution-only colleagues over whom they take on as clients, and you may find it hard to gain access to a good one if you are a small investor. Should you be in this category, you may do better to seek your broker in a provincial rather than a London broking house.

Even if your choice appears limited, select your broker carefully. A list of some brokers is available from the Association of Private Client Investment Managers & Stockbrokers' (tel: 020 7247 7080, and Web site at www.apcims.org), but inclusion in this list is no guarantee of suitability for your purposes.

Investigate the advisory broker's background

Ask prospective advisory brokers for how many years they have worked in this industry and in what firms. Inquire their track record for making clients money, their investment philosophy, if they have any, and the size of stocks or sectors in which they specialize. Be wary if a broker is only really interested in small companies as these can be highly speculative.

Do not expect brokers to have achieved much in the way of professional qualifications but ask about this all the same. The only requirement for them to trade is the Registered Persons' exam, which is extremely basic. Owing to experience in the market, they may have been exempted from taking even that.

Your broker may also have achieved the Securities Institute diploma. This is taken in three sittings and is represented as the industry's highest qualification. In terms of rigour the diploma does not hold a candle to the professional qualifications of solicitors, accountants, etc. Nonetheless, about 50 per cent of candidates fail some of the exams.

There are other financial qualifications your broker may or may not have. All of these can be checked, but remember that the broker's job, despite its advisory element, is essentially trading in shares, which does not in itself require qualifications. Although the analogy is not perfect, you don't expect a fruit and vegetable stall-holder to do the job better if he or she has a degree in horticulture.

In some cases, the broker is responsible personally for stock selection, which can benefit from an ability to read accounts and from other areas of expertise that may be assisted by industry qualifications. But such qualifications in themselves are no guarantee of success, and no prerequisite for it.

Choose your stockbroking firm carefully

In selecting your stockbroker, you may prefer a firm that specializes in areas of investment interest to you. For instance, Ellis & Partners specializes in the small companies sector. Teather & Greenwood is particularly good on AIM listed companies, while Raphael Zorn specializes in insurance companies. Alternatively, you may go for a less specialist firm.

Either way, make sure you deal with a firm of reasonably good reputation, even if this means that the dealing commissions are higher. Read a firm's brochures and look up its Web site (if it has one) on the Internet to get an overall impression.

The Web site often reveals a lot. For instance, in this way Ellis & Partners provides details of some of the companies it brings to the market. Redmayne Bentley offers a newsletter on the Web giving an invaluable daily market commentary. In the US, Fidelity offers through its Web site whole pages of sound advice on investment strategy, penned by investment big gun Peter Lynch.

Assuming that through your researches you find a suitable broking firm, be sure to feel comfortable with the individual representative who would be handling your portfolio. Individual brokers can vary widely in talents and approach, even when they work for the same firm.

Check your broker's information sources

An advisory broker should have at his or her fingertips up-to-date share prices as well as information, statistics and news flow about companies. You can be as well served, or almost so, at home by subscribing to *REFS* and/or using an electronic service such as Market Eye.

Meanwhile, scrutinize any quality equity research that your broker uses as a basis for his or her recommendations and that he or she will make available to you. You can get your own up-to-date brokers' research via the Internet, but this can work out expensive. A useful site for this is that of Investext Group, a division of Thomson Financial Services (www.investext.com), which does at least tell you how much an individual item of research will cost you and lets you look at the contents before committing yourself.

In the future, brokers' research may become accessible more cheaply and, at the time of writing, a few investment banks are pioneering free access to their research material. At this stage, if your own broker can make available to you either its own or other brokers' research on a timely basis, this is a definite plus point. Greig Middleton is a rare example of a stockbroker that produces its own very high-quality research, and yet will deal with private clients.

Sadly, many so-called half-commission brokers – who operate on a split commission deal with their firms and have no basic salaries – have access to no research facilities, and, for this reason, you should be wary of their recommendations. Some of their firms produce dubious recommendations based on 'crunching the numbers' of many companies through their computer. To provide these statistics, they rely entirely on the (sometimes outdated) research of the larger brokers.

Meet your broker and assess his or her image

When you deal with your broker, you must find not just the right firm, but the right person. Of course, clients tend to find brokers who have a compatible outlook, but a good match is not always made immediately. It is important for you to feel comfortable with your broker and there are some warning signs you should heed.

As a financial journalist, I have specialized in writing about financial sharp practice for some years, and would draw to your attention a favourite saying amongst US financial services industry regulators of my acquaintance: *Beware of financial consultants bearing gifts.*

Take this on board and you should not be too impressed if your broker takes you out to lunch in a really posh restaurant. His or her clients are paying for that lunch. If your broker wears tailor-made suits, drives a Bentley and has a Rolex watch, beware too.

Some brokers have made their money the easy way – by duping the gullible, while others on the make are broke but dress to impress. At the risk of blowing my own trumpet, I would mention that Chapter 8 gives you the best inside guide to spotting dubious promoters of small company shares that you will ever be likely to come across.

That is not to say that you should opt for a shabby-looking broker. If your broker's suit is threadworn and his watch is cheap, his money-making abilities may be limited. If he cannot make money for himself, how can he ever do so for you?

There is worse. You should normally avoid the firms that specialize in pushing penny shares. They are the sure descendants of the erst-while dealers licensed by the Department of Trade & Industry that pushed mostly unsuitable shares on gullible private investors in the late 1980s and beyond (see Chapter 8).

In the mid to late 1990s, several of these firms shut up shop, volun-tarily or otherwise, after failing to obtain regulation under the Financial Services Act from the recently formed self-regulatory organi-zation The Personal Investment Authority (PIA). Many had been found to have breached regulations in the way they operated.

The surviving penny share specialists are extremely clever in the way that they operate. Their telesales pitches are tape-recorded for 'everybody's protection'. In the firm's brochures, it is pointed out boldly that you can lose all your money on penny shares, that the spreads are wide and the liquidity limited, that you should only invest with spare cash, etc.

The dealers make their profits from the difference in the price at which they buy the penny shares as principals and that at which they sell to clients. The shares have often been offloaded on them in bulk by another party who badly wanted to get rid of them. Even if the shares are in a quoted company and are being offered at the current market price or less, this is no guarantee that they are a good buy. If you must buy quoted penny shares, do so from a broker that is – and check this – a *bona fide* member of the London Stock Exchange.

While the right broker can help you in buying shares, the right inde-pendent financial adviser (IFA) can help you with your other invest-ments. But, like brokers, independent financial advisers vary widely in quality. You can assess them initially by looking at their Web sites.

To track down some IFAs on the Internet, use the Internet directory for UK financial services at www.find.co.uk.

How to work the financial services sales system

The way to work the financial services sales system is to fix appointments with several IFAs in turn. They will each in turn assess your circumstances, and come up with recommendations on a no-obligation basis. You can sometimes learn from their advice, but ultimately you will probably not be buying through their firms. Do not stress that you are conducting your research in this way or they may stop dealing with you immediately. You need say no more than that you are keeping your options open.

Far more dangerous than IFAs are tied agents, who, by definition, represent a single insurance company. They are often ignorant of products other than those pushed by their own firm, and are notorious for high-pressure selling (see Chapter 15). Even nowadays when regulations have tightened up, many such salespeople are here today, gone tomorrow. You could visit tied agents for research purposes, but never buy from one unless he or she is exceptionally clued up and has the right product for you, at the right price.

Once you are ready to buy, do not automatically do so through the IFA. Similarly, do not bother in most cases to go directly to the company that provides the product as, this way, you would be charged as high a commission as if you went through an IFA.

Instead, your first port of call should be the discount brokers, which are accessible on the World Wide Web through the Internet directory for UK financial services at www.find.co.uk. They do not offer individual advice – except sometimes on request as an extra service for which you would be charged – but you will by this stage have obtained an advisory service – for what it was worth – from the IFAs who previously gave you free consultations in the hope of attracting your business.

The discount brokers, by not offering you advice, can give discounts, typically between 1 and 5 per cent, on the *upfront* commission payable as part of the standard retail price of financial products. Be prepared to pay any *annual* commission in full.

The discount brokers offer you the cheapest deals

Provided that you know which product you want, discount brokers, if they stock it, will offer you the cheapest deal. For example, as I started writing this book, The Pep Shop Ltd in Nottingham was offering the Fidelity Triple Performance Pep at a 3 per cent discount to its usual retail price, and was recommending this for value investors. There are no longer new Peps on offer, but the principle is illustrated. The savings can be small, but, if reinvested, will benefit from compound growth over a period.

Realistically, consider the discount for a given financial product in relation to any residual upfront charge and any annual charge, which you will still have to pay. In the case of some products with high commissions payable but where big discounts are on offer, you would pay higher overall charges than for certain other products where the discounts are smaller but which have lower commissions. Meanwhile, the level of rebate for the same product can vary, so you should always obtain quotes from several of the discount brokers. For a list of some of these brokers, turn to Appendix 4.

Above all, remember that the quality and suitability of the underlying investment is more important than the level of discount you receive on the purchase price. First and foremost, check a fund's track record, either with an IFA, or in the pages of *Money Management* or another financial magazine that provides comparative performance tables. Alternatively, check the statistics of the fund online at the Web site of Micropal (www.micropal.com). Also, keep an eye on news flow that may indicate, for example, a change in management of a fund, as this may affect its future performance. I will refer in more detail to the procedures required in Chapter 10.

Such research takes an effort, which is doubtless why people do not flock to use the discount brokers. Disconcertingly for lazy or uninitiated investors, these brokers do not offer individual advice and do not tout for business by cold-calling. To buy from one of these firms, you have to conduct your own research and make your own decisions.

If you do not intend to do this, you may be better off buying tracker funds, which simply replicate the market and, in so doing, outperform the vast majority of funds. The tracker funds vary slightly in weightings and performance, but all have lower management charges than specialist funds (see Chapter 10). At the time of writing, the most successful tracker fund is the Close techMARK index tracking fund (details at www.trackerfunds.com, and in Chapter 7).

If, in general, you try to buy from any IFA or tied agent without contacting several of the firms and getting a feel for the market, the chances of your acquiring the wrong investment are significant. Recently publicized scandals over the misselling of pensions and endowment policies are only the tip of the iceberg. In broad terms, how may the IFAs and tied agents pull the wool over your eyes? First, by selling you unsuitable products; second, by charging extremely high commissions.

While writing this book, I visited an IFA in London, shortly before the stock market entered a heavy correction phase in mid-1998. The salesman breezily advised me to invest a very substantial sum in a particular unit trust, which paid him a much higher commission than most.

I protested that the stock market seemed grossly overvalued and might go down. The salesman had the nerve to pooh-pooh this responsible argument. 'We can't second-guess the market', he said. He argued, not incorrectly, that equities had outperformed less risky investments over any given period of years.

Nonetheless, at this point in the cycle, shares were absurdly over-valued, and it was a dangerous time to buy unit trusts. The salesman must have known this but, like many in his line of work, he clearly cared only about his commission.

To the great amusement of my investment banking colleagues, this character kept ringing me up in my office where I worked and trying to hard-sell me his product. The IFAs are not always so 'independent' as they make out, although they have been found to be more so when advising on a fee-paid basis. If you want independent financial advice for a fixed fee, it may be worthwhile checking out the Web site of Sort (www.sort.co.uk).

If you do buy through an IFA – perhaps because a discount broker does not offer the precise product that you want – find out how many companies' products it promotes. Check what qualifications your adviser has, and for how long he or she has been working in the field. If the firm specializes in certain areas, make sure that *you* can benefit from this.

In addition, ask your IFA for a rebate on part of the commission on the products that you would buy from it. It *may* begrudgingly provide this, particularly if such a rebate is available elsewhere, but you will usually have to ask. If, for whatever reason, you want to buy from the

IFA without doing this, at least ask how much commission it will receive from the deal. Should it decline to tell you, take your business elsewhere.

Such drastic action is unnecessary if you deal with fee-paid IFAs who will receive no commission on sales arising from your consultation with them. But the fee-paid IFAs can be as ignorant about the market place as their commission-paid counterparts and will similarly never recommend a company that only sells directly to the public. Do not say you have not been warned.

Golden rules covered in this chapter

Rule 7   Execution-only brokers vary widely in efficiency, breadth of service and charges. Avoid online brokers that have unreliable Web sites or inadequate telephone backup services.

Rule 8   Avoid penny-share dealers.

Rule 9   To find a good advisory broker that will deal with small clients, look for a provincial rather than a London firm.

Rule 10   Investigate a potential advisory broker's background, meeting the individual with whom you would be dealing. Check the reputation of any broking firm with which you are considering dealing, and the quality of its research services.

Rule 11   Make use of IFAs for research purposes, without necessarily buying from them.

Rule 12   Avoid tied agents except under exceptional circumstances.

Rule 13   Buy from discount brokers and save on commission.

Rule 14   If you buy from an IFA, ask for a rebate on commission.

3

How to invest like a City insider

Buy stocks when they are out of favour

Buying of stocks under the Bargain Hunters' Investment FlexiSystem is based firmly on common sense, as well as on the application of the rules that are revealed in this book. The main point is that as a medium- to long-term investor, you will be buying stocks when they are cheap and, for that reason, out of favour.

How do you measure value in this sense? This chapter explores various streetwise methods used in the City, and it must be read in conjunction with Chapter 4, which focuses on accounting ratios.

Famous London-based speculative investor and accountant Simon Cawkwell has claimed to the press that textual analysis – defined as company statements and responses from company directors to his questions – and information not generally known to the market are more important than the accounting figures for successful stock market investment.

Take this opinion whence it came. Cawkwell, who has operated under the nom-de-plume *Evil Knievil* (sic), is not known as a long-term value investor. He specializes in short-selling, which involves the selling of shares in troubled companies that he does not own, then hopefully buying the shares at a lower price and keeping the difference before he delivers the certificates. He has made much money from this practice but it is not recommended except sometimes to traders (see Chapter 13 and, for details of Cawkwell's own book, Chapter 17).

Users of the Bargain Hunters' Investment FlexiSystem who are interested in medium- to long-term investment should buy and hold shares rather than selling short. In this context, timing of purchases, although not so important as with other trading, should not be ignored.

With an eye to good timing, some users of the Bargain Hunters' Investment system buy shares when there is a lot of business in the related call options. These options give buyers the right to *buy* the underlying share within a given time period at a fixed price. The call option activity indicates that some investors think the share price will rise and so enable them to exercise the option and buy the underlying shares for less than their market value.

On a more basic issue of timing, you should try to avoid buying at the top of the market. For instance, in May 1998, when the FTSE 100 index was bubbling merrily – if a little shakily – above the 6,000 level, economists and analysts were cautioning that world stock markets were riding too high.

As night follows day, the market correction came in mid-1998 and, by September, the FTSE 100 index had dropped below the 5,000 level – a technical 'correction' that many strategists felt was too steep.

This, paradoxically as it may seem to the uninitiated, was good news for the astute value investor who had held back from buying stocks until such a time as this. For every misfortune, there is an upside, and it is when the market is down that there are bargains to be had.

The views of City analysts matter

No matter how depressed or volatile are current market conditions, you should continue to take an interest in what City analysts say about an individual stock or the direction of the market, and you should sometimes be ready to act on their advice.

We have examined the role of analysts cursorily in Chapter 1. Here, I would add that analysts not only proffer stock recommendations, they help make them true. For further free analysts' consensus forecasts updated daily, consult Hemmington Scott's UK Equities Direct service on the Internet (www.hemscott.com).

Of course, if an investment bank is corporate broker to a company, its analyst may tirelessly promote the shares as a buy, at which point doubt may legitimately be shed on the objectivity of his or her advice.

On the other hand, the corporate broker to a company knows a good deal about its strengths and weaknesses, and for this reason should at least be listened to carefully.

Obviously analysts are not the only source of information to assist your investment decisions. In the rest of this chapter we will look at three main areas. First, how to obtain your information for successful investment; second, company-specific issues you should consider; and third, the macroeconomic perspective.

On the information front, a few of the world's top fund managers boast that they do not bother to keep much of an eye on day-to-day financial and economic news. But most do, and oblivion to news flow is a luxury that you cannot afford.

The importance of keeping up with company news

You should be particularly attentive when quoted companies make carefully prepared statements about past and future trading as they release their interim or full year results. At this point, all the companies – even the small ones – vie for press coverage.

At around this time, City analysts are often jogged into changing forecasts. Fund managers act on these changes when buying or selling shares perhaps for several million pounds per transaction. All this will affect the price at which you buy or sell your shares, particularly in any of the FTSE 100 companies, which are by far the most actively traded in the UK. So keeping an eye on news flow is vital.

It is without doubt a good idea to read the *Financial Times (FT)* – preferably daily but, if not, on Saturdays. This is Europe's most influential business newspaper (available on the Web at www.ft.com), and is worth taking to scan, amongst other things, the *Lex* column, which provides critical comment on individual companies across Europe. You can obtain the *Lex* column, and a dedicated archive, online at www.ft.com/hippocampus/lex.

Lex – written by a dedicated team of journalists who make regular contact with leading City analysts on an anonymous basis – can send the share price soaring or plummeting. It is a window on the current thinking about a stock in certain leading City brokers, although there are always alternative views.

You should also read the financial pages of a quality daily newspaper such as the *Daily Telegraph*. The electronic version is available on the Internet, complete with a useful archive service (www. telegraph.co.uk.). Meanwhile, do not ignore middle of the road tabloids like the *Daily Mail*. Company chairmen like to get news into these papers because their wives read them, according to the founder of one leading City PR agency. You can gain access online to the news archives of the *Daily Mail*, *Mail on Sunday* and *Evening Standard* at This Is Money (www.thisismoney.com).

To obtain City news on the morning it happens, coupled with the latest share prices of major UK quoted companies (updated every 20 minutes), I strongly recommend you use the City pages of the *Evening Standard* online (www.thisislondon.com).

Generally, for results news in the national press, the reporting companies – fronted by their PR agencies – set the agenda. The companies wine and dine journalists and (separately, with a more in-depth approach) analysts, take them on expenses-paid trips around sites, and deliver carefully prepared speeches that represent the company in a favourable light.

The PR agencies often take the lead, although from behind the scenes. The story you read in the press may represent a major company in a better-than-deserved light – usually thanks to the machinations of a spin doctor in the course of a long-term campaign on its client's behalf.

What you really want to read is a newspaper report on a company or sector that digs a little deeper, uncovering something more than the glossed-over picture presented by the companies and their PR agencies. You sometimes get this in the *FT*. You also get it in the quality Sunday press, where journalists have often had the luxury of time to do some spadework.

Whatever you read in the newspapers about a company, do not take the implications at face value. Ring up analysts, which is relatively easy if they are quoted in an article as you will then have their names and their firms. Ask them for their opinions on the company. Ring up the company's registrar and obtain the accounts, which you can then read carefully with the help of Chapter 4 of this book, discovering actual or potential problems and strengths.

Subscribe to *Investors Chronicle* and to its more recently established rival *Shares*, and take note of the information reported. Both magazines sometimes get their recommendations wrong but they are a useful source of ideas. *Investors Chronicle* has a particularly useful section that summarizes investment recommendations from the

City's major brokers. It also has a useful Web site (www. investorschronicle.co.uk), where you have access to FAQs, and to the magazine's archives. For further advice on tipsheets worth reading, turn to Chapter 17, and consult the Web site of Tipsheets.co.uk (www.tipsheets.co.uk) for formal details, and facilities for subscribing.

Reading between the lines

In press reports about quoted companies, news that is presented as depressing in broad terms may, paradoxically as it may seem, be considered beneficial for shareholders. The following example demonstrates this.

At one point, Shell Transport & Trading put out a gloomy trading statement. The press carried shock-horror stories about job losses expected to arise from Shell's planned office closures.

However, some leading oil industry analysts were looking at Shell's strategy positively from the point of view of shareholders. Shell's cost-cutting measures, including the shutting down of some offices, would enable higher returns and stimulate growth. This was likely to provide a fillip to the share price, they argued. Of course, not everybody in the City came to such an optimistic conclusion.

Sectors can be inter-linked

In considering such company-specific news, you should view it in the context of the relevant sector. In addition, sectors can be inter-linked, and good news in one sector may have an adverse or other effect on another.

For example, insatiable demand from retailers for prime sites at urban shopping centres has led to constantly rising rents on the renewal of their leases every five years. While this is a burden on retailers, it is excellent news for their landlords – quoted property companies.

Sometimes, events can have the same effect on more than one sector. For instance, at the time of writing and earlier, merger activity in Europe's banking sector has been sending up the share price of insurers as well as banks. This is partly because banking mergers typically involve a 'bancassurance' element.

When the markets are volatile, buy stocks in a defensive sector

Financials, like other major defensive sectors, withstand volatile markets like nothing else. For instance, in the aftermath of a recent severe market correction, the share prices of mortgage banks such as Halifax, Alliance & Leicester and Northern Rock had held up startlingly well.

This made sense as the mortgage banks were viewed by the market as a safe haven. Mortgage lending had historically not been too badly affected by an adverse economic climate. On the bear side, analysts in a number of firms noted that mortgage banks had lower margins and less fee income than clearing banks, with the result that their gearing into bad debts was higher.

In comparison, the share prices of clearing banks had fallen by a sector average of about 25 per cent at that point, and so were looking cheap. National Westminster Bank in particular looked good value, given that it was yet to reap the benefits of its ongoing cost-cutting measures.

Another example of a defensive sector is that of brewers. Beer is always in demand, and it has the benefit of low fixed costs, excise duty becoming payable only after the beer has been sold. But some brewers are more vulnerable to an economic downturn than others because they have diverse interests. They are typically exposed to the not-so-defensive hotel industry and other leisure outlets, diluting the defensive nature of their brewing interests.

Even when a sector is almost wholly defensive, such as pharmaceuticals, the investment value of companies included in it will vary enormously. Although people buy drugs whatever the economic climate, they are more likely to favour some manufacturers than others. Check which pharmaceutical companies are market leaders and which are losing market share in crucial growth fields such as asthma treatment or HIV-related therapy, and you may find surprisingly wide differences.

Unsurprisingly, some pharmaceutical companies that are weak in certain areas go to enormous lengths to obfuscate this and, unless you have a specialist knowledge of the sector, you are best off getting hold of a top analyst's research material to assist your investigation.

These examples from the banking, brewing and pharmaceutical sectors show that it not enough to select indiscriminately from defensive sectors during a declining stock market. You need to select the most undervalued and recession-proofed stocks within your chosen sector, and you cannot do this without a little detective work. Even then, be prepared to wait for your profits.

Take a long-term view

From a value investing perspective, the more willing you are to take a long-term view on a stock, the better you will be rewarded, although there are, of course, some exceptions to this rule. Few will be prepared to ride out a slow recovery in a stock for the partly valid reason that distant benefits are always less certain.

But long-term benefits can seem probable, as at one low point they did for Marks & Spencer. The legendary UK-based retailer had invested substantially in overseas expansion. However, the market had not given the retailer's share price credit for benefits likely to result from the move, bullish analysts argued.

The bears on Marks & Spencer disagreed, and this is nothing new. In the City, analysts from different broking houses, even if fed with more or less the same information, as is usually the case, are famous for disagreeing on a company's prospects. In this case, in the period that ensued, the bears seemed right. However, the story on Marks & Spencer is not over yet, and some retail analysts see the company as a candidate for takeover, which could send the share price soaring from the extremely low level that it has hit at the time of writing.

When making your own investment decisions in such cases, it pays to consider both sides of the argument. For this reason, and given potential biases arising from corporate brokerships, you should never rely blindly on the views of a single analyst, particularly when they are strong.

In another example, the composite insurer Guardian Royal Exchange, while it existed under that name, had two camps amongst City analysts: those who recommended the stock as a buy and those who categorized it as a sell. The bull case for GRE was that it was undervalued compared to its peers when compared with the strength of its assets, while the bear case was that it was significantly invested in equities with all attendant risks (as well as rewards), and had a disparate business.

GRE's share price had fallen badly at one point in 1998. Later, it soared as GRE became the subject of takeover speculation, leading in early 1999 to a successful cash bid from French insurer AXA through its UK subsidiary Sun Life & Provincial.

Buy on merger or takeover speculation

When a company is seen as a potential target for a takeover or merger, the price can stay buoyed, even if the share's underlying value is not so great. For example, insurer Norwich Union has not always been a runaway favourite amongst City analysts, arguably because it has been highly priced on value criteria.

However, Norwich Union, despite its high market capitalization, was constantly seen as a prospective takeover target, and it is arguably this that kept the share price steadier than that of some other insurers.

When the takeover possibilities crystallize into action, even at a very preliminary stage, the target company's share price may soar. Competing predators may raise their bids if earlier offers have been rejected. If the takeover deal proceeds but is not considered particularly good, the acquiring company's shares could fall sharply.

Of course the target company's shares may similarly fall if the proposed takeover fails, particularly if there is no other in the offing. It is at this point that you may like to buy. If the company has been subject to takeover speculation once, there is a good chance it will eventually be so again. Similarly, the price is often unjustifiably weak following a profit warning.

Alternatively, you should try to spot a takeover candidate before any predator has shown its hand. This is a matter of spotting a company when it is vulnerable. For instance, companies that lose and do not immediately replace their Chief Executive are potential targets. For instance, telecommunications group Cable & Wireless has been seen by some as ripe for takeover since the departure of its Chief Executive Dick Brown.

If there is a whiff of takeover interest in a stock, others in the sector stand to benefit. This is particularly so if the takeover actually happens. For example, when US-based Web portal provider Yahoo in late January 1999 announced the takeover of Geocities, shares of both companies soared and so did those of many other Internet stocks.

Profit warning and scandal: a buying opportunity.

After a company issues profit warning or news of accounting discrepancies, the company's shares may plummet as much as 75 per cent or more, and frequently at least 25 per cent. This is often the cue to pick up stock. At one point, MFI fell 75 per cent in less than a year.

There are plenty of similar fallen angels that, at depressed levels when out of favour, can represent exceptionally good value. In some cases, you should buy the depressed shares, sit tight on them, and forget about them for up to a few years.

But before committing your money, make sure that the bombed-out stocks have plenty of assets, not too much debt, and the potential for regaining their strength and climbing the ladder once again. Some companies will have been hit so hard that they will take many years to get their second wind, if they ever do. The penny share universe is full of such dogs.

If you are looking for shares whose price may be hyped up by frenzied buying from institutions, and promotional activities by investment banks, look no further than new issues or, as they are known in the US, initial public offerings (IPOs).

New issues

New issues often take the form of an offer for sale, under which shares are offered to the public. Alternatively, there may be an offer for subscription, where the company sets a minimum subscription level. If this level is not reached, the offer may be scrapped.

Alternative forms of a new issue of shares include a placing, under which the company's broker privately allots shares to its clients, or an introduction, under which shares are already held by many investors, and the company requires permission for the shares to be dealt on the market.

Whichever way it is organized, a new issue will frequently make private investors a quick profit – if they have bought it early, at or near the opening price. But even if you make an immediate paper profit from investing in a new issue, you may be better off holding on to the stock rather than 'stagging' it, ie selling very quickly after you have bought.

The flip side of the coin is that new issues can flop – particularly in the case of astronomically overpriced technology companies, although in market conditions at the time of writing most of these are ending the first day of trading at a fat premium to the issue price.

In the case of the failures – which do not always show themselves in their true colours on the first day of trading – one major problem is that investment banks promote new issues hard, and their analysts can be duly over-optimistic about the company's potential.

In some banks, brokers are penalized if buyers of new issues resell too soon. It is typically the private investors whom they try to keep well loaded with stock. But the story for private investors is not entirely one of grief. When, for instance, it comes to share restructuring, you are treated in the same way as institutional investors.

Share splits and scrip issues

Once you own shares, you may find that they are restructured under a share split or scrip issue, increasing the number of shares in issue and lowering the share price.

Under a share split, the nominal (also known as par) value of a share – as distinct from its price – is split, with the result that the shares are proportionately multiplied and the share price is to a similar extent diluted. For instance, a company with a share price of 60p may split its nominal value of 10p in two. In this way, the new nominal value per share is 5p, the number of shares in issue will have doubled and the new share price is 30p.

A scrip, or capitalization, issue is sometimes wrongly confused with a share split. In a scrip issue, free shares are issued to existing shareholders. This is an accounting exercise involving a transfer within the company's reserves, all of which are owned by the shareholders, so, in principle, nothing is gained.

Following the scrip issue, the price of shares is reduced so that, theoretically, the total new holding is of the same value as the old one. For instance, one share priced at 60p may, as a result of a scrip issue, be changed into three shares priced at 20p each.

In practice, a company's share price will often rise on news of a planned share split or scrip issue. Investors prefer to have low-priced shares than high-priced ones. They believe illogically that they are in this way getting more value for their money, and this can become a self-fulfilling prophecy.

Rights issues

In a separate initiative, a company may ask its shareholders for more money by announcing a rights issue, which gives them the right to buy new shares at a specified price. For instance, as a shareholder, you may be offered a 1 for 4 rights issue, giving you the right to buy one new share for every four you already hold.

The new shares are cheaper than your existing shares. For this reason, after the rights issue has taken place, the share price evens out to a level slightly below that of your original shares. If shares are sold to you 'cum' a rights or scrip issue, this means they are with it. If the shares come 'ex' the issue, they are without it.

A rights issue can sometimes be good value as it enables you to buy shares without paying a stockbroker's commission. Your decision on whether or not to participate should depend on how the company plans to use the capital so raised. If, for instance, the company seeks funding from a rights issue for an unwise acquisition or for ill-conceived expansion plans, do not get involved. The magazine *Investors Chronicle* offers advice on whether to take up rights issues.

Warrants

Another way in which new share capital may be created is through warrants. These are sometimes given away with a new issue, perhaps in the ratio of one warrant for five shares. The warrant will give you the right to subscribe for an extra share at a fixed price on a specified date perhaps several years ahead. If it is not exercised, the warrant becomes worthless.

The subscription price is usually set above the current price of the shares, so any value in the warrant is time value. If the share price soars, the lower-priced warrant will rise similarly in percentage terms, but by a larger actual amount, and will similarly fall by more if the share price declines. In this way, warrants are highly geared.

Warrants have often been compared with traded options, but differ in that they give the right to buy a *new* share, while the option gives the right to buy an *existing* share from its owner. Warrants can be bought and sold in their own right, a potentially lucrative although risky area of investment.

In relation to a share restructuring or otherwise, the more informa-tion you have about a company's plans, the more easily you will be able to decide on whether to buy or sell its shares. The company should of course play its part in keeping you in the know.

Some companies are insufficiently communicative to shareholders

Against their own long-term interest, some companies are notoriously uncommunicative to brokers as well as to shareholders and the press. As a result, the market may assume the worst, and the share price may underestimate the group's long-term prospects.

For instance, the chairman of one particular major quoted company notoriously refuses to give interviews, and the company has severely under-performed in comparison with its peers. For obvious reasons, I am not going to name this or any of the other offenders in this book. But if you come across an uncommunicative company, think carefully before investing. Amongst the more severe problems the company may avoid addressing properly in public is that of debt.

Check out a company's exposure to bad debt

When you are buying stocks in volatile markets, you must pay careful attention to a company's exposure to bad debt. For example, when the rouble virtually collapsed recently, UK banks seemed less badly hit than some had feared owing to their limited Russian exposure. In contrast, they remained extremely vulnerable to Asia's ongoing financial crisis.

Besides looking at company specifics, you should take into account macroeconomic trends and you should assume an international perspective in selecting your investments. We will conclude this chapter with a brief investigation into these two areas.

The markets are affected by economic trends but these are hard to predict

Bottom-up investors scrutinize company specifics first and foremost.

Included in their number is US stock market guru Peter Lynch who has famously not set much store by economics in his incredibly successful stock selection procedures. In contrast, *top-down* investors look at the macroeconomic picture first, followed by the relevant sector and, only then, at the company's financials.

City investment houses usually incorporate strong elements of both the bottom-up and top-down approaches, and this can lead to conflicting recommendations. It is not uncommon for the strategists of a major investment bank (who scrutinize, amongst other things, the macroeconomic picture) to disagree with its analysts (who are more concerned with particular companies) on the desirability of investing in a particular sector.

To cover their backs, strategists keep revising their forecasts as economic conditions change. This means their trailing forecasts may be worth very little in terms of predicting the future, even if they show insight into the current state of the economy.

It only adds fuel to the flames that, at any given time, economic statistics present a conflicting story when called on to assist forecasts in the areas of, for instance, inflation or interest rates. The more skilled the analyst or strategist, the more contradictions he or she will notice. The analyst terms these complexities.

For instance, in the second half of 1998, manufacturing was depressed but consumer spending was quite buoyant. Unemployment was rising – good news to combat inflation – and interest rates looked likely to fall slightly in the medium term on the back of expected US interest rate cuts following hints to that effect by US Federal Reserve chairman Alan Greenspan.

Was the country going into recession or not? A case could be made either way. At any given time, economic problems in Asia – responsible for depressed prices in so many stocks – could worsen or (less likely) improve. The same was true of Russia's financial crisis.

At this point, the status of US president Bill Clinton had been called into question over a sex scandal, and this was adversely affecting Wall Street and, by proxy, other major world stock markets. The oil price was depressed and there was speculation – but, of course, no certainty – that it had reached rock bottom.

The markets, true to form, were like a child – reacting exaggeratedly to even the slightest upheaval on the economic or political world landscape. The biggest upheaval to come was, of course, a new unified Europe.

Develop an international perspective

The key issue to remember about Europe is that it represents the future of investing for all of us. The UK is already perceived as part of a broader European investment universe, although it hung back from joining the first participants in EMU.

Logically, European stock markets are now tending to move in unison although they of course retain country-specific idiosyncrasies. You can get a feel for how it all works by keeping up with European stock market news. One major issue at the time of writing is standard-ization of company reporting across Europe.

Given these trends, you can no longer afford to ignore the knock-on effect that price movements in a given sector in one European country have on stocks in the same sector in the rest of the continent, an area we will look at in more detail in Chapter 13 (on day trading).

If, for example, you are keen to invest in telecoms companies, you should be looking at not only the UK incumbents but also Telecom Italia, Portugal Telecom, France Telecom and Deutsche Telekom. Some of these companies have been seeking alliances across European boundaries.

If you want to go the whole hog and spread your investment risk across Europe, you may find problems obtaining information about individual companies. If, at this stage, you invest in Europe through UK stockbrokers, the deals will be expensive, but you will be protected by the Financial Services Act – no matter where you invest. As most overseas companies issue bearer certificates, which do not carry your name, you will need a custodian – usually a major bank – to hold the shares in safety.

With the advent of online trading as well as Europe's greater promi-nence in the investment arena, it will only get easier and cheaper to buy and sell Euro stocks. The foundations were laid when, in 1998, the London Stock Exchange announced its plans for an alliance with the German Stock Exchange to form a pan-European bourse that would initially trade about 140 stocks. Italy's Borsa Italiana and Spain's Madrid bourse subsequently announced their plans to join the new grouping, and, in January 1999, the French and Swiss exchanges announced that they would form their own alliance.

It was a major breakthrough when, in September 1999, the chief executives of the eight European exchanges agreed on a common basis for trading in European blue chip shares, and on one electronic interface. The agreement, which will be fully implemented by November 2000, marks the establishment of an integrated cross-border market for major European stocks.

As an investor in Europe, it may take you a while yet to feel comfortable with buying continental stocks. If so, you may prefer to invest in unit trusts rather than in individual stocks. Should you follow this route, the same broad rules apply as for buying any unit trusts (see Chapter 10). Consult the magazine *Money Management* or Micropal online to compare their past track records and select funds that regularly hit the top quartile in terms of performance, ideally buying into these at a reduced charge from a discount broker.

Where angels fear to tread

Bolder users of the Bargain Hunters' Investment FlexiSystem are sinking large sums of money into local stocks in more esoteric areas of the world than Western Europe. A favourite territory has been Asia.

When I began writing this book, Asian markets had started rallying from the severe lows to which they had plunged. The economic crisis that had caused the lows was not entirely over and some expert opinion went so far as to suggest that this was a prolonged sucker's rally – a prelude to worse market declines.

For users of our system, stock selection is more important than timing and, without a doubt, the Asian crisis created the scenario of many stocks trading at prices far below their net asset value. For *bona fide* value investors prepared to take a calculated risk, it has been a feast.

As this book goes to press, Japan's stock market is enjoying a boom, and should rise further, given that it is an upturn in its early stages compared with the prolonged Wall Street and London stock market bull markets. On a long-term historical perspective, the Japanese stock market has proven itself capable of soaring to great heights.

If you buy *any* Asian stocks, be prepared for volatility in their price movements. There is a thin market in some of the shares. In Hong Kong, for instance, shares available to the public have at times represented only half of the $240 billion local stock market's capitalization.

To maximize gains on your Asian stocks in volatile market conditions, you will either need to cultivate a trading mentality – broadly covered in Chapter 13 – and have access to real-time prices and news flow, or you must be prepared to be patient.

In early 2000, the most attractive Asian investments were technology stocks, but some of these are not cutting-edge, and you need to be selective. Hong Kong Telecom, for instance, has been judged under-appreciated in terms of its Internet value, and search engine provider Yahoo! Japan is acknowledged as a clear market leader in its field. For relevant up-to-date news flow and research, go to the Asian pages of the Web site interactive investor international (www.iii-asia.com). For financial statements of Japanese companies (English language version), go to japanfinancials.com/.

Buying ADRs

If you are buying shares in markets outside the US or Europe, it is a good idea to pick them up in the form of American Depositary Receipts (ADRs) where these are available. ADRs are US domestic securities representing ownership of a foreign stock, and are available through brokers that deal in US shares.

ADRs work out slightly more expensive than the underlying securities, making this market unpopular amongst some institutional investors. However, ADRs give you access to proper reporting information and fast news flow, and, as an ADR-holder, you will be notified of dividends and structural reorganizations – services sometimes denied to those who buy shares in exotic home markets.

In total, more than 1,600 ADRs from more than 16 countries are listed in the US. They are usually backed by a US bank where the original shares are deposited, and may be listed on any US exchange. To find out more, I would recommend you visit via the Internet the highly informative ADR Web site of US investment bank J P Morgan (www.adr.com).

Golden rules covered in this chapter

Rule 15   When purchasing shares, do not ignore timing.

Rule 16   Keep an eye on news flow and read between the lines.

Rule 17   Note that sectors can be inter-linked.

Rule 18   When the markets are volatile, buy stocks in a defensive sector.

Rule 19   New issues can be risky.

Rule 20   Take a long-term view on stocks.

Rule 21   When making investment decisions, it pays to consider both sides of the argument.

Rule 22   Buy on takeover prospects.

Rule 23   If a stock falls massively owing to a profit warning or scandal or similar, there is likely to have been an overreaction and it may be a good time to buy. But first make sure that the bombed-out stock has plenty of assets.

Rule 24   Check out a company's management policy.

Rule 25   Check a company's exposure to bad debt.

Rule 26   Investment houses can give fickle or contradictory recommendations.

Rule 27   Develop a pan-European perspective in your investment activities.

Rule 28   If you are investing in exotic markets, buy ADRs where possible.

4

The magic of ratio analysis

In Chapter 3, we looked at the broad investment issues that you must consider, as a professional investor would, when you carry out the Bargain Hunters' Investment FlexiSystem. In this chapter we will focus on accounting specifics. Accounting is the language of business, and by the time you have read this chapter, you will have a grasp of its basic principles and how to use ratios culled from the annual report and accounts in making your investment decisions.

You do not need to work out the ratios yourself, although, to understand what they mean, it helps to know how they are calculated. Some ratios are listed with the share prices in the newspapers, but your best sources for the UK stock market are either online or in up-to-date editions of *REFS* or, failing that, *The Estimate Directory*. It is largely by comparing the main ratios that you will select stocks for your portfolio.

Your share portfolio should include blue chips, and perhaps some growth companies, the proportions depending on how risk averse you are, which in turn is influenced by your stage in life and your personal circumstances. Whatever the make-up of your portfolio, you will find the ratios covered in this chapter relevant in selecting its stocks.

Experienced readers who are *au fait* with working their way through a set of company accounts may wish to skip this chapter but others should read it carefully. If you don't take it all in at the first reading, do not worry. You can always refer back to it.

Getting to grips with a company report and accounts

You will use the ratios defined in this chapter for evaluating quoted companies against both their own past years, and competitors in the same sector. These ratios are made up from figures that you can take from the latest company report and accounts.

Most UK-quoted companies issue accounts twice a year in some form. After the first six months, whose starting date will vary, an interim statement is published. The first-half profits reported on are not necessarily a pro rata indication of the full year profits. Soon after the full year, the company publishes full year figures, known as preliminaries, followed by the official audited annual report and accounts.

It is the official annual report and accounts that are of the most use to you. The main part of these accounts is the profit and loss account, the balance sheet and the cash flow statement and we shall briefly survey all of these in the next few paragraphs. In each case, this year's figures are shown alongside last year's for comparison purposes.

The profit and loss account records the company's profits, and how they were reached, over the previous year. It starts with turnover, which represents all income received by the company. Cost of sales follows, and other expenses, with the net total deducted from turnover to give a trading profit figure. Pre-tax profits – which take interest payments into account – are cited.

Net profit is after tax and dividends due to preference shareholders. The net profit margin, which is net profit divided by sales, will hopefully be rising year by year. The earnings per share is the net profit, divided by the number of shares in issue.

Most companies pay out some of their net profits in dividends and invest some in the business. However, companies in trouble may pay out all their net profits and may even use their reserves to keep up a satisfactory dividend payment. If so, this should serve as a warning that the company may be suffering from problems.

The balance sheet represents a financial snapshot of the company on just one day of its year. For this reason, the picture it presents may not be typical for the year as a whole. The balance sheet shows the company's assets less liabilities, and the net total of these is balanced by shareholders' funds.

The top part of the balance sheet shows assets and liabilities. First there are tangible fixed assets, such as land and machinery. Land is often undervalued owing to historical valuations, and machinery is sometimes overvalued. Intangible fixed assets, if any, are shown next. They typically include goodwill[1], which is the difference between the purchase price of an acquired company and its net asset value, and brands, which are controversial due to disagreements on fair valuation.

Next come current assets, which are split into stock, debtors and cash-in-hand. The valuation of stock is not always reliable and debtors can be slow to pay. Cash is the most reliable current asset.

After assets come liabilities, which represent what the company owes. Current liabilities, ie payable within one year, include trade creditors' overdrafts and tax. Current assets less current liabilities are current net assets (or liabilities).

Next shown is the total of all assets less current liabilities. From this figure are deducted long-term liabilities, consisting of loans that do not need to be paid within a year.

The company's total assets less total liabilities on the balance sheet amount to its net assets. The net assets are 'balanced' by various kinds of capital and reserves – described as shareholders' funds – in the bottom half of the balance sheet. The figures must balance, with net assets invariably equal to shareholders' funds.

The cash flow statement is important as it shows how much hard cash is available to the company and may reveal some accounting manipulation. A company's net operating cash flow cannot be fudged and may therefore be much less than the trading profit.

The chairman's statement – also included in the accounts – can contain a lot of hype and you must learn to read between the lines when assessing this, as well as to heed any warnings issued.

The auditor's report normally tells you that everything is true and fair. But auditors can have a cosy relationship with companies and, in a few well-publicized cases, have missed indications of fraud. If the report is in any way qualified, be extremely wary.

Otherwise, the nasties are often concealed in the notes to the financial statements, and it is worthwhile sifting through these notes with a fine-tooth comb. Watch out in particular under 'Contingent Liabilities' for potential high expenses that the company may face if, for example,

---

1 Under FRS10, which applies to accounting periods ending after 28 December 1998, goodwill must be capitalized as an intangible asset and amortized over a period. It was previously possible also to write goodwill off to reserves.

it loses a forthcoming legal case. Watch too for a change in the method of depreciation, which would affect both the life of assets and the hit to the profit and loss account.

These are the bare bones of a set of accounts and, coupled with the ratio analysis techniques explained in the rest of this chapter, will be enough to get you started reading them. Some of the highest-calibre analysts and corporate financiers in the City argue that the plainer the annual report, the more likely it is to be useful, and they find that lavish colour pictures of smiling personnel feature most in the company reports of operations with something to hide. For guidance on further reading related to understanding company accounts, turn to Chapter 17.

Earlier in the 20th century, interpretation of ratios culled from the annual report and accounts was *virtually the only skill that mattered* in value investing as defined by Benjamin Graham, the founder of investment analysis.

The Benjamin Graham approach to valuation

Benjamin Graham was a US-based mathematician and classics enthusiast who developed his value investing system in the 1920s. The value investor, as defined by Graham, acquires sound securities that sell for no more than intrinsic value and then holds them until there is a strong reason for selling.

In 1926, Graham formed the Benjamin Graham joint account, a pooled account that he managed in exchange for a profit share. His method of investing in shares for the account proved highly successful. Over a 30-year period, Graham's clients earned an average 17 per cent return.

Graham taught his investment techniques at an evening class at Columbia University. He advised his pupils that investment was based on thorough analysis, promising safety of capital and an expected satisfactory return. He dismissed as speculation any financial decision that was based only on forecasts for the stock market as a whole.

Graham's star pupil at the Columbia classes was the young Warren Buffett. In the years to come, Buffet was to prove himself America's most successful investor by using investment techniques that were largely but not exclusively Graham's.

There is a so-called *Buffetology* industry today, including books published on Buffett's investment techniques, tipsheets that have claimed to apply his principles to stock selection, and, at the time of writing, a day-long conference in London devoted to Buffett's investment techniques, although sadly the master himself was not attending.

I do not propose to lend my own voice to Buffett's adulation here. Suffice it to say that while Buffett and a few other masters of investment have made Graham's principles work for them, most investors have not.

There is an excuse. In today's markets, the late Graham's principles are so stringent that there are sometimes, particularly in bullish times, no stocks available that he would have approved for purchase. So what are Graham's investment criteria?

According to Graham, a value investor buys shares with the same approach that he or she would use for buying the entire underlying company. You should buy only if the company's total market capitalization (ie share price multiplied by number of shares in issue) is two-thirds or less of the company's net current assets (ie current assets, excluding stock, less current liabilities).

Under Graham's criteria, you should sell when a company's market capitalization has reached 100 per cent of its net current assets' value. Meanwhile, if the accounting is questionable, the securities must be shunned, no matter how safe they may appear.

Graham had other similarly stringent investment criteria and, in 1934, he published his entire system, with Professor David L Dodd as co-author, in his classic textbook *Security Analysis*. The book was seen as radical in its time. It has had several updates – with other authors involved – and is claimed to be read by numerous investors today. The purists are said to prefer Graham's original edition, and copies of this tome pass hands amongst collectors at premium prices.

Security Analysis is very hard going, even for many investment professionals, and most of my colleagues in the City of London would appear not to have read it (although some have made a spirited attempt). It is without a doubt possible to be a highly rated securities analyst, and never to have read Benjamin Graham.

More readable than *Security Analysis* is Graham's book for the man in the street, *The Intelligent Investor*, which has similarly achieved the status of a classic. Buffet described it as 'by far the best book on investing ever written'.

If you want to get to grips with Graham's ideas, you do not need initially to read the master's own words, a task that can be demanding and time-consuming. Instead, start by reading a summary of them. For more details on where to find this, turn to Chapter 17.

We will now leave Graham's criteria alone and will instead look at how you should apply certain valuation ratios under the Bargain Hunters' Investment Flexisystem. Of these ratios, the best known – and probably the most widely used – is the price/earnings (PE) ratio.

The PE ratio

The PE ratio is a yardstick for assessing how a company is rated against its peers. It also tells you at current levels for how many years' profit you will have to pay in purchasing the shares. The PE ratio consists of the share price, divided by the earnings per share (eps). The eps is defined as profits after tax divided by the number of shares in issue.

Both the historic PE – based on last year's eps – and the prospective PE are relevant. In either case, if a company's PE is high compared with the sector and/or market average, the shares could be over-valued, but could still shoot higher for a while (particularly in a short-term trading situation, as covered in Chapter 13).

If the PE is low, the shares could be undervalued, although this might be for a very good reason. The experience of those who use the Bargain Hunters' Investment FlexiSystem shows that, for large companies, a low PE ratio means that the share price is likely to beat the market, at least in the medium to long term[2].

In comparing PE ratios, make sure that you are setting like against like. A company's historic PE (using last year's eps) should be compared with the same for another company or the sector as a whole. Similarly, the prospective PE (using next year's consensus forecast eps) should be compared with the same.

The historic PE will be listed in the newspapers, and to find the sector and market averages for comparison purposes, you should look at the FT's Actuaries Share Indices (The UK Series) in Monday's *Financial Times*. The indices also show the gross yield, net yield, net

2 US fund manager David Dreman found from his recent researches into the Standard & Poor's database a strong correlation between a low PE ratio and out-performers amongst large companies. Conversely, US investment guru William O'Neill has found from his own surveys that a low PE ratio is no indication of future out-performance.

dividend cover and other figures for all sectors in the London stock market.

So, for example, on 23 November 1998, the net weighted average PE ratio for the insurance sector, included in this table, was 19.3x. Any insurer that had a PE below this figure would have been deemed to have a below-average multiple.

Another way to find a comparative PE is in *REFS*. This lists the prospective PE – based on the next 12 months' consensus forecast eps – comparing it to the sector and to the market as a whole. The prospective PE has the merit of being more up to date than its historic counterpart in that it takes the future analysts' consensus earnings forecast into account.

Predictably, analysts' earnings forecasts that make up the consensus vary widely and are often wrong. The charitable explanation is that unforeseen macroeconomic or company-specific events arise and change the direction of expected profits.

If the company knows in advance of a major change in earnings expectations, it should give some warning to analysts. Failing this, analysts will rightly blame the company for not keeping it informed if it turns out that, for this reason, their forecasts had been significantly misplaced. Of course, a company's profit warning typically sends the share price plummeting.

Bear in mind also that the eps may have been worked out differently by companies and, if so, earnings comparisons between the companies are misleading. The eps is, you will recall, used to make up the PE ratio. For instance, when the eps is calculated on an FRS3 basis (referring to the relevant accounting standard), unusual or one-off items are included in the after-tax profits calculation. On this basis, the eps figure could be very different from when it is calculated on a 'normalized' basis, ie excluding unusual items.

In a hastily written brokers' research note, for instance, it is not always made clear on what basis the eps has been calculated. Some City professionals, as well as most financial journalists, are vague about the distinctions.

Even if the eps is calculated in the same way for two companies being compared, the figure is open to manipulation. Some of the most blatant abuses in company accounting over the years have resulted in the massaging of earnings.

In implementing such creative accounting, the aim of the finance directors of quoted companies is not always to enhance earnings as much as possible in a given year. They prefer to present the eps as steadily rising year on year, as this is what the City rewards.

Before FRS3 was implemented in the early 1990s, one of the most outrageous ways of manipulating the eps figure was by arbitrary selection of items to be included above the line as exceptional items or below the line as extraordinary items.

This loophole was closed by FRS3 but other ways remain to massage the eps and so, ultimately, the PE ratio. Tax losses will benefit the eps, until they are used up, at which point the upwards trend of the eps over the years can dramatically reverse. Until the bubble bursts, the creative accounting can be incredibly difficult to detect. City analysts are sometimes incapable of understanding the nuances in accounting, and nor do they always want to, as recent surveys have corroborated.

As a variation on the simple PE ratio, analysts often prefer to look at the PE relative (PER), which reflects the PE ratio of the company in question in comparison with that of the market as a whole. The figure is expressed in percentage terms, with a PER of 100 representing that of the market as a whole. By comparison, a PER of 65 would be significantly lower than the PER of the market, while a PER of 135 would be proportionately higher.

But you must also compare the PER of a company with that of its sector. If, for instance, the sector is growth-orientated, all the companies in it may have high PERs. In that case, a high PER for one company within the sector does not make it stand out from its peers.

The PE ratio, whether expressed in relative terms or not, has limitations. One man who has acknowledged this publicly is private client stock market guru Jim Slater. His own contribution to the literature of investment ratios is the PEG (price earnings divided by growth) ratio, which takes the PE ratio one step further. For his own explanations of the PEG, and his related investment philosophy, you could not do better than turn to his own excellent Web site (www.global-investor.com/slater/index.htm).

The PEG ratio

Many in the City are sceptical about the PEG ratio, but it is, nonetheless, used as an extra weapon in the professional investment analyst's armoury in the analysis of growth stocks in particular. It does not work so well for cyclical or recovery stocks for instance.

The PEG shows the PE ratio in relation to the company's earnings growth rate. It is defined as the prospective PE ratio divided by the prospective average eps growth. Another version – the Fool ratio – based on the criteria of the US-based *Motley Fool Investment Guide*'s team (see Chapter 17 for details of the UK book) is similar except that it is based on a trailing 12-month historic eps growth figure. Either way, the PEG should be significantly less than one if it is to represent value, it has been argued.

Insisting normally on a low PEG for selected growth stocks, Slater has in the past made some excellent share tips in the *Mail on Sunday* and, later, despite some severe short-term fluctuations, in his tipsheet *Jim Slater: Investing for Growth*. But Slater's investment system has other stock selection criteria than just the PEG, some of which require human judgment. How far others can use the Slater system as successfully as its creator is open to question.

If you want to try the Slater system, get to grips with the *REFS* directory (see Chapter 17), which was compiled by the master. Use Slater's so-called filters in selecting stocks from the statistics compiled in *REFS* and good luck to you. Otherwise, as a Slater aficionado, you could just buy what the master recommends.

If you do, buy on a long-term basis and be prepared sometimes to pay a marked-up price. On Mondays, after subscribers have received the latest issue of *Jim Slater: Investing for Growth*, stocks tipped have been known to rise say 12 per cent on the day, and sometimes much more in the days that follow.

Slater's tips sometimes give the share price a fillip in this way, simply because there is a narrow market in some of the small stocks he recommends, and he has plenty of devoted disciples who will buy immediately on his advice. Be warned that some of Slater's tips have been known to flop.

The lazy man's way to capitalize on the Slater methods is to pick up unit trusts in the Slater Growth Fund (www.global-investor. com/slater/slater-i.htm) marketed by fund manager Charles Fry in the UK. The fund specializes in small, undervalued companies with defensive qualities as well as growth potential. In the long term, it has been a top performer, although, at some stages, its return has looked disappointing. The fund is managed by Mark Slater, Jim's son, who, when I interviewed him for *The Sunday Times*, confirmed that he makes significant use of his father's company selection techniques, including the requirement for a low PEG ratio.

However, do not rely too much on the PEG in your own stock

picking, as the ratio's component parts are fraught with uncertainty. A low PE ratio, which would contribute to a low PEG, does not reliably indicate an undervalued stock – particularly in the case of small companies – and recent eps growth, the other contributor, sometimes subsides unexpectedly. Prospective eps growth – as used in Slater's PEG – is based on analysts' consensus forecasts, which may well be wrong. More widely used than the PEG ratio – although not directly comparable – is the return on capital employed (ROCE).

Return on capital employed

The ROCE is a useful yardstick for assessing management performance. In its simplest form, it is calculated as profits before interest payable and tax, divided by capital employed. The profits figure, which, as defined, excludes elements outside management control, can be taken from the profit and loss account. The capital employed may be defined as year-end total assets less total liabilities excluding long-term loans, which may be culled from the balance sheet[3].

The higher a company's ROCE, the better the company is using the assets at its disposal, and, ideally, the figure should be rising year on year. The ROCE can be increased either by producing higher pre-tax, pre-interest profits, or by reducing the level of capital employed. The latter reduction is often made by returning cash to shareholders, so reducing the cash element of the company's assets.

In certain sectors such as retail, some analysts have found an extremely high correlation between changes in the ROCE and the trend of the share price. On this basis, quoted retailers who organized share buybacks would be improving their share price as well as their ROCE.

The profit figures used in the ROCE, as elsewhere, can be rigged by use of a little creative accounting. Cash flow cannot be manipulated in the same way. For this reason, analysts sometimes give cash flow much higher priority than profit ratios, particularly in sectors where it is crucial to a company's ongoing viability.

---

3 A not dissimilar ratio is return on equity, which is net earnings, divided by the total assets less total liabilities. In algebraic terms, the ratio may be broken up into ratios representing profitability, turnover in relation to assets, and borrowings.

EV/EBITDA – a cash-flow-related measure

In assessing capital intensive stocks such as in the telecoms sector, the EV/EBITDA ratio, ie the enterprise value (market capitalization + debt less cash) divided by EBITDA (earnings before interest, tax, depreciation and amortization), is sometimes preferred by analysts to the PE ratio.

The EBITDA figure can be particularly flattering to companies that write off substantial amortization every year after acquiring purchased goodwill as a result of a takeover. The figure, estimated for future years on the basis of discounted cash flows, ignores the impact of amortization, while the eps takes it into account.

In this way, Vodafone may be represented more positively on the basis of the forecast EBITDA than eps over the next few years, owing to its early 1999 acquisition of Airtouch, which involved significant purchased goodwill.

While such use of the EBITDA is widespread in the City, it is recognized that it would not be fair to compare stocks on an EBITDA basis across international borders if the respective countries' tax regimes differ. The reason is that the EBITDA excludes tax. In the telecoms sector, for example, Telecom Italia has a consolidated tax rate of more than 50 per cent, and so cannot realistically be compared on an EV/EBITDA basis with Swisscom, which has a tax rate of less than 25 per cent.

It is no small wonder that the EV/EBITDA multiple is not recognized in accounting terms. For this reason, some analysts ignore it and concentrate on the traditional PE ratio or other earnings-related criteria.

While we will not be using the EV/EBITDA ratio under the Bargain Hunters' Investment FlexiSystem, it is constantly cited in today's analysts' reports and you should be familiar with its usage.

Share price/cash flow per share

The share price/cash flow per share is similar to the EV/EBITDA ratio, although there are some differences. The ratio is defined as the stock's market value, divided by total cash flow (profits plus depreciation and amortization).

A price/cash flow per share ratio that is lower than eps/share is a strong indicator of value, and this is something you should look for.

Discounted cash flows

Meanwhile, a company's discounted cash flow per share is increasingly used by analysts to find out the net present value of future earnings. The analyst calculates whether the return on capital (ie net present value of future earnings) is more than the weighted average cost of capital (WAAC). Only if so is the company considered profitable, but the methods of calculation are far from straightforward. The discount rate used by analysts in calculating the net present value will vary, and a slight difference in this rate can affect the final result enormously.

To calculate the cost of capital, analysts usually use the Capital Asset Pricing Model (CAPM). This involves making a 'guesstimate' of the risk premium for investing in equities over bonds. It also involves using a stock's so-called beta as a measure of the share's volatility and, therefore, investment risk in comparison with that of the market as a whole. The beta is an historic figure and so is not a reliable indicator.

Generally, there are at least three major schools of thought as to how cash flows should be discounted, and we touch on the basics in Chapter 16. At this stage, be aware that forecasts for stock price performance derived from discounted cash flows are based on uncertain assumptions and so are unreliable.

A frightening example of this may be cited. Analysts of some investment houses were promoting Dialog, the supplier of online information, as a good investment up to November 1998, based on discounted cash flow valuations. In mid-November, the company issued a profit warning and the shares more than halved in value. At about this point, the *FT's Lex* Column suggested somewhat unkindly that the company would be known by its nickname Dial-a-dog.

Current and quick ratios

A vital check on a company's liquidity is the current ratio, defined as current assets divided by current liabilities (figures available on the balance sheet). To be really comfortable, the current ratio should be over 2, but companies in some sectors do not need as high a figure as those in others. The quick ratio (acid test), which is current assets less stock and work-in-progress divided by current liabilities (all figures again on the balance sheet), should be over 1.

If liquidity, as demonstrated by the current or quick ratio, is too low, the company may react by cutting its dividend. To measure the current level of dividend, look at the dividend yield.

Dividend yield

The dividend yield is the gross annual dividend expressed as a percentage of the share price. Like other valuation measures, a company's dividend yield is best measured against that of its peers. Alternatively, examine the company's dividend yield relative. If this is higher or lower than 100, it is to that extent above or below the market average.

The City seeks dividends that steadily increase every year. When a large company fails to increase its dividend or, worse, cuts it, and is not overtly planning to use the extra retained profits to finance expansion, the reason is likely to be that it needs cash for its own survival. Under such circumstances, the share price is likely to overreact – downwards.

As a company's share price falls, its yield rises. A high yield is seen as advantageous for value investors as it suggests an out-of-favour company – which may, however, be facing business problems. Users of the Bargain Hunters' Investment FlexiSystem have found that the largest blue chip companies with high dividends are likely to show more capital gain – particularly with, but also without, dividends reinvested – than smaller companies with similarly high yields.

Dividend cover

A useful measure to assess a company's financial soundness is dividend cover, ie eps divided by dividend per share. If dividend cover falls below the level of 1, the company faces problems as, by definition, it will not be able to pay its dividend out of current earnings. A dividend cut may well be in the offing, which is likely to be reflected in a declining share price in advance.

Sometimes, it is the less popular ratios that have been shown to be particularly useful. The price/sales ratio falls into this category.

Price/sales ratio

The price/sales ratio (PSR) is the total market value of the company divided by the previous year's sales (figure available on the profit and loss account). There is some sentiment against the PSR in the City. Sceptical analysts stress that a high level of sales is of no use without profits.

Despite these reservations, users of the Bargain Hunters' Investment FlexiSystem have found that a low PSR (less than 1.5 or, in some cases, less than 1.0 or 0.75) is one of the very strongest indicators of value. In substantiation of this finding, a stock with a low PSR is unlikely to have a high PE ratio. For more on the symbiotic relationship between these two ratios, read *Super Stocks* (Irwin, 1994) by US fund manager Kenneth Fisher.

In this book, which is substantially about technology stocks, Fisher explains that the PSR is of value because the sales portion of the ratio is more stable than most other variables such as earnings. He says that stocks should be priced by investors on causes, not results, and the results, including eps, flow from there.

According to Fisher, the price/research ratio (PRR) can serve as a valuable cross-check to the PSR. The PRR may be defined as the market value of the company divided by its corporate research expenses for the past year. The ratio may be used to assess only those companies that have high research expenses – typically in technology sectors. Broadly, Fisher finds the PSR more useful than the PRR.

Fisher is not the only investment professional to see a predictive value in the PSR. In his best-seller *What Works on Wall Street* (McGraw Hill, 1998), fund manager James O'Shaughnessy examined the effectiveness of the PSR and a lot of other ratios, based on his research into the Standard & Poor's Compustat Active and Research database from 1951 through 1996.

In his research, O'Shaughnessy found that low PSRs *beat the market more than any other value ratio and did so more consistently.* I strongly recommend to you his excellent book, which destroys a lot of assumptions prevalent amongst investment professionals.

Share price/net asset value per share

Meanwhile, the share price/net asset value (NAV) per share is a ratio far more widely used by investment professionals. The NAV per share is calculated as follows. You take the total assets less total liabilities, and you divide the figure by the number of shares in issue. The relevant figures are available on the balance sheet.

While the share price/NAV per share is not always useful in evaluating growth or technology companies, it is a crucial measure in the case of property companies, investment trusts and composite insurers. Typically, insurance analysts wax lyrical if composite insurers trade at a low price/NAV compared to their peers as this makes the companies seem undervalued. The reason for the low ratio may be that the insurance sector is out of favour or the stock market is in a downturn. There is often a company-specific reason too.

From a low point, the price/NAV ratio can sometimes rise substantially. There is often a backlash as the share price starts declining from new highs, thereby reverting to its previous norm. Of course, some companies with a high share price/NAV buck the trend and remain highly priced.

For instance, Lloyd's investment vehicles (LIVs) were at one recent point trading at high prices in relation to NAV (in one case, 4.5×), reflecting exceptionally strong recent share price rises. Some analysts predicted that the trend would continue. Despite being highly priced, the LIVs were arguably good value given that they were in the process of becoming integrated insurance companies. The shift towards integration could significantly enhance profits, subject to an above-average performance from the companies' managing agencies, it was felt.

If you want to invest in Lloyd's of London, choose a Lloyd's investment vehicle. Think carefully before becoming a Lloyd's name in your own right as you would then be liable to your last cuff link and could be ruined. This has recently been the fate of many who had been too greedy or naive to know what they were letting themselves in for. If you want to know the risks you run from being a Lloyd's name – particularly without having specialist knowledge of the syndicates with which you are involved – read one of the books on Lloyd's of London in which impoverished names are interviewed and allegations of misconduct are aired (see Chapter 17).

Gearing

In addition to using value ratios discussed in this chapter, you should check a company's level of borrowing, for which the technical term is gearing. The so-called gearing ratio may be defined as interest-bearing loans and preference share capital, divided by ordinary shareholders' funds, all expressed as a percentage. The figures are again available from the financial statements. Ordinarily, gearing should be a cause for concern if it is over 50 per cent.

Assess a company by a number of yardsticks

Obviously a stock may appear good value on the basis of one ratio, but poor value on the basis of another. For this reason, use a number of ratios in analysing a stock, and look for some level of consistency in the story they tell.

Which ratios are the more important indicators of value? Researchers have used sophisticated computer models to assess which ratios have produced consistent outperformance and at what levels. In different countries and over varying time spans, tests have produced different results.

But many researchers have corroborated the position of the Bargain Hunters' Investment FlexiSystem, which is that a company in which you invest on value grounds should have a low PE ratio, a low PSR, a low price/cash flow and a high and rising ROCE with strong discounted cash flow projections from a number of analysts.

The largest companies with the highest dividends offer a combination of high value and low risk. Meanwhile, avoid stocks with very high PE ratios and do not rely on a company's recent rises in eps being sustained.

In general, if a company has shown a strong rise in share price, this is likely to continue. Avoid buying into a company that has shown price deterioration as this will be likely to continue (unless there is a strong reason for improvement).

Of course, even if the ratios tell a consistent story, there may be other factors weighing on the share price. For instance, the company may be adversely affected by internal politics or changes. The industry in which it operates may be entering a slump.

It is not for nothing that fund managers visit companies and talk with their management. You too can get a taster of what is going on by attending a company's annual general meeting. Better still, visit the company yourself, which can be easier to organize on a group basis as members of an investment club (see Chapter 1).

I will give you an example of why it is important to build up a picture of a company in which you plan to invest. Recently I was very interested in investing in (and recommending for investment) a quoted company called Independent Insurance. I ascertained from the insurer's report and accounts that it had an outstanding record of underwriting profits, and steady eps growth over the previous few years.

However, I felt it right to query why Independent Insurance was trading at 2.5× NAV, which seemed high. After conducting some basic research, which included talking to the company, I came to realize that the price/NAV was irrelevant as Independent has been historically a growth company. The impressive eps growth record and the low PE ratio were in this case the best indicators of quality and value.

Unlike the composite insurers, Independent Insurance was not involved in life assurance, and was no longer partaking to any great extent in high-volume, low-margin business such as household insurance, which had been marketed so heavily by direct (telesales) insurers. Instead, Independent Insurance concentrated on the niche areas of property and liability insurance. It had entered innovative long-term agreements with brokers, and, separately, with its reinsurers.

Owing to its not inexpensive but thorough risk-selection process, Independent had enjoyed an excellent underwriting profits record, and it was investing funds conservatively. This seemed a good bet for investment.

When you are assessing companies for investment purposes, you too should conduct some research into the *practical* aspects of its business in addition to analysing ratios. More about how to go about this in the way professionals do is explained in the next chapter.

Golden rules covered in this chapter

Rule 29   Avoid companies with a high price/earnings (PE) ratio for medium- to long-term investment purposes. For large companies, a low PE ratio is a strong indicator of value.

Rule 30   When comparing PE ratios of companies, make sure that you are setting like against like.

Rule 31   A company's return on capital employed (ROCE) should ideally rise each year. There is sometimes a high correlation between the ROCE and the share price.

Rule 32   The EV/EBITDA ratio (ie enterprise value/earnings before interest, tax, depreciation and amortization) is used by some analysts to measure the profitability of capital-intensive companies.

Rule 33   Do not rely entirely on discounted cash flow calculations made by analysts, as they are based on uncertain assumptions.

Rule 34   A low price/sales ratio is a strong indication of value.

Rule 35   Use several ratios at once to evaluate a company.

5

How to make a killing out of boring blue chips

A proven technique for selecting under-valued major blue chip companies for investment

While the market is volatile, you are going to step in and buy major blue chips as part of your portfolio, using the Bargain Hunters' Investment FlexiSystem. Major blue chips, which for the purposes of this book we are confining to those with market capitalizations (ie share price multiplied by number of shares in issue) of around £6 billion or more, are safer than the majority of quoted companies.

These 'biggies' have the resources to withstand a recession and do well when the economic climate improves. There is a further safety net in such companies in that they are automatically bought by index tracker funds, keeping prices to some extent buoyant.

For these reasons, if you are a beginner in investment, you should make sure that at least half of your shares are in such companies. With that proviso, under the Bargain Hunters' Investment FlexiSystem, *you* choose the proportion of your investment portfolio that you invest in major blue chips, depending on much risk you are able or willing to take.

You could put the rest of your money in any combination of invest-ment,s which include shares in more blue chips or in smaller growth companies or, to be cautious, bonds. Always keep a small reserve, perhaps £5,000, in an instant access account with your building society for the proverbial rainy day.

Blue chips with high dividend yields are your staple

The key to buying blue chips under our proven system is to select out-of-favour companies with a large market capitalization, a low price and, above all, a high dividend yield.

In the formative years of value investing, the late Benjamin Graham had endorsed the use of dividend yields as one of the major criteria for selecting cheap shares. The Bargain Hunters' Investment FlexiSystem requires you to reinvest the dividends on an ongoing basis to maximize your profits.

This technique for buying undervalued blue chips is rooted in a tradition of 'contrarian investing' in out-of-favour stocks with high dividends. To reduce the risk for you, the Bargain Hunters' Investment FlexiSystem adds some proven refinements to such methods used by investment professionals in the past.

You will apply basic ratio analysis, as covered in Chapter 4, to candidates for inclusion in your portfolio. In addition, you will pay attention to the timing of your investment, a factor that some other high dividend blue chip share buying systems may ignore at their peril.

The risk is reduced further for you by using a stop loss in your investments. Crucially, your purchase of blue chips is part of a broader investment strategy. The Bargain Hunters' Investment FlexiSystem obeys the first law of successful investing, which is that you do not put all your eggs in one basket.

In the final analysis, our system – unlike a good many other stock market systems that simply do not work – requires some input from yourself, which is no bad thing. You are ultimately responsible for your own investment decisions.

Before we look at how to invest in blue chips under the rules of this system in detail, we will examine the history and theory of investing in high yield stocks. This will serve as a solid foundation for getting to grips with the practical steps outlined towards the end of the chapter.

US influence

The O'Higgins legacy

To demonstrate how profitable investing in high-yield, low-priced blue chips can be, we will first look at the O'Higgins legacy. Michael

O'Higgins is a fund manager based in Albany, New York who has popularized such investment techniques in his book *Beating the Dow* (HarperCollins).

In this book, O'Higgins claims that investment need not be complicated and that investing in a portfolio of out-of-favour Dow stocks has consistently beaten the Dow Jones Industrial Average index, which other fund managers have failed to do.

To implement the system explained in his book, O'Higgins advises readers to open a discount brokerage (ie execution only) account, dispensing with a broker's expensive advisory services. He advises investing in the 10 highest-yielding Dow stocks or, alternatively, in the five of these that have the lowest closing prices. In addition, he suggests that the second-lowest-priced stock of the 10 highest yielders can be a good investment risk in itself. Once a year, the stocks are replaced where new ones qualify. Very importantly, all dividends are reinvested.

For readers who are interested in reading more about the O'Higgins theory, to which it is impossible fully to do justice in these few pages, I would strongly recommend buying *Beating The Dow*, which has sold 250,000 copies to date. Although the book is now a little dated, its principles are timeless.

The broad arguments cited by O'Higgins in favour of investing in high-yielding Dow stocks have proved applicable to the UK market. He says that the companies making up the Dow are strong and resilient due to size and asset strength. In his view, they include 'the most viable business enterprises on this earth'. Similarly viable, users of the Bargain Hunters' Investment FlexiSystem have found, are major companies included in the UK's FTSE 100 and FT 30 indices.

Where these companies' shares are high yielding, this is usually an indication that they are out of favour, and the share price will be correspondingly low. In the US, O'Higgins argues that the major blue chips on the Dow that are out of favour and sell at bargain prices will soon return to their true value.

Meanwhile, high dividends reinvested are a significant part of the overall return on shares in an out-of-favour company, O'Higgins stresses. In the US markets particularly, companies keep up their dividend payments if possible to retain investors' confidence.

Examining the evidence of out-performance

The O'Higgins principle sounds logical, but has it beaten the index over a period? In the US, statistics over the period 1973–91, cited by O'Higgins, reveal that the five highest yielders with the lowest share prices on the Dow Jones out-performed the index for 15 out of the total 19 years. Clearly, this is an impressive track record[1].

While past performance may not be repeated, particularly in the stock market, which is governed by human behaviour, it is the only guide that we have. The O'Higgins system seems a good bet for beating the Dow in the future. Others have cottoned on to the underlying principle. Another advocate for buying large-cap high-dividend stocks is US investment guru James O'Shaughnessy.

The O'Shaughnessy contribution

In his book *What Works on Wall Street*, O'Shaughnessy concludes that the effectiveness of high-dividend yields as an indicator of future out-performance depends largely on the size of companies bought.

The book explains how, in scrutinizing the Standard & Poor's Compustat database, O'Shaughnessy found that the returns, including dividends, of the 50 high-yielding stocks (excluding utility stocks) drawn from an *All stocks* group failed to beat it over the 49-year period from 1951 to 1996. In contrast, the 50 highest-yielding stocks (also excluding utility stocks) drawn from a *Large stocks* universe did almost twice as well as their group over the period.

As a result of these findings, investors who want to use yield as the only factor in choosing stocks for investment should select large companies, O'Shaughnessy said. Significantly, under the Bargain Hunters' Investment FlexiSystem, you will be using the high-yield criterion for selecting only major UK blue chips.

When it comes to stock selection, O'Shaughnessy suggests that models beat human forecasters because they consistently apply the same criteria, whereas humans use intuitive methods. However, in the experience of users of the FlexiSystem, a hunch about a company can still be very useful in assessing the quality of its management, the feel of its operation, etc.

---

1 O'Higgins has written a new book, *Beating the Dow with Bonds*, which recommends switching between high-dividend large-cap stocks and high-yielding bonds to suit market conditions.

When Wall Street sneezes, London catches a cold

The findings of O'Higgins and O'Shaughnessy have clearly carried weight for savvy Wall Street investors. However, the case must be examined as to how far these findings transfer to stock markets in London or the rest of Europe.

In broad terms, there is no doubt that when Wall Street sneezes, London catches a cold. Every morning, if the Dow Jones has been down overnight, the FTSE 100 is likely to open down in similar proportions. The copycat pattern is similar if the Dow was up.

The rest of Europe, with the occasional exception, normally follows suit. As we observed in Chapter 3, European stock markets, including London, are marching increasingly in harmony.

Let us not underestimate the vast influence of Wall Street world-wide on sectors as well as index performance. For instance, technology stocks Europe-wide have often taken a beating simply because one major IT company in the US announced lower-than-expected results.

On the copycat principle, would not systems of investing in high-yield blue chips that have consistently beaten the Dow be likely on the same principle to beat the major UK indices? Fortunately for bargain-seeking investors in UK markets, the issue has been put to the test.

The *Financial Times* contribution

The *Financial Times* (*FT*) tested out the O'Higgins system in the UK by applying it to the FTSE 30 share index. Between 1979 and 1992, the *FT* found that £10,000 invested in the 10 highest-yielding shares in the FTSE 30 rose to £130,000, with significant gain attributable to the rein-vestment of gross dividends. In comparison, the same sum invested in the FTA All-Share index reached only £81,540.

The *Investors Chronicle* contribution

Similarly, test portfolios based on high-yield investments have been monitored by UK investment magazine *Investors Chronicle* (*IC*). The criteria for inclusion are explained by former *IC* editor Gillian O'Connor in her encyclopaedic tome *A Guide to Stockpicking*.

An *IC* portfolio would consist of the 30 highest yielders available, subject to the following further criteria. The yield on shares included must be more than that on a chosen index, while the shares must be at least as highly priced as at a year earlier. Smaller companies are excluded owing to marketability problems.

Shares are removed from the portfolio only if the yield falls below that of the FTSE Actuaries index and the share price has fallen below the previous year's level. Over a 40-year period the *IC* portfolios have normally – but not always – beaten the market significantly, according to O'Connor.

The Dreman contribution

US-based David Dreman, who manages the market-leading Kemper-Dreman High Return fund in the US, has similarly advocated the purchase of high-yielding blue chips. After conducting tests on the largest 1,500 US companies on the S&P Compustat database for the 27 years ending 31 December 1996, Dreman found that the quintile (fifth) of stocks with the lowest price/dividend ratio provided a 16.1 per cent annual return, almost half of which derived from the yield itself. The strategy with dividends reinvested beat the market, as Dreman demonstrates in his excellent book *Contrarian Investment Strategies* (Simon & Schuster).

However, other investment strategies produced a higher return than investing in the quintile of stocks with the lowest price/dividend ratio, according to Dreman's tests. Buying stocks in the quintile with the lowest PE ratio gave a 19 per cent annual return. Stocks in the quintile with the lowest price/book value ratio returned 18.8 per cent, while stocks with the lowest price/cash flow produced an 18 per cent return.

Out of the various high-yield investment systems, it is the O'Higgins method that initially interested private client stock market guru Jim Slater, although he was later to be influenced by David Dreman's findings.

The Slater contribution

Jim Slater recommends a UK version of the O'Higgins system in his book *Pep Up Your Wealth* (Orion), which was published in 1994. In the book, he explains how he approached UK fund manager Charles Fry and worked with the company in researching the application of the O'Higgins principle to the UK market.

The results of Charles Fry's research are reported in *Pep Up Your Wealth*. In the 10-year period ended December 1993, the 10 highest yielders in the FTA All-Share index showed a compound annual total return of 22.4 per cent, against 18.8 per cent from the index as a whole. The five lowest priced of the top 10 highest yielders gave a 26.1 per cent compound return over the period, 7.3 per cent more than the FTA All-Share index.

In his book, Slater presented further evidence that seemed to substantiate the O'Higgins thesis. According to a Micropal survey, investments in the average UK equity growth unit trust over a 10-year period significantly underperformed the equivalent in the average equity income unit trust. Separately, research by stockbroker Capel Cure Myers suggested that portfolios with an average yield that was 25 per cent above that of the market average usually substantially out-performed the FTA All-Share index.

On the basis of such evidence, Slater recommended in *Pep Up Your Wealth* that private investors should use a UK version of the O'Higgins principle to select and invest in out-of-favour blue chips. Charles Fry duly introduced a collective investment scheme tailored for the purpose.

Cannily, Slater foresaw a possibility of the system's failure and he warned that there was no guarantee it would continue to work in the future. In late 1998, Slater advised newsletter subscribers not to carry out the system in the prevailing volatile market conditions. In the short term, some UK versions of the O'Higgins system have certainly failed. Whether the principle continues to work in the long term remains to be seen.

Recently, I have seen investment professionals lose thousands of pounds on paper almost immediately by implementing a UK version of the O'Higgins method, as recommended by Slater, at a short-lived peak of the bull market.

How a UK version of the O'Higgins system lost thousands on paper for my investment banker friend

In the early months of 1998, Jacob, an investment banker who was a friend of mine, was keen to implement a UK version of the O'Higgins principle after he had read *Beating The Dow* and *Pep Up Your Wealth* respectively. Using Slater's UK version of the O'Higgins principle, Jacob singled out the five lowest-priced stocks amongst the 10 highest yielders selected from the top 30 stocks by market capitalization in the FTSE 100. He also focused on the FTSE 100 index's second-lowest priced of the 10 high yielders. None of these stocks seemed to be high performers at the time, but the theory behind investing in such out-of-favour blue chips, coupled with evidence of how well the method had worked in the past on either side of the Atlantic, seemed convincing, and Jacob decided to give it the benefit of the doubt.

In July 1998, Jacob duly invested up to £3,000 in each of the following stocks: Royal & Sun Alliance (663.5p), Shell (424p), J Sainsbury (526p), BAT (720p), M&S (538p). These were the five lowest priced out of the 10 highest-yielding stocks in the FTSE 100. In addition, he invested £3,000 in HSBC (1643p), which was the FTSE 100's second-lowest-priced high yielder. The stocks were acquired through an execution-only broker to save on commission costs.

In making his investments according to the O'Higgins principle, Jacob was going against much of the advice from top sector analysts in his own and other investment banks. For example, some banking analysts recommended selling HSBC owing to Far East problems. BAT was seen by many as less good value than certain other tobacco companies, and Marks & Spencer was seen by most as significantly lacking in short-term prospects.

Jacob was not worried by the failure of analysts to endorse his stock selections. He knew that City analysts constantly disagreed with each other, and often made wrong, biased, or poorly timed recommendations, which they might change later if it suited them.

As soon as Jacob had bought his stocks, the market dipped into a correction. The FTSE 100 fell 14 per cent in the following six weeks or so owing to currency problems in Russia, an ongoing recession in Asia, and panic selling of over-priced stocks on Wall Street.

The warnings about over-priced global stock markets had been constant from strategists around the globe but Jacob, at the height of the bull market, had ignored them. Under Slater's version of the O'Higgins principle, or indeed the original principle itself, the index's dangerously high level had not been cited as a major issue. Now Jacob was on paper losing serious money.

In the period from 20 July 1998 to 30 August 1998, Royal & Sun

Alliance had fallen from 663.5p to 502p despite positive brokers' recommendations, while Shell was down from 424p to 316.25p, largely due to brokers' downgrades. J Sainsbury was down from 526p to 515p and BAT was down from 720p to 587p. HSBC had fallen from 1643 to 1239 as Hong Kong's Hang Seng index had proved volatile, while Marks & Spencer was down from 538p to 515p.

By November 1998, Marks & Spencer was down to 401p, and would later fall significantly further. Aggravatingly for Jacob, some blue chips not recommended under the O'Higgins system were rising in value.

The O'Higgins system can only be judged on a long-term basis but, nonetheless, Jacob fervently wished that he had paid more attention to brokers' forecasts, which provide momentum for the share price even if, in some cases, they are little more than guesswork[2]. He also wished that he had not ignored market timing. In *Beating the Dow*, O'Higgins argued that while some market timing methods have some success, once they have become popular, they never work quite so well again.

Perhaps so, but as an investor, you cannot completely ignore market timing. Having said that, do not fall into the trap of relying excessively on technical analysis, ie trying to read the charts in your efforts to time the market (for more on the risks of this, read Chapter 9).

Instead, apply common sense. When the market is too high, you will know it. Most stocks will be overvalued on fundamentals. There will be plenty of pundits giving you warnings in the newspapers and on television. If all these people are ignored by the investing public, you will know that the time may have come for you to sell out. Similarly, alarm bells should ring when your local newsagent owner or your taxi driver is boasting of his or her paper gains from investment in the latest hot stocks. A bull market can roar ahead for only so long.

The best time for you to buy is after a market correction, when stock prices have fallen considerably and nobody else is daring to buy. This is where you step in and select your blue chips in accordance with the Bargain Hunters' Investment FlexiSystem. Here are the steps that you must follow:

---

2 Analysts' consensus forecasts are more reliable if the individual forecasts from which they are made up are numerous and do not deviate much from each other.

Your master plan

Step 1

Always buy stocks after a market correction when prices are depressed. Granted there is a risk that the market may decline further, but you would still be better off than if you had bought at the height of a bull market.

Step 2

Select the 10 highest yielders from the top 30 stocks by market capitalization in the FTSE 100, which is one of the techniques recommended by Jim Slater for implementing the O'Higgins method (our system has major differences). The business section of *The Sunday Times* lists the top 200 stocks every week with details of the share price and market capitalization, and this is ideal to use as the source for your selection.

Step 3

Out of the 10 highest yielders selected, narrow down your choice. Initially, throw out any companies that have recently had, or may be facing, much in the way of analysts' downgrades (details available in *REFS*) or that have serious internal problems.

In addition, look for good news ahead for the company and/or its sector and never be enticed only by the shareholder perks available for investing in certain large companies. Generally, in deciding on which stocks to avoid, you must rely on your own judgment. In order to come to the right decision, your research may involve checking out a company's services for yourself, or simply keeping abreast of current events affecting its business.

If, for instance, you had managed to buy shares in British American Tobacco when it started trading in early September 1998, you could have locked into a massive 10 per cent yield. In addition, the group clearly had a stable business with strong cash flow and good brand names. But you may have had reservations on the grounds that the group might not be immune from the wider impact of US anti-tobacco litigation.

Once you have got rid of what you see as the dubious candidates for your portfolio, you will need to apply a little ratio analysis to remaining stocks using theory covered in Chapter 4.

A large company in which you are considering investing should ideally have at least 2× dividend cover (eps/dividend per share) to reduce the risk of a dividend cut. Cash flow per share should be higher than eps, and gearing not higher than 50 per cent. In addition, look for a low PE ratio (ideally on a historic and prospective basis) compared to the sector and the market as a whole.

You should also look for a low price/NAV and low price/sales value. If the share price has recently risen more than the market as a whole, so much the better. You will probably not win on all of these criteria but should do so on at least some.

I repeat the point made in Chapter 4 that it is unnecessary for you to calculate your own ratios. Unless you have the resources of my City colleagues, you are best off obtaining the required ratios from the financial press or a reference source such as *REFS*.

Given favourable ratios are in place, you should give preference to *lower-priced* stocks as they are, for psychological reasons, more appealing for investors. After you have screened the potential candidates for your portfolio on these grounds, you may be left with only a few companies. It is in these that you should invest.

Step 4

Once you are fully invested, set a stop loss of 20 per cent below the mid-price of your shares as at the time that you bought them. Your stop loss must trail share price gains. If the share price rises, the stop loss must rise with it, always staying 20 per cent below the previous day's mid-price at close of business. If a share falls more than 20 per cent below the trailing stop loss, you must sell immediately, with no exceptions.

To implement the stop loss thoroughly, you will need to monitor price movements in your shares on a daily basis. As these particular investments are major blue chips, they will be listed in any quality national newspaper or on Teletext.

Such a stop loss should allow leeway for day-by-day price fluctuations as your stock hopefully soars in value over the medium term. The value of the dogs of the FTSE 100 that make up your portfolio will very likely fluctuate significantly, so be prepared.

This stop loss system will sometimes save you a fortune, although it may also occasionally mean that you sell a good stock prematurely. For what it is worth, *Daily Mail* share tipster and former deputy City editor Michael Walters found a not dissimilar stop loss system of his own concoction the most effective tool for private investors that he had come across in his 35 years as a financial journalist, and he has covered it in detail in his recent book *How to Beat the Bear Market* (Batsford).

As an alternative to using a stop loss, you could, under the Bargain Hunters' Investment FlexiSystem, use options to limit your potential losses to 10 per cent of your total investments. To implement this safeguard, you must buy an option for each of the companies in which you have invested that guarantees that the shares can be sold at a specific price within a clear time period up to nine months.

If, for instance, you have a share worth 200p, and you buy an option to sell it for 200p at any time in the next three, six or nine months, you can keep the shares if they go up, and your profits will then have been reduced by only up to 10 per cent, ie the cost of the option. If the shares go down, you can sell them for 200p, and so will avoid any loss at all, except the outlay for your options.

The longer the period for which you hold the options, the more expensive they are. If you want to use options in this (or any other) way, make sure first that you thoroughly understand the concept. Contact the London International Financial Futures & Options Exchange (LIFFE) (tel: 020 7379 2580, Web site at www.liffe.com) for detailed information.

Step 5

On the same day every year, you will reinvest any dividends received from your blue chips and will review your portfolio. During the year, you should have saved your dividends in a high interest earning account so that you can reinvest them at once, which is cheaper than reinvesting in several instalments throughout the year.

Of course you need not reinvest your dividends if the job is done for you. A few FTSE 100 companies offer a dividend reinvestment plan under which they use the conventional cash dividend to buy shares in the market, which they then allot to shareholders. While shareholders are charged for this service, they will pay less than if they had reinvested the dividends themselves.

It is still more cost-effective for shareholders to receive scrip dividends, where companies *issue* extra shares instead of paying a dividend. Over the years, companies have favoured scrip dividends as they have not been required to pay Advance Corporation Tax (ACT) on these, as they would on conventional dividends. For this reason, companies with ACT difficulties have sometimes offered enhanced scrip dividends, worth more than the dividend in value. However, in April 1999, ACT was abolished, which has made scrip dividends less attractive for companies.

Once your dividends are reinvested or you have acquired an equivalent payout in the form of shares, you must implement again the share selection process outlined in rules 2 and 3. You will buy any stocks that fit the criteria outlined in these rules, and will sell any that no longer do so.

Step 6

If there are firm indications that you are at the height of a bull market, sell out of your portfolio at the first serious signs of a market correction. It is unnecessary to weather the bear market, which at this point or soon after is likely to ensue. You can always repurchase your shares at bargain prices when the market is low.

Generally, do not be afraid to sell. Take a leaf from the book of the world's most successful investor. In 1969, Warren Buffett could find no shares worth owning and sold everything in his portfolio. In the bear market that followed, he held cash. He bought shares again four years later, when they were going cheap.

Step 7

Invest the part of your money not used to buy out-of-favour blue chips in keeping with the level of risk you are prepared to take. If, for instance, you have some years of working life ahead of you, you should balance your share portfolio with some growth stocks selected according to the broad criteria explained in Chapter 4 and elsewhere.

Conversely, if you are approaching retirement, you will want your money in, for instance, government bonds or cash, as you are less able to afford the risks of an equity market downturn. More about your broader investment strategy will be discussed in Chapter 10.

How the method described in this chapter draws on the investment wisdom of the ages

When implementing our method of buying out-of-favour blue chips, you are focusing on companies that are likely to have been over-penalized by the market. You are attributing great importance to the timing of your investment purchases, to avoid the kind of paper losses that my investment banker friend Jacob incurred. In addition, you are investing in well-established companies with large market capitalizations. For this reason, they will be resilient against adverse market conditions or internal problems.

To further limit potential losses, you are looking for favourable ratios where possible on your selected companies. You are also running a trailing stop loss system, and are ready to sell your portfolio on signs of a market correction. To maximize the upside, you will review your portfolio regularly, and make any required changes.

You are not putting all your eggs into one basket. Buying high-dividend large-capitalization blue chips is only one of the proven share-buying and other investment techniques incorporated into the Bargain Hunters' Investment System.

Golden rules covered in this chapter

Rule 36   If you are a novice investor, make sure that at least half of your shares are in major blue chips.

Rule 37   When buying blue chips, you should select high-yield, large-capitalization stocks from the FTSE 100 index according to criteria specified.

Rule 38   Throw out blue chips that face problems or analysts' downgrades, or have too many unsatisfactory ratios.

Rule 39   Operate a trailing 20 per cent stop loss system on the blue chips or, alternatively, use options as an insurance against major share price falls.

Rule 40   Review your blue chip shares every 12–18 months.

Rule 41   Sell out your blue chips at the first signs of a market correction.

Rule 42   Once you have bought blue chips, invest the rest of your money to suit your risk profile using principles described in this book.

6

Small is not always beautiful

To include small companies (with a market capitalization of under £200 million) in your portfolio is not compulsory under the Bargain Hunters' Investment FlexiSystem, but, if you are seeking capital growth and are in a position to take risks, it is advisable.

You should select most of your small company investments from the constituent companies of the FTSE SmallCap index, which are each capitalized from around £20 million to £350 million. The FTSE Fledgling index, which includes some still smaller companies, is a secondary hunting ground.

In a volatile market, there are often plenty of bargains amongst the constituents of these two indices. This is because the stock market will at times have fallen exaggeratedly, leaving many companies priced at well below fair value.

In the case of most small companies in which you are considering investing, look for a low price/sales ratio, coupled with a recent rising share price and excellent business prospects. Be prepared to hold through volatile markets until the stocks have reached a fair price. Cut your losses but not too soon (it can help to set a stop loss, as explained in Chapter 5) – and run your profits.

Specifically for small companies, users of the Bargain Hunters' Investment FlexiSystem have found that a low PE ratio is not likely to rise, and should be taken as a sign of likely sluggishness in the company's share price. At the other extreme, avoid companies, small or otherwise, that have a very high PE ratio – unless you are trading – as the share price will later typically fall sharply. A major exception is to be found in Internet stocks, which, if profitable at all, tend to have very high PE ratios (see Chapter 7).

How much should you invest in small companies?

Generally, how much of your capital should you risk investing in small companies? At any given time, some brokers are arguing for investing more while others argue for investing less. Despite the ease with which supporting statistics can be manipulated, it is demonstrably true that, over decades, small companies have out-performed their larger counterparts.

Bucking the trend from the start of 1995 until early 1999, the UK's FTSE SmallCap index had consistently under-performed the FTSE 100 and the FT All-Share indices. In a slow or deflationary UK market such as when I started writing this book, small companies are a disadvantage because they have greater exposure to the domestic economy.

The small companies cannot compete on economies of scale enjoyed by larger companies. In addition, they do not have so much support from institutional investors owing to their lack of liquidity. The disadvantages are often reflected in the share price.

For this reason, many small companies at such times are much better value than the larger counterparts, and the management may also have stronger incentives to make a success of the business. Although you will find it harder to research small companies, if you invest wisely or luckily in the sector, the shares may soar perhaps 50 or 100 per cent within months.

In such cases, the company should arguably retain its earnings for growth, rather than pay them out in the form of high dividends. Share buybacks can be instead used with impunity to enhance shareholder value.

For the future, the December 1998 introduction of the FT All-Small index, which represents a new benchmark for performance analysis, may whip up more enthusiasm amongst institutions for the small company sector, with the likely exception of penny shares.

The penny share minefield

Penny shares are those below a certain price, set by some at 50p, by others perhaps as high as £1. The monetary threshold is not important. Penny shares tend to have seen better days and are high-risk investments. They need a good reason to start soaring in price, such as new management or involvement in a reverse takeover. Even then, the shares may not respond.

The problem is that there are fewer bargain penny shares than you may think, and the bargains are certainly not always graced with the lowest share price, or with the recommendations of tipsters or promoters. Do not subscribe to an investment newsletter in this field without checking that it is independent and has a reasonable track record.

On the other hand, penny shares are relatively immune from the ups and downs of the market's fortunes, tending to rise and fall more for company-specific reasons. If you select the right penny share, you may be lucky enough to make a good paper profit on it, despite a large spread – the difference between the buying and selling price of the securities. Some users of the Bargain Hunters' Investment FlexiSystem have succumbed to buying quoted penny gold-mining stocks, gold being seen as a safe haven in volatile market conditions.

But unquoted gold mine or other companies are a different ball-game. If you are to follow the Bargain Hunters' Investment FlexiSystem to the letter, avoid *all* unquoted companies, including those listed on the Off Exchange Market (OFEX) or Alternative Investment Market (AIM).

A few practitioners of our system have broken this rule and have invested successfully in unquoted shares. In case you should decide to follow suit, we will take a brief look at the OFEX and AIM markets.

The OFEX casino

The OFEX trading facility, in the words of John Jenkins who runs its single London market maker J P Jenkins, is the 'Wild West' of investing territory. As this book goes to press, there are a total of 191 OFEX companies, with a combined market capitalization of £2.891 billion, and demand for Internet shares on this exchange is so high that telephone problems have arisen.

Despite the investment risks, a few who implement the Bargain Hunters' Investment FlexiSystem have made money from investing in carefully selected OFEX stocks. If you have a yearning to follow their example, first research your market. Free seminars about the OFEX market are available in London and the provinces at various times throughout the year. To register for this, go to the OFEX Web site (www.ofex.co.uk).

In checking out a specific OFEX company, your first port of call could be *The Hambro Company Guide* (tel: 020 7278 7769), which includes their statistics. For details of new issues, consult the OFEX Web site. John Jenkins advises that your OFEX shares should make up no more than 10 per cent of your portfolio.

Ideally, spread your risk, perhaps splitting a £10,000 investment into £1,000 in each of 10 OFEX companies. In such small amounts, it will be easier to resell the shares when it suits you but you must be ready to hold the shares for at least a year. Of the 10 companies chosen, two may soar in value, five may go nowhere and three may go bust, John says. J P Jenkins has vetted every OFEX company, although not primarily for the benefit of private investors, looking for an exciting product and directors who have a track record.

J P Jenkins favours OFEX company sponsors that have a reputation for picking winners. As a potential investor, you would do well to talk with the sponsor – usually an accountant or solicitor – about the company. Avoid companies where the shares are tightly held by a minority group. If a stake was sold, the price could move sharply against you.

Shares are often traded on a matched bargain basis, which means that, for every seller, a buyer must be found. Even in good times, OFEX stocks can suffer from a lack of liquidity, which means you may not be able to get your money out when you want to. At the time of writing, perhaps 60 per cent of OFEX stocks are at or above their issue price but not all could be easily sold.

Once you have bought your OFEX shares, you can follow the prices of those stocks that have paid for a listing in the *Financial Times* and the *Evening Standard*. Contrary to popular belief, OFEX is not so volatile as the main market and may follow its trend only after several months have passed. The time lag is partly because OFEX only has one market maker and there is no price competition. As OFEX companies grow, they often plan to join the AIM, and some have made the leap.

The Alternative Investment Market (AIM)

The AIM is a market created and regulated by the London Stock Exchange, which at the end of November 1999 had a total of 337 companies. More than 50 companies have progressed from the AIM on to the main market, and the market is currently proving a springboard for some Internet companies that make sky-high returns for early investors.

The regulatory requirements for the AIM are less than for companies that have a full listing. For this reason, the AIM attracts many high-risk start-up companies, which should be valued at a discount to more mature companies in their sector. The AIM's future is uncertain in a climate where there is much talk of convergence between small company exchanges in Europe.

Do not buy shares in an AIM company without checking its accounts and talking to its official sponsor (who may also be the market maker in the stock). Check the background of the directors, and, in the case of new issues, look for restrictions on how quickly they can sell their shareholdings.

In addition, check which broker is backing the AIM company that interests you. The better the broker's track record for successful new issues, the more likely its latest offering will attract institutional backing, which in itself can send the share price soaring.

Even when the AIM stocks of your choice look good, be prepared for extreme volatility. In 1998, for instance, the top performer on the AIM was Peel Hotels. It was issued at 25p in March, and closed the year up more than 500 per cent at 151.5p. At the other extreme, Desire Petroleum ended 1998 down 85 per cent on its issue price. Both stocks had looked promising on issue.

In buying AIM stocks that show such swings and roundabouts, it is obviously helpful if you can get your timing right. In general terms, it makes sense to buy when the small companies are increasingly undervalued compared with blue chips. To keep up with more company-specific timing issues, you may find it useful to subscribe to *The AIM Newsletter* (see Appendix 7). You can find more details of this publication, and view a sample issue at the Web site of its publisher Newsletter Publishing (www.newsletters.co.uk). Also, check out AIM information at the London Stock Exchange Web site (www.london-stockexchange.com).

As an investor in OFEX or AIM stocks, you are often entitled to tax incentives. But you should never for this reason buy an investment that does not stand up in its own right. In the 1980s, I saw many investors in companies that qualified for tax relief under the Business Expansion Scheme (BES) – replaced now by the Enterprise Investment Scheme – investing only for the tax advantages. They did not inquire too deeply into the quality of company in which they were investing. Some of the companies were dubious and investors in these lost fortunes.

Golden rules covered in this chapter

Rule 43   Select small companies for investment initially from the FTSE SmallCap index.

Rule 44   Do not buy small companies with too low or too high a PE ratio.

Rule 45   Exclude unquoted shares from your portfolio, except as an extra.

Rule 46   Do not invest for tax incentives unless you are also happy with the underlying investment.

7

Profit from the Internet revolution

As this book goes to press, users of the Bargain Hunters' Investment FlexiSystem have been throwing speculative cash at Internet and other technology stocks, with astonishing rewards. In 1999, technology stocks were the top performers in the UK stock market, as well as in the preceding decade, according to an end-of-year survey by Primark International, the Information Services group.

Users of the FlexiSystem have struck gold from investing in Internet stocks in particular, where they have applied tried-and-tested share selection techniques to this specialist sector. You will find these methods set out here for your own use.

Internet companies

Usually loss-making but with fast-growing revenues, Internet companies have sometimes seen their share price rise by many times, within weeks or even days of flotation. Institutional investors have rushed to secure stock, with private investors bringing up the rear.

In 1999, the gold rush was tacitly encouraged by the US Federal Reserve and other Central Banks, which pumped money into the credit and money markets to offset concerns about potential computer glitches at the start of the year 2000.

The millennium concerns proved misplaced as, towards the end of 1999, an anticipated panic sell-off of stocks never took place. On the contrary, extra money was put into Internet and other technology shares. Experts, including Intel chief executive Andrew Grove, have suggested that, in five years' time, the Internet will be so freely used that the concept of an Internet company *per se* will no longer exist. Of course, in the race for market share in Cyberspace, there will be many also-rans and some losers as a backdrop to the few serious winners. Some areas of Internet business are clearly more successful than others.

What is an Internet company?

An Internet company may be involved in a number of areas, including e-commerce, online content, and back-up services. Undeniably, the companies that benefit most from the Internet are using it not just for communication but also for e-commerce. Online transactions enable major cost savings.

Business-to-business e-commerce

Within e-commerce, business-to-business has high potential as it dispenses with the need for a middleman and can exploit the Internet's order-taking and service facilities. Significantly, Ford Motors and General Motors in the US have said that they plan to buy goods and services from suppliers on the Internet.

Consumer-to-consumer e-commerce

Similarly, consumer-to-consumer business has high potential. Via the Internet, consumers buy and sell items from each other, and the company acts as match-maker, raking in revenue without holding inventory. On such a business model, US-based online auctioneer eBay has been profitable since it went public in the autumn of 1998, bucking the loss-making trend of most quoted Internet companies in their formative years.

The consumer-to-consumer model is flexible. For example, US-based Price-line.com has developed a 'demand collection' system for its auctions by which it helps to bridge the gap between prices offered and prices asked for. Under this arrangement, a buyer may be allowed to pay a lower price for an item if he or she will also buy another at the standard price, creating a combined margin acceptable to the seller.

Business-to-consumer e-commerce

Across the spectrum of e-commerce, the business-to-consumer model is the least proven, and companies in this field risk being squeezed out by the price competition. Online retailers must buy items from producers and store them, so paying for use of a middleman, for inventory space, and for extra administration. In this field particularly, it pays to be a market leader.

Online content companies

Online content companies, which specialize in the collection and production of online content, have attracted much interest from investors, but the business model is unproven. People who will pay for newspapers or TV have to date declined to pay for similar material on the Web.

For this reason, online content providers rely for revenue both on advertising and on online promoters to whom they send user lists. Many companies in this field are loss-making, with US search engine Yahoo! being a frequently cited exception.

Invest in non-dot.coms

You can invest in the Internet sector at less risk via companies such as software developers that benefit indirectly from the Internet's growth. Such companies are rated highly by the market, but differ from most pure Internet players in that they have early profits and a track record. Invest also in companies that offer, for example, Web page design and Web-based support, which will be in demand regardless of how their client companies' strategies for e-commerce fare in an increasingly competitive market.

If you invest in companies that are only partly involved in the Internet, such as publishers with an online division, the risks are lower, but so are the rewards. These players will benefit from the Internet only in proportion to their involvement.

As an investor in Internet companies, you are entering a high-risk arena

Whichever type of Internet stock you are buying, accept that you are entering a high-risk arena. Federal Reserve Chairman Alan Greenspan has described Internet company valuations as pie-in-the sky, while Microsoft boss Bill Gates has said that he does not recommend Internet stocks to people who 'don't like massive risk'.

Even UK retailer Dixons, which launched Freeserve as Britain's first free Internet services provider in 1999 and has since retained an 80 per cent market share, sees the Internet as risky for investors. It admitted that investors in Freeserve were taking a gamble on the future of the Internet and e-commerce, and the company's position in these.

In its first quarter to September 1999, Freeserve showed an operating loss of £5.2 million before tax, as well as £3.6 million of exceptional losses related to its flotation, and it is not expected to be profitable until 2003. Despite this, Freeserve has proved a highly successful, if volatile investment for its loyal shareholders. One City analyst has compared the task of valuing Freeserve to a game of chance, like throwing darts at a board.

This is an extreme view, and it is in fact possible to narrow the odds of successful investment in Internet stocks by careful stock selection, as explained in this chapter.

Give more priority to the business's quality than the numbers

Some experts are saying that we have entered a new era of the stock market when valuations are at a new high, and that the value of an Internet stock is simply what somebody will pay for it, assuming that the seller will accept the offer.

Given the inflated prices being paid for Internet stocks as this book goes to press, discounted cash flow (DCF) analysis is often set aside by analysts specializing in the sector. After all, cash flows for the next few years may be declining owing to a company's ongoing reinvestment, it is reasoned.

Nonetheless, the various forecast ratios in use for valuing Internet stocks, including that of price in relation to earnings, sales, subscribers and so on, are simply a derivation of the DCF analysis technique. In the next few pages, we will be looking at the most important ratios in more detail.

But for Internet businesses, ratios make only one contribution to the valuation puzzle. For stocks in this king of growth sectors, you will be looking more at the company's business prospects, its strategy, its market share, and its strength of management. In addition, you will be looking closely at the company's backing, and the proportion of stock made available in a share offering.

Look for a leader

First movers amongst Internet companies have a major advantage, as Amazon has demonstrated by its outstanding share price performance in recent years. But leadership must be retained. While competitors were trying to copy Amazon, Jeff Bezos, Amazon's billionaire founder, was initiating a pioneering associates' programme that created a vast team of Amazon sales agents across the Internet.

Sometimes to be first is not enough. CD Now was popular in 1994, when it was launched, but it was overtaken by Amazon in 1998 within a period of three months, although it has since developed its business much further.

Sound backing is a sign of strength

In the case of a new Internet – or any other – company, you must always check which parties are involved, information that is available in the company prospectus. Backing from 'smart money' means that the company has been vigorously vetted, lending respectability and status. You will come to recognize some of the backers to watch for. For example, Sequoia Capital backed the highly successful Yahoo!, while Benchmark Capital backed eBay.

You should also look for a top investment bank as manager of an IPO or secondary stock offering. If, for instance, Merrill Lynch or Morgan Stanley Dean Witter is involved, it can be a good sign. Such leading investment banks will not risk tarnishing their reputations with a dud share offering if they can help it. That said, they can make mistakes, and Morgan Stanley Dean Witter was global coordinator to the disasterous flotation of lastminute.com, an Internet retailer, in early 2000.

A strong brand name

A strong brand name represents a major advantage for an Internet company, and creates barriers to entry by competitors into the company's specialist business. To build a brand name requires extensive marketing. For this reason, Internet companies put much of their revenues into marketing and so have a high burn rate – the rate at which they get through cash – and usually heavy losses for a few years. There are exceptions – earlier in this chapter, we have looked at eBay's early profitability.

The case for eyeballs

The case is often made that eyeballs alone – numbers that visit the Web site – are what matters for a growing Internet company. A related factor is 'stickiness' – how long eyeballs stay fixed on a site. But eyeballs alone cannot make a business viable in the long term, much as they can help its growth. Within a few years, a viable Internet business should have the potential to show an operating profit.

The 'eyeballs' case is that an Internet company must first build up its business by attracting visitors to its site. To support this argument, it is noted that leading US Internet search engine Yahoo! was initially loss-making, and became profitable only after it had built up its business.

Sadly, not all Internet companies have the potential of Yahoo! in its salad days. Some companies can achieve a high level of sales, but lack the infrastructure to fulfil orders, as happened with some online retailers of toys in the run-up to Christmas 1999.

More usually, the problem is that people visit a site without parting with money. Undeniably, advertisers – a major source of revenue – are attracted by the number of visitors to a site. However, as the supply of Web pages increases, advertising rates are coming down – except for some market leaders such as Yahoo! which in 1999 was actually able to increase its rates due to its large number of users.

Except in such untypical cases, the weakest players in this increasingly competitive market place are the Web sites that offer free services, as they are spending without taking in revenue. The strongest players, in contrast, are those that sell high-margin products such as financial services on the Web.

Gross margin is the key to survival

For all players, marketing costs are rising as Internet companies face increasing competition in luring customers to their sites. The key to an individual company's survival is a high gross margin, which is the part of revenue that remains after subtracting production costs, but before advertising costs.

Expert opinion suggests that an Internet company needs a gross margin of between 35 and 45 per cent. A decent gross margin is most easily achieved by the market leaders. For instance, eBay has a gross margin of at least 75 per cent, and need spend less on marketing than its rival online auctioneers.

The operating margin goes one step beyond gross profit, and represents the part of revenue that remains after marketing and production costs, but before interest and tax. A small operating margin – perhaps just 5 per cent or thereabouts, given the large market capitalizations of Internet companies – is seen as desirable within the foreseeable future.

How do you measure operating profit?

So how do you measure operating profit, prospective or otherwise, in an Internet company? In the case of mature Internet companies where earnings are available and acquisitions have been made, City analysts have sometimes valued the company on the basis of a ratio that emphasizes cash flow – enterprise value (market capitalization plus debt less cash), divided by EBITDA (earnings before interest, tax, depreciation and amortization).

This measure has seemed more appropriate for Internet companies than the standard price/earnings (PE) ratio, which measures the number of times the price covers the company's net earnings per share. But financial journalists are often fixated on PE ratios. They cite the sky-high PE ratios of the profitable Internet companies as a warning that such stocks are overvalued, but they do not look hard enough at the growth rates. In December 1999, the PE ratio of Yahoo! was a stratospheric 1,400, but, every quarter, its revenue had been up well over 100 per cent year-on-year.

For most young Internet companies, the PE ratio is inapplicable as they have no earnings. Sales are the most common basis for valuing an

Internet stock, even if the company is selling a loss-making product. Some have taken a cynical view of the matter. UK magazine *The Economist* on 30 January 1999 queried whether it was too implausible to imagine 'Dollar.com – a company that sells dollar bills for 90 cents and makes money from advertising'.

True to form, in early 1999, a Californian company offered to give away 10,000 Compaq Presario computers, complete with modem and monitor, to individuals that were an attractive demographic fit, provided that they agreed to be confronted with advertisements every time they turned on the PC for at least two years, and to let the free PC track their online habits. The company's business model assumed that eyeballs were worth more to advertisers than the $600 price of the PC.

Price/sales is the most common ratio for valuing Internet stocks

The City gives sales the same priority, and the price/sales ratio (PSR) – the current market capitalization of a company divided by the last year's sales – is duly the most commonly used ratio for valuing Internet companies. Within the sector, the PSR is only relevant when used to compare companies in the same area of business.

In Chapter 4, we looked at how technology recovery stocks can often be a good buy on the basis of a low PSR ratio, ideally less than 1. In many non-Internet-related sectors, the PSR might be 3 or 4 for market leaders. For Internet companies, the PSR is typically much higher. For instance, Freeserve was valued at a PSR of 123 times forecast sales at flotation.

At the time of writing, in the US, e-commerce and online content stocks are valued at between 6 and 15 times next year's revenues, while the so-called infrastructure stocks – including search engines – are valued at between 40 and 200 times next year's revenues. In the City, next year's revenues are forecast on the basis of previous earnings. Owing to the exceptionally fast-moving nature of the Internet sector, the City often prefers to forecast future annualized revenue on the basis of the previous quarter's figures, rather than on the figures of the previous year as a whole. But revenues will far overreach forecasts if the company makes an unexpected acquisition.

Acquisition potential

Internet companies seek scale of operation, which is why Yahoo! took over GeoCities in early 1999. But savvy Internet companies are understandably cautious about seeking to take over companies. In making an acquisition, the trick is to avoid any significant overlap of businesses, and perhaps to increase the acquiring company's own potential as a candidate for takeover. Takeover rumours can send a share price north, as indeed can stock scarcity.

Stock scarcity and share offerings

Share prices of Internet companies in the early stages rocket owing to stock scarcity, which is usually orchestrated. In her online column (www.mrscohen.co.uk), self-made private client stock market guru Bernice Cohen dubs high-tech stock scarcity the Van Gogh factor. As about 75 per cent of all paintings by Dutch artist Van Gogh are housed in the eponymous museum in Amsterdam, only the remaining few are available to private collectors, and, for this reason, the prices are high. In a similar vein, lack of availability forces up the price of high-tech stocks.

The limitation on available shares is created by the initial share offering where, typically, only 10–20 per cent of the share capital is made available to the public, creating a shortage and so pushing up the first-day premium on the purchase price. By comparison, in the early 1990s, a company would sell as much as 30–40 per cent of its share capital at the offer stage.

The inflated first-day premiums from Internet share offerings are reported in the media with great fanfare, and, when the next share offering takes place, the company's owners and initial investors can get away with selling less of the stock to raise the required level of capital. The share offering is seen as the major event, with the quality of the company coming a very poor second.

In the rush to secure a slice of the action at share offerings, retail investors are not the main beneficiaries. Particularly in the case of hot offerings, they are unable to get shares in any great quantity, if at all, and must make do with buying at an inflated price in the aftermarket.

Some brokers are experimenting with fairer systems of distributing shares. W R Hambrecht, an online investment bank, has promised to create a 'fairer and more efficient market system' using the Web. It used the open initial public offering (IPO) system, based on the Dutch auction model designed by Nobel prize-winning economist William Vicrey, to price the 1999 IPO of Andover.net, which runs Web sites connected to the free Linux operating system. Generally, the effectiveness of this model has been called into question.

Whichever way the share offering works, the main beneficiaries are the companies that are floated. The proceeds from the share offering may prove a lifesaver in lean years ahead. For their part, venture capitalists and initial investors sell out their stakes in young Internet companies as they reach the market, knowing that the bean feast may not last.

Sometimes, the various parties involved in promoting an Internet company are loaded to the hilt with options, warrants and shareholdings. Already, some major advisers to Internet company flotations, including lawyers, accountants and management consultants, will consider taking share options in lieu of fees.

The pickings seem potentially vast. For instance, US computer operating systems company VA Linux went public in December 1999 with its shares priced at $30, and closed on the first day of trading at a record 700 per cent premium. In the same month, UK-based JellyWorks, a fledgling Internet incubator fund, rose tenfold on its first day of trading on the AIM from a placing price of 5p. Within eight days of trading, the share price had hit 122.5p.

But not all Internet company flotations are ultimately successful, and a surging share price can plummet on bad news, leaving early subscribers out of pocket. The real test is the company's performance beyond the first day of trading, and, except in exceptional cases, during a bull market the technology premium may settle at between 30 and 100 per cent. Be prepared for extreme volatility in the share price at all times.

Adapt to Internet time

The exciting thing about Internet stocks is that they move in 'Internet time', which is somewhat accelerated. Within days, a stock's value can soar by 10 to 20 times, but volatility can be tremendous. For instance, America Online fell 75 per cent in value during Summer 1996, as a result of which the US media blithely dubbed it 'America Offline', and brokers wrote off the stock as overvalued.

Media criticism can be a good sign

Paradoxically, media warnings that an Internet stock is overvalued can be a buying signal. Financial Web site The Motley Fool has suggested rightly that press comments about a high growth stock being overvalued can be a reason for buying it.

Undeniably, the press makes knee-jerk reactions to day-by-day stock movements, and is the naïve mouthpiece of stock market professionals with an agenda. The best Internet companies often trade at sky-high valuations that discount substantial growth rates and profits, and remain the best. The trick is to take an informed view on when the valuation is justified.

Put these valuation techniques into practice

The valuation techniques covered in this chapter have been gathered by much trial and error, and are proven to work. Using these techniques as a basis, you should feel confident about investing in Internet companies, but use your common sense. If, for example, the market for Internet companies crashes, wait until it has reached an obvious low before you buy.

As a user of the FlexiSystem, I practise what I preach. I will show you how I selected one of the highest-performing Internet stocks for investment at an optimum time. In this case, I got it right, but if I had got it wrong, so what? You should never invest too much in one Internet stock initially, so that if you do get wiped out, you will have the resources to start again.

In late November 1999, I singled out for investment an Israel-based company called Geo Interactive Media. The company, quoted on the London Stock Exchange, was clearly on to a winner with its key product, a worldwide patented technology called Emblaze. This product enabled easy and fast delivery of video and audio material, known as rich media, via any Internet protocol network (Internet, intranet, or extranet) on to PCs or other platforms such as cellular phones.

I was keen on this company because its Emblaze product was so timely. Delivery of rich media on the Internet has been a disastrous area until recently, which is understandable as the Web was designed for what Geo Interactive Media describes as 'short bursts of textual messaging'. As a result, Webmasters have had problems putting rich media on to a Web site, and the user has needed special plug-ins to download it.

I ascertained from Geo Interactive's own Web site that the company's Emblaze product uses streaming technology to enable the transfer of rich media without the need for special plug-ins by PC users. The risk for the business was that Emblaze would not remain in the forefront of technology. True, Geo Interactive did have some major competitors, but the market for streaming media products was expanding rapidly. An agreement between Geo Interactive and a cellular phone company was pending, and a NASDAQ listing was planned.

Note that I selected this company for investment mainly on the basis of its strong position in an expanding field. Less important were the numbers, which was just as well. In the interim results released in October 1999, Geo Interactive had shown a loss of $8.1 million, which was largely unchanged from the previous six months, on sales of just $300,000.

Nor did it seem significant that, shortly after transferring from the AIM to a full listing on the London Stock Exchange in 1998, the company had seen its share price fall from 187p to 16p as a result of issuing warnings about falling revenues. The shares were hovering at around the 160p level and looked cheap, even if they had previously been many times cheaper.

At the time, I recommended the stock in a prominent market newsletter, *Vanguard Investor*, and my own ethics prevented me from buying a stake myself. Shortly after I had delivered my article to the newsletter's publisher, I received a phone call from the managing editor. The share price had more than doubled to around the 330p level before they had even gone to press. Was it still worth recommending this stock?, he wanted to know.

I said yes, and the stock proceed to climb from around 160p in late November to 1,235p on 20 December 1999. It was a spectacular performance. Overall in 1999, Geo Interactive was the second-best performer on the London stock market, having been up 4,111 per cent in the year.

In November 1999, just as I was recommending Geo Interactive, various online message boards on the Internet – which contain views and information from a variety of investors who use the Web site – made encouraging noises. For instance, various techies using the UK Motley Fool message board were avid fans of Geo Interactive's technology. How do these message boards work?

The incredible value of online message boards

As you use the Internet to research not just high-tech but any stocks, do not neglect the online message boards. These represent space on a Web site available for investors to communicate with each other. The message boards are usually indexed by stock or sector, with an A–Z index for speedy access. The messages include views, questions, answers, insights, copies of articles, or information, about stocks, dealing facilities, or the market as a whole. Anybody registered can contribute.

These message boards are responsible for much volatility in share prices, and are making the market more responsive to sentiment, at least in the short term, than to fundamental values. You – in common with many City professionals – should find these message boards of great help in making your investment decisions, provided that you do not take the messages too literally.

At present, the US message boards offer more sophisticated dialogue than the UK equivalents, but the Internet is helping us to catch up on know-how. On the boards, many minds are working at once in dissecting a stock, which leads to better informed conclusions than if you are working in isolation.

The downside is that there are dubious postings from more than a few winsome folk who hype up a stock that they hold for the wrong reasons. Some go so far as to post wrong information, and rumours are rife. City regulators have raised the alarm that the message boards may be used for ramping stocks – causing them to rise on speculation that may be ill-founded – or insider trading, which is against the law. But not everybody is crooked (or wrong) all the time, and a consensus of views – as expressed on the message boards – often reaches sound conclusions.

Apart from the information you glean this way, message boards make investing a less lonely activity. To use the message boards is akin to meeting regularly with scores of fanatical investors in your local pub, and hearing their comments and insights. Some analysts are already speculating that the next step may be for 'message board communities' to trade stocks with each other, so dispensing with the need for a broker.

Your choice of message boards

Which message boards should you use? My favourite is the UK Motley Fool message board (www.motleyfool.co.uk), where you can look up individual shares on an A–Z index, and follow the threads. The input into the board is supplemented by well-argued contributions from the Motley Fool writers.

But do not confine yourself to one message board. Here is a tip. Go the following Web address: www.freeyellow.com/members6/scottit/page7.html, and you will find yourself on a page with links to message boards of Market-Eye, Hemmington Scott, UK Shares, and Interactive Investor International. If you want to check out the message boards of one of these, you can just click on it, and follow instructions, returning to the link page when you would like to try one of the others.

To contribute to a message board, you will need to register, which will involve you typing your proposed user name and password on to a form online. You must offer a user name that is not already in use, or your application will be rejected. I suggest you try your own name spelt backwards *and* with some letters missing.

Other online sources of information about Internet stocks

As you invest more in Internet stocks, you will need an information flow. At the time of writing, the financial press is full of news about the Internet revolution. The *Financial Times* carries Internet-related news every day, which is read (and acted on) by the City professionals who influence share price movements. The online version is available at www.ft.com, and, once you have registered with the site, you can get news delivered to you by e-mail.

In terms of general coverage in magazines, I have found particularly useful some of the features in *Shares*, a stock-tipping magazine that has focused extensively on high-tech stocks. For information about the range of available sites, I would also recommend an easy-to-read and informative magazine, *Internet Investor*, whose first issue was published in January 2000 (www.internetinvestor.co.uk).

If you want share tips based on an expert perspective, subscribe to *Techninvest*, which is widely acknowledged as the best tipsheet for

Internet and other high-tech stocks. For subscription details, see Appendix 7.

Otherwise, your most productive source of information on Internet stocks will be the World Wide Web itself. Most investors in Internet stocks are also avid users of the Internet, so join the vicious circle.

For access to informed opinion on high-tech stocks generally, it is worth checking out the message boards, newslinks and features at Silicon Investor (www.techstocks.com). Check the news and features at online technology magazine Red Herring (www. redherring.com).

In addition, register free with the Web page of Richard Holway Ltd, which specializes in coverage of high-tech and Internet-related stocks www.holway.com). You will then have free access to the System House 'hotnews' page, which gives an up-to-date informed commentary on high-tech stocks. The service does not tip stocks, but it provides valuable perspectives. It believes that the Internet 'pick and shovel' stocks – involved in, for example, support services to the Internet – are a better bet than the 'dot coms'.

In addition, you should visit the Motley Fool US Web site, which offers extensive and well-informed ongoing coverage of Internet stocks (www.fool.com). Do not be put off by the US emphasis of the coverage. In the case of Internet stocks, as in other sectors, it is Wall Street that leads, and the City of London follows. In addition, the Motley Fool UK Web site (www.fool.co.uk) offers coverage of UK Internet stocks.

Here is a further tip. Excellent free research relevant to Internet stocks is at the time of writing available online from investment bank Durlacher (www.durlacher.co.uk./research). You should also visit the Web site of Wit Capital, which bills itself as the world's first online investment banking firm (www.witcapital.com). The site provides free access to significant quantities of high-quality research about Internet stocks, which is of a standard suitable for institutional investors.

But perhaps the stock selection process is too much for you. If you are too busy, lazy or risk averse to invest in Internet stocks directly, you could go for a collective investment. You should compare technology funds on the basis of track record (over a very short time period in some cases), country weighting, stock selection techniques, track record of fund managers, size of fund, and so on. In the next few paragraphs, I will highlight some of the most promising funds at the time of writing.

Collective investments in Internet and other high-tech stocks

If you are interested specifically in Internet stocks, it is worth considering investing in the Framlington NetNet fund. To select the fund's stocks, fund manager Framlington Group draws on the skills of its US partner Munder Capital Management, which manages one of the largest Internet investment funds. In April 1999, the NetNet fund was launched at 50p a unit, and by 23 December of that year, it had nearly doubled in value to 98.7p, with plenty of volatility en route. The fund includes highly valued Internet stalwarts such as Amazon, AOL, Intel, Yahoo! and Freeserve.

If you are interested in high-tech stocks generally, a unit trust constantly in the top quartile of its sector – an important filtering test for collective investments – is Aberdeen Technology. Since its launch 17 years ago, the fund has given investors an average return of 22 per cent per year. Alternatively, go for the SocGen Technology Unit Trust, which by 23 December 1999 had risen 200 per cent from when it was launched in May 1998.

Another option would be to invest in the Close FTSE techMARK Fund, set up to track the new techMARK index, which includes small to medium-sized high-tech companies listed in the UK. Between its launch in early November 1999 and 23 December 1999, the fund has achieved a more than 50 per cent gain for investors.

You should, if at all possible, buy your technology funds from a discount broker where you will save substantially on commission, at the expense of receiving financial advice. The above funds, for instance, are all available from leading London-based discount broker Seymour Sinclair Investments (www.seymoursinclair.co.uk).

Tracking down research and news on the Internet

Finally, make sure that you use the Internet to research any company or market in which you are interested – not just Internet or high-tech stocks – and to track related news flow. In Appendix 8, I suggest Web sites useful for this purpose.

In general terms, I would suggest that for free information on a share, including a five-year summary profit and loss account with balance sheet, share price movements, major shareholders and similar, you should go to the Hemmington Scott Web site (www.hemscott. com/EQUITIES/INDEX.HTM).

For daily business news, tailored where required to specific stocks, go to Bloomberg news (www.bloomberg.com/uk/markets/index. html). It is also worth checking out Yahoo's business news pages (UK.news.yahoo.com/s/). For a summary of news stories in last Sunday's quality press, go to the Web site of Financial News Digest (www.pigeon.co.uk).

Setting up your own portfolio

The Internet can also be used for setting up your own portfolio. Many online brokers offer this service, but if you are not registered with one of these, there are other free outlets.

I would recommend the portfolio management services of Interactive Investor International (www.iii.co.uk/portfolio). Through this source, you can have your individual shares listed on screen with up-to-date prices and last closing prices. At the click of a button, you will receive recent news flow or (in some ways, more valuable) access to message boards where other investors give opinions about relevant stocks.

Conclusion

The Internet is here to stay, and is the single most important innovation of the 20th century. If you are serious about investing, you cannot afford to ignore it. As this book goes to press, users of the Bargain Hunters' Investment FlexiSystem – in common with many other private investors – are starting to deal online, and making good use of the Internet as a medium for message boards and news flow, for research and statistics.

Some investors have made serious money very quickly from buying and selling Internet stocks. If you follow the advice in this chapter and get your timing right, there is no reason why you should not do the same.

Golden rules covered in this chapter

Rule 47   Give more priority to the quality of an Internet business than the numbers.

Rule 48   Look for a leader, with sound backing and a brand name.

Rule 49   Revenues can be more important than profits.

Rule 50   Internet companies should eventually show an operating profit.

Rule 51   Price/sales is the most common ratio for valuing Internet stocks.

Rule 52   Acquisition potential can increase the value of an Internet company dramatically.

Rule 53   Be prepared for volatility in Internet stocks and welcome media criticism.

Rule 54   Keep abreast of gossip on relevant message boards.

Rule 55   Consider collective investments in Internet and other high-tech companies as an easier alternative to your own stock selection.

Rule 56   Set up and follow your own portfolio on the Internet.

8

How to get the better of dubious share pushers

A recap on the principles we have learned to date

To make your fortune in a volatile stock market, you will pick what appear to be the most undervalued stocks using the simple but time-honoured value principles outlined in this book, making only a few exceptions – for example, of high-tech stocks when the sector is in favour.

In addition, you will keep your eye out for news flow that may affect your investments. Ideally, you will sell your shares when the market is high and buy when it is at rock bottom.

The above programme, to which this book introduces you, is not hard to follow. You do not need more than a basic knowledge of accounting to calculate the ratios on which you will largely base your buying decisions, and Chapter 4 shows you how to go about the required analysis from start to finish.

Almost whatever such stocks you buy, provided you get them at a price that is substantially below their true value, and are prepared to hang on to them until they reach a fairer price – a proven gravitational tendency of companies quoted on major stock markets – then you should make money.

If you select your shares sensibly, and buy in enough quantities, and have the patience to wait, you could easily make your fortune. The sole aim of this book is to help you do this.

As in anything related to investment, there are no guarantees. To take the worst scenario, unforeseen events could drive a company into liquidation. Of course, such a disaster is unlikely to hit your entire portfolio.

If you spread your risk during a volatile market by investing in a range of undervalued stocks at once, your chances of eventually coming out very much on top when the eventual upturn inevitably occurs are high indeed. If you make it a rule not to invest in unquoted stocks, this will protect you against the cowboy promoters.

Dealing with the cowboys

As a further protective measure, you should never buy shares from unknown and unchecked salespeople. The stock promotion in question will usually be a set-up and, if you fall for the share pushers' patter, you will lose your money.

It is a giveaway sign that stocks pushed by these cowboys are neither quoted on any recognized exchange nor even available on OFEX or the AIM. They may, however, be quoted on the US-based National Quotation Bureau's so-called 'Pink Sheets', which have no regulatory barriers and include stocks indiscriminately. Alternatively, they may be quoted on the US-based OTC Bulletin Board.

It is important to understand that the companies quoted on the Pink Sheets or the OTC Bulletin Board are not subject to the full reporting requirements of Nasdaq stocks and, in some cases, have proven highly dubious. If you are an active private investor who gives out a telephone number, we can almost guarantee that you will get pestered by pushers of such high-risk stocks and worse.

They will have obtained your name from old share registers, or from lists of people who have bought/inquired about investment publications, or from lists of high net worth individuals. Most investors' names are perpetually rented out or sold as part of lists, and some of the list renters are sharks.

As a private investor, you will be particularly vulnerable to these winsome share pushers when the market is volatile. This is partly because you will be in an uncertain state of mind. '*Should I buy, should I sell, or should I sit tight*', will be the range of questions buzzing in your head in these trying periods.

The shark share pushers may well be the only ones coming up with the firm answer that you should buy shares in such bearish market conditions. In contrast, your regular stockbroker may be telling you to sit tight.

Your regular broker may be scared to recommend you to buy owing to the risk of further short-term falls in stocks – even if it is in your interest to buy for the long term on value grounds. Broker know that if they appear to get their recommendations wrong, they may lose you as a client, and, if they are worth their salt, they are interested in the long-term relationship.

On the other hand, often brokers will not want you to sell your shares either, as such a move would reduce the capital invested in your portfolio. They would obviously prefer that you do not take your money elsewhere.

Brokers know that they have competitors. From your point of view, the main caveat is that some of them are not entirely scrupulous. In times of volatile markets, the shark share pushers proliferate.

You will recognize dubious share pushers by their tendency to sell hard and persuasively and glibly, in a manner that smacks more of selling second-hand cars 'off the back of a lorry' than of giving investment advice. The pusher may ring you often, sometimes at evenings and weekends, to the point of leaving you feeling trapped.

While this sales approach differs from your *bona fide* broker's perhaps more in degree than in kind, it remains true that if you are feeling pressurized and manipulated, you are almost certainly being 'pitched' by one of the many shark share dealers.

If this is the case, experience shows you are best off putting down the phone on such salespeople. Do not worry about being rude. These people are incredibly thick-skinned and, within two seconds, will have forgotten you and will be ringing up another potential punter.

In practice, enormous numbers of private investors do not put the phone down on the share sharks. They are being pitched by professionals, get greedy, and often buy. As a result they lose all their money almost immediately.

You may say it cannot happen to you, but this fate befalls so many private investors that it is essential that you have a more detailed knowledge of what you are up against. You don't want to make your fortune using the principles outlined in this book, only to have all your money spirited away by some smooth-talker peddling virtually non-existent shares. To find out what such operators really think of their clients, and how they treat them, turn to Appendix 10, where I have included songs that have circulated their training floors for years.

The background and training of share sharks

In many cases, the 'old hands' operating (or selling for) the rogue share-pushing operations across the world received their basic training as youths working for licensed dealers in securities and similar firms in the UK up to the late 1980s and beyond. In other cases, they received similar training from equivalent firms abroad.

Licensed dealers in securities in their original form are extinct, although, as this chapter will show you, some of the old operations still operate in a modified form. This is particularly dangerous as the firms can actually now be regulated under the Financial Services Act.

History recalls that licensed dealers in securities – so called because they were licensed by the Department of Trade and Industry – were, in many cases, the bucket shops of the securities industry.

The trick was to establish such a licensed (or in some cases unlicensed) dealer, sell dud shares for a few months (or maybe years), then to cease trading, leaving thousands (in one notable case, tens of thousands) of clients stranded with major or total losses.

The principals behind these firms – often also behind the companies whose shares they were pushing – would then start up another dealing firm. They would hire staff partly from the new firm's defunct predecessor, and the entire process would start over again. 'Burnt out' clients who had lost fortunes at the previous firm would be persuaded, in many cases to reinvest.

Some clients would, of course, refuse to be duped all over again, although their number was always surprisingly few. From the point of view of the firms, this did not matter. The key to their entire recycling process was that new clients were constantly 'discovered' to supplement the diminishing supply of existing ones.

A major source of such new blood was in the form of inexperienced investors lured into the stock market by government privatizations. Undoubtedly the Thatcher government did these investors no favours by making sure that they made easy profits on their privatized shares such as British Gas and British Telecom. The experience gave them an unjustified confidence in the stock market and, as a result, they fell prey to the share sharks.

Experienced salespeople working for the licensed dealers would sell the punters' privatization shares on their behalf, often at a better price than available elsewhere. The money would often then be reinvested on a salesman's urgent recommendation in dubious high-risk stocks.

The process was rampant not just in bull markets but also when the market was depressed or volatile. Following the market crash of the late 1980s, thousands of investors were advised to sell out of quoted blue chips and to avoid investing in more blue chips at then bargain prices. They were instead being cajoled into investing in worthless small companies. Do not make the same terrible mistake.

It is important to realize that most of the salespeople who implemented these scams – just like their counterparts nowadays – had no real financial knowledge, no real interest in the stock market, and no commitment to making money for you as a client.

These salespeople came from any kind of background. Some had been waiters or taxi drivers, others clerks or librarians, and many hailed straight from the dole queue. Here were mercenaries who knew or cared for nothing except making a quick buck. It made them ideal employees of the bucket-shop share dealers.

These firms never cared about anything except getting your money, and had no interest in building a long-term relationship with you as a client. The principals of these operations knew that they were living on borrowed time owing to constant client complaints and ongoing regulatory investigations.

They used skilled lawyers to stall the dissatisfied while they paid their salespeople ridiculously high commissions to offload dubious stock quickly. Money coming into the company was promptly filtered out through various dubious channels and, as soon as the game was up, the company would be placed into liquidation.

In the late 1980s most of the share sharks in the UK were, as stated earlier, licensed by the Department of Trade & Industry (DTI). Others were licensed by the Financial Intermediaries Members and Brokers Association (FIMBRA) or, in the case of futures dealers, the Association of Futures Brokers and Dealers (AFBD). These last two bodies were, from February 1988, recognized as so-called self-regulatory organizations under the newly implemented Financial Services Act (FSA). Other share sharks remained unregulated, in some cases temporarily. But in the UK, regulation would eventually be a legal requirement for every kind of financial services company.

Where the share sharks operate now

Since the FSA came into force in early 1988, it has no longer been possible for share-dealing firms to be licensed by the DTI. In addition, many unlicensed firms have been stopped from operating in this country and have been driven abroad.

Under the government banner, some of the regulatory bodies have changed shape and some FSA regulations have been modified. FIMBRA has recently been merged into the Personal Investment Authority. Long previously, the AFBD had been merged with The Securities Association – which regulated *bona fide* stockbrokers – to become the Securities and Futures Association (SFA). Further mergers of regulatory bodies are being planned.

While, undeniably, regulation of the securities industry has been tightened up to some extent, the cowboys are still operating, and it is crucial that you understand this if you are not going to lose thousands of pounds to their manipulative salespeople.

The dangerous thing nowadays is that dubious individuals are now operating from apparently respectable and regulated firms. Sometimes they are sitting in the basement of a stockbroker of apparent high standing, peddling dubious shares in their capacity as a self-employed 'consultant' or associate.

More often, the entire firm is dubious. It is not safe for you to rely on the fact that a firm is regulated under the FSA. Such firms are sometimes expelled from membership of their regulatory body – too late.

But the real loophole in the system is when regulatory bodies change form, and previously regulated firms are forced to reapply for regulation under the new body. They do not make it because their standards are so low. Instead of capitulating, they enter a drawn-out appeal process, and, during the months or even years that this lasts, they carry on dealing.

In this period, the firms will often legitimately claim some kind of 'provisional' or interim authorization. In the meantime, they will be raking in as much money as possible, knowing that they are living on borrowed time. The primary victims are private clients.

Obviously, if a firm is severely held up in getting permanent regulation, this should serve as a likely warning. But for legal reasons, the regulators are not allowed to reveal dubious ways in which these firms may operate, and so unless the press can get wind of it, there is no real way you can find out. In some cases, the regulators have turned out to have been unhealthily close to the firms.

Meanwhile, dubious share pushers without any licence whatsoever are operating from abroad. They will typically set up offices in Costa Rica, Marbella, Malta, Dublin, or in certain US states. The ideal from their point of view is to find a territory that encourages new businesses to set up, and does not care about their practices so long as nationals are not being ripped off.

The switching office

Even so, as a double precaution, these businesses still use 'switching offices'. By this means, the share pushers will be operating from a secret office based, for example, in Latin America. However, their letterhead and phone number will tell of an entirely separate office, perhaps in Paris.

By this chicanery, you as the investor will believe the dealers are based in Paris, whereas, in reality the Paris office is nothing more than a front to prevent the whereabouts of the dealers being known. That way, if there are complaints or police investigations, the dealers can disappear without being caught.

Fortunately, with the help of this book you will easily be able to detect the switching offices, which are, by definition, only used by dubious firms. If you are rung up by a salesperson claiming to be working in Paris who recommends you buy some shares urgently, you could tell him or her that you want to discuss this purchase right now with your investment partner, and that you will ring back in a few minutes.

If a switching office is in use, you will find that the salesperson is reluctant to give you a phone number at all. If he or she does give you a Paris number, you should try it out. If every time you ring, the Paris office switchboard says that the salesperson in question is in a meeting but will ring you back themselves, you will be able to guess quite accurately that they are not based at that office.

The procedure is that messages will be passed to the salesperson in their Latin American hide-out. He or she will then call you back from Latin America, pretending that they are based at the Paris office, in the hope of closing a deal.

The most notorious of these share-selling pirates almost always operate under false names. They may assume double-barrelled surnames that have a safe, old English ring to them. It is all part of the process of soft-soaping you into parting with thousands, ideally tens of thousands of pounds in a single first transaction, and the process has then only started.

Given that there have been some international crackdowns on these dubious share-dealing firms, the risks of getting caught are higher for the salespeople, and the commissions that they are paid for their work are correspondingly high. It is not unknown for the salespeople to receive up to 60 per cent of any money they rake in from clients.

This means that, if you are foolish enough to agree to buy £10,000 worth of shares from such a company, £6,000 will go straight into the share salesman's pocket, and the rest indirectly to the promoter. Do not expect to see a share certificate from this firm, whether you have 'bought' shares in an unquoted company or in a blue chip company. In reality, you will not have bought anything.

The pressure on you to agree a purchase will often be immense. For example, if you try to fob off the salesperson with the line 'I'll have to ask my wife/husband if I can go ahead with buying these shares', the standard sarcastic retaliation in the past has been: 'You do that, and I'll have to ask my wife/husband if I can sell them to you'.

The salespeople who introduce you to the firm's 'services' are known internally as 'loaders', and once they have 'opened up' a client with a first deal, his or her details are passed to another salesperson who tries to do other deals. Only when the operation has milked you for as much money as it can, does it lose interest. At this point, you will probably never hear from it again.

The same game, broadly speaking, is played by many sellers of gold coins and jewellery, of whisky for investment, of foreign exchange products, of futures funds, of bank notes and of phoney art. The firms are often run by the same international crooks operating far behind the scenes. These string-pullers often have criminal records, and a track record for ripping off private investors as long as your arm.

Share pushers in Cyberspace

Internet stocks are the latest offerings from the dubious international share pushers. Avoid buying shares in companies with names like Wealthbuilder.com or billionaire.com, and be sceptical of supposed deals that they claim to be negotiating with well-known computer manufacturers or similar. The claimed deals are a hook to get your money and are completely invented.

In one case, a less-than-substantial Internet start-up company has raked in outrageous sums from investors on the basis of its proposed launch of a 'new virtual country' where one should be able to sightsee, shop, travel in virtual buses, etc. Here is a today version of the classic type of colourful story that has seduced stock investors over decades. In the case of Internet companies in particular, investors must be forgiven if they find it hard to distinguish the wheat from the chaff.

The dubious Internet companies operate on extremely tight margins, depending mainly on volumes of trade and advertising revenue. They are invariably loss-making. But similar attributes may be found in many genuine Internet companies (see Chapter 7). They cannot be assessed by normal valuation measures, and the share price may soar despite the continual lack of earnings.

To convince potential buyers further, huge numbers of newsletters are made available on the Internet or by direct mail, promoting the dodgy Internet company, often amidst talk of the well-known successful Internet stocks, which lends spurious credibility to their claims.

In the US, from where most of the dubious Internet companies emanate, stock tipsters are obliged to declare if they are paid by the companies that they promote. In practice, they are often not open about this but instead try to pass themselves off as impartial advisers.

While some of the Web sites that promote the dubious stocks are amateurishly constructed with a writing style that is over the top, others are thoroughly professional and convincing and it is of course these that are the most dangerous.

On the World Wide Web, like elsewhere, *caveat emptor* prevails when it comes to buying stocks. In an international marketplace in particular, do not rely on the UK's Financial Services Act to protect you.

However, some help is to hand in policing the dubious Internet stock promotion industry, even if it has so far proved to some extent shutting the stable door after the horse has bolted. The Securities & Exchange Commission, which regulates the securities industry in the US, recently announced that it had charged 44 individuals and companies in five cities with Internet fraud after they had promoted penny stocks via electronic newsletters and bulletins without revealing that they were paid to promote these companies.

Fortunately, Internet use means that such fraudsters leave a record of these operations. Nonetheless, if you are going to buy a stock as a result of reading promotional blurb on the Internet, download a copy of the relevant Web page and print it out so that you have a firm record in case it turns out that you have been duped.

For general guidance on dubious Internet stocks, the World Wide Web offers you Stock Detective, a tough vigilante Web site from the US (www.stockdetective.com). The site analyses dud stock offerings –

more often than not Internet companies – and also provides a wealth of back-up educational features. For more details of this Web site, turn to Chapter 17.

Sometimes in the early days after an IPO (US jargon for new issue) of a dubious stock, the share price will soar. In the case of an Internet start-up company, the price may rise 15 times or more within days, but this sadly does not always mean that you will be able to realize 15 times your money.

In the case of a set-up, involving a dud stock, the gain is short term and, for most investors, strictly on paper. The price is initially ramped not just by misleading promotional initiatives that prompt a stampede to buy the shares, but also by bent insiders who buy huge quantities of stock cheap, only to sell out after the share price is at its highest. This is what Stock Detective refers to as the 'pump-and-dump' routine, and once the insiders have sold out, other investors too rush for the door, causing a rapid deceleration in share price.

If, before the stock is dumped, the average small investor tries to sell out of his or her own investment at the prevailing inflated price, he or she will find it almost impossible. The market is thin, the dealing spread – the difference between the buying and selling price – is often vast, and liquidity may be non-existent. The stock promoters may simply be unavailable to take sell orders.

For anybody who has been at the sharp end of the dubious share pushers who operated in the UK in the 1980s and early 1990s, this story will have a painfully familiar ring to it. It is now over 11 years ago since I documented their crafty sales techniques, including artificial ramping of stock prices, in my book *The City Share Pushers*. (For further details of this book turn to Chapter 17.)

The UK press as a whole is inefficient in exposing these crooks. An exception is to be found in the financial problem pages run by Tony Hetherington, currently writing for *The Mail on Sunday* and for *Moneywise*. He is probably the country's leading expert at investigating those who try to dupe private clients into buying dud investments.

It would also be worth reading the books of Michael Walters (see Chapter 17) who has reported on many of the less than straightforward share dealers in his years as deputy City editor for the *Daily Mail*. These two investigative journalists can boast of having shut down many a dubious operator in the UK – and sometimes outside it.

The UK firms today

While UK firms do not usually, these days, sell non-existent shares, they have been known to sell penny shares of uncertain value. These may be in either quoted or unquoted companies. The dealing firms have offloaded the shares in bulk at a high price to private clients.

The share salespeople (or dealers, as they prefer to be known) are paid perhaps 10 or 15 per cent commission on the value of deals. They will often slip in recommendations for dubious penny stocks amidst broader cover-up recommendations of *bona fide* blue chips.

Usually, such salespeople are regulated and so will operate under their own names, and will be accountable for their actions under the FSA. But it can be difficult and expensive for you to pursue the dealers for misrepresentation in the courts, and this almost never happens.

However, should a company regulated under the FSA go bust, you do have access to a Compensation Fund. So regulation does offer you some protection and should stop you suffering as, for instance, did initially the hapless victims of the Barlow Clowes fraud.

As a streetwise private investor, it is important to realize that a firm, even if regulated under the FSA, or in the process of applying to be regulated under a new body, may not operate with integrity.

Although it very difficult to find this out if you are not an insider, such firms are often deeply entrenched in the culture of the original licensed dealers. They will sometimes be staffed with the former henchmen of the worst bucket shops in the 1980s.

Staff of these dealing firms may speak with public school accents and be incredibly charming, belying an extreme contempt for the client that they do not trouble to conceal on the dealing floor amongst themselves. They may be happy to discuss in detail the shares currently in your portfolio with the sole aim of finding out the maximum cash to which you have access for investment with their firms.

If they sell you out of existing shares and into new ones purely to generate commission, this is called 'churning' and is forbidden under the FSA. However, the salespeople are up to all sorts of tricks to get round this. One way is when they praise a new stock enormously and then say to you: 'If you want to come out this stock and into the new one, it is up to you. It has to be you who approach me about it.' If you fall for this one, they cannot be technically accused of the misdeed.

Such tactics are more likely to be deployed by the less scrupulous but regulated stockbrokers, where the brokers are trying to stay within the rules of the FSA, than by the out-and-out rogues working for certain share dealers that are unregulated, or not regulated by the Securities & Futures Authority (SFA). The rogues will more blatantly churn your portfolio.

In a case known to the author, one UK-based stockbroker has employed as 'associates' – paid entirely on a commission basis – a succession of people who had previously been employed as dealers in some of the worst bucket shops in London. Unsurprisingly, they sought to obtain business by getting up to their old tricks.

To start with, they would acquire new clients by sending out a letter offering a free research report on a company in which the recipients had invested. If the punters sent back the letter requesting the report, a relationship had technically been formed. This is because the letter included details of the broker's terms, which are agreed to by returning the letter.

From that point, the brokers could not, under Section 56 of the Financial Services Act (1986), be accused of cold-calling when they subsequently rang up these people and pushed them into buying shares. Here is a loophole in the strict rules against cold-calling new private clients that the greedier stockbrokers ruthlessly exploit.

In the case of this firm's operations, the associates' subsequent business with the newfound clients led to complete disasters. Two of the broking firm's associates ended up in prison for separate offences, while others ended up with debt problems.

Amongst *bona fide* stockbrokers, which are, by definition, regulated by the Securities & Futures Authority (SFA) – the relevant regulator at the time of writing – it is certainly those that employ associates that you should check out most thoroughly before doing business with them. While many such firms are respectable, a few are less than careful about the quality of associate they take on. They are instead more concerned about levels of business achieved.

Often in such firms, the associates have limited access to specialist information about stocks, and may get substantial amounts of their information from the *Financial Times*, or from more substantial brokers' research (received late). You need to question whether they are adding anything of value for you in return for their dealing commissions.

In this book we advocate making your own investment decisions as far as possible, and it is far better to use an execution-only dealing service than a potentially dubious stockbroker – obviously not just because of the reduced commission rates.

The mark of the beast

How to distinguish the dubious stocks

In Chapter 4, we took a clear look at company accounts. We examined some useful ratios that may be gleaned from them to throw light on profitability and liquidity. We also looked at how to extrapolate trends in these areas.

Such principles are applied, sometimes in a more sophisticated way, by professional security analysts and investors. They make sense, but only in the case of *bona fide* companies with some kind of track record.

Even then, as we have seen, fundamental analysis of this kind in isolation is not always a reliable way to predict share price performance. This is particularly so for companies that place great store on future performance. For such companies, professional analysts work out discounted cash flows over a period of years, and, after reading Chapter 4, you should understand the broad principles by which these are calculated.

In this way, you will avoid being taken in by false cash flow projections based on nothing more than the creative imagination of the promoters of dud companies. Many of the unquoted companies that are offered to UK private investors project amazing profit growth over the next few years, but have not yet produced any of this profit. Even if they have shown a profit, this may be due to creative accounting, a still-flourishing scandal that we have touched on in Chapter 4 and elsewhere.

Usually, the accounting information behind the dubious unquoted stocks gives every indication of any fraud. This is because the promoters of these shares do not bother to dress up the accounts too much. They know from experience that most private investors, even when quite sophisticated, are too lazy to seek out accounting information, even if they would be capable of understanding it.

Most private investors look instead for some element of inside knowledge relating perhaps to a forthcoming deal that will send the share price soaring. The dubious salespeople play on this craving on the part of investors and promise huge prospects. It is here that private investors get caught. Be sceptical.

For example, one dubious US-based high-tech company, quoted only on the US Pink Sheets, was represented by salespeople as being about to employ a major public figure as its chairman. The company was also claimed to be on the verge of an alliance with one of the largest blue chip high-tech companies in the US.

The salespeople quoted the names of the prospective chairman and the business partner in hush-hush tones, urging clients on this basis to invest all the money they could rustle up into this international public offer. Many private clients fell for what turned out to be an outrageous fraud.

Sometimes the salespeople make such a deal sound more attractive by emphasizing the short-term nature of the expected profits. 'In the next 60 days, we expect that you will make a 25 per cent gain on this stock, so empty your building society accounts, and sell your unit trusts to maximize your investment now', they may say. After you have invested, the salespeople may even pretend that the share price has gone up to fob off your suspicions. In reality, if you were stupid enough to send in a cheque, you will probably have lost all your money.

The lesson to be learned is, if a salesperson claims that a company of which you have never heard is linked with, for instance, a blue chip operation, check out the story. Follow investment guru Robert Beckman's advice of not buying the shares immediately.

Of course, it may be hard for you to get hold of anybody at the company in question (if it exists) who will speak to you. If you do, the person may not be prepared to make a categorical statement on this rumour, confirming any suspicions you may harbour that, perhaps, there is something in the story after all. The salesperson is banking on such a lack of clarity arising. Do not have faith in his or her claims.

Similarly, do not fall for the fact that the company being pushed by these salespeople is in a currently fast-moving industry. In this respect, we have already looked at the dangers of investing in dubious Internet stocks. At the time of writing, financial stocks, telecoms stocks and, to some extent, high-tech stocks are also in favour, while the rest of the market is down. Some dubious share pushers are taking advantage of these fads to push small companies in the favoured sectors.

However, just because quoted stocks in these sectors are doing well, it does not mean that unquoted stocks will do so. What counts far more than the sector is the intrinsic quality and the track record of the company concerned. If these are not clear to you, or if they are not good, steer clear.

Often the key to detecting dubious companies is when the salespeople do not send you anything in writing as a preliminary to any potential deal. They may promise to do so, but the literature does not arrive. Later, they will ring you up to tell you the share price has risen while you dithered, and that they sent literature but it must have got lost in the post. Do not fall for this.

If you do actually receive written literature about companies in which you are invited to invest by suspected share pushers, examine this carefully. Company prospectuses are sometimes full of the most incredible and meaningless waffle.

Be suspicious too of newsletters produced by such dubious share pushers. You will find that they are usually of a very low standard in terms of analysis, but are full of optimism about the prospects for smaller companies. There is often substantial commentary about blue chip companies (often cribbed from a respectable publication and reworded), with little puffs for dubious small companies slipped into the text here and there. It is the smaller companies that the firms will be pushing.

If you have not heard of the company whose shares are being recommended, and have not read about it in the financial press, check its details with your broker, accountant or bank manager and show them any prospectus or written material provided. If he or she has not heard of the stock either, warning bells should be ringing in your head.

By this stage, it should stick out a mile if something is wrong. However, should you want further evidence, why not check the accounts of the company whose shares are being pushed and/or the share-dealing company? This is easiest if either is based in the UK, in which case you can obtain the information from Companies House, either by visiting it directly in London, or through one of the many services that will conduct the visit on your behalf for a small fee.

Be wary if you find that the directors of share-dealing firms double up as directors of the companies whose shares they are promoting. Also be wary if the directors of the share dealers have astronomical salaries (plus dividends).

Finally, if you do deal against your better judgment, if it has been with a possibly dubious firm abroad, do not necessarily feel obliged to stick to the oral agreement. Check out the firm and, if it is one of the many con-outfits in operation, it will not chase you for your money. However, share promoters in the UK that are regulated under the FSA often tape phone calls and, if you commit yourself to buying on the phone, they may be able to prove it and you could find it difficult to wriggle out of the deal.

Remember, one of the hardest parts of successful investing is hanging on to your money once you have made it. If this chapter helps you do this, it will be worth to you a great many times the cost of this book.

Golden rules covered in this chapter

Rule 57 The con artist sells shares glibly and promises quick profits. He or she receives up to 60 per cent commission on every deal. As a buyer of his or her shares, you will never see a share certificate or your money back.

Rule 58 If you can never reach your share salesman by making a phone call, this indicates that a 'switching office' may be in operation to keep the share-pushing outfit's whereabouts secret. The salesman may assume a double-barrelled name to impress you.

Rule 59 Check a share salesman's story and do not buy immediately.

Rule 60 Do not be seduced into buying shares simply because the underlying company is in a fashionable industry such as high-tech. Be wary in particular of worthless Internet stocks whose prices are temporarily ramped to attract naive investors.

Rule 61 If a share salesman promises to send you literature about a company and it does not arrive, be suspicious.

Rule 62 Be wary of newsletters that include hype for shares in small, unknown companies.

Rule 63 Check the accounts of UK share promoters and of the companies whose shares they are pushing. Be wary if the directors are the same for both.

Rule 64 Avoid investing in companies of which neither you nor your accountant/broker/bank manager have heard.

Rule 65 Put the phone down on dubious salespeople. But if you deal against your better judgment, do not necessarily feel obliged to stick to the oral agreement.

9

Prophets, fools or charlatans? The world of technical analysis

The importance of timing

As a medium- to long-term investor, you will not be paying as much attention to market timing as to stock selection. If you buy under-valued stocks, they should eventually rise to their true value whatever the overall market conditions.

Of course, if you manage to time your investment decisions well, you will be buying still greater value. To achieve this, you will want to buy ideally when the markets are at the bottom but about to go up.

But timing the market is easier said than done. In a bull market for instance, stocks typically get to the point where they are overvalued but the market is still rising. It is a danger sign, but you have to be very strong-willed to liquidate your portfolio in a such a market, and, should you do so, you may find that the stocks you had, until recently, owned continue for a while to increase in price.

However, it is better for you to sell your shares ahead of a major market correction too soon than too late. Remember that a market correction can easily develop into a dangerous bear market. As we have discussed earlier, the market pundits will tell you, via the business pages of quality newspapers and TV business programmes, when the market is over-stretched, at which point a correction is only a matter of time.

In the small matter of fine-tuning the timing of your investment decisions, a small band of enthusiasts in the City and on Wall Street believe they have the answers. These are the technical analysts, known in their more extreme form as chartists (the two terms are often used interchangeably). Although chartists have something to offer traders (see Chapter 13), be sceptical of any claims on their part that they can predict future share price movements.

The far-reaching claims of technical analysis

Technical analysts believe that, by looking at charts of share price and market movements, they can predict future trends based on the past. The more cautious like to know which stock or market is represented by the squiggly line on the chart they will be using for their forecasts. The purists amongst their number, in contrast, are happy to play the soothsayer on the basis of *unidentified* squiggles.

As a group, technical analysts have a reputation for being quite learned and having a good grasp of statistics. They can run rings round some of their fellow professionals in their mastery of computer software. When they talk at length about their recommendations, it is with a jargon that sounds impressive.

Although chartists sometimes make clumsy attempts to deny it, they take it for granted that patterns read off the charts showing past share price or index movements will repeat themselves in a similar form.

It does not help their image that technical analysts make notoriously little money from their black art. Their salaries do not stand up against those of equivalent-level fundamental analysts, or salespeople. The cliché of the technical analyst walking round hunched in a dirty mackintosh and eating tuna sandwiches in a workmen's cafe for lunch has not vanished from City of London and Wall Street folklore for very good reasons.

But nobody would openly accuse technical analysts as a group of being insincere (although some have that unworthy suspicion). Most technical analysts are an earnest, dedicated lot. They are totally blinded by their art, and believe they have got it right even when they blatantly have not.

When I pursued a course at a London-based university recently, which was designed to lead to the Society of Technical Analysts examinations, the tutor never attempted to justify technical analysis. He took it for granted that he was preaching to the converted.

Throughout the course, chartist techniques that made huge assumptions about past patterns repeating themselves were presented with remarkable confidence in their insuperability. I was presented with many ways to draw and interpret squiggly lines. But I did not have my basic doubts about the entire concept even addressed, let alone quashed. It is not as if I kept my mouth shut either.

I did find, however, that there were not many people on the course, and that some dropped out. On the part of the students that remained, who came from varying backgrounds and in some cases had never worked in the City, there was an extraordinarily uncritical acceptance of what we were taught.

Technical analysts generally, including those fledgling practitioners who were my dedicated fellow students on the above-mentioned course, often get pained if their ideas are challenged. In *Where Are the Customers' Yachts?*, his classic book about Wall Street in the 1920s, Fred Schwed Jr wrote: 'I once suggested to a chart reader, who was explaining his theories to me, that since I wasn't a customer he should slip me the wink on this tripe. It was a social error; he was as deeply offended as if I had said something gross about his religion – which, I suppose, I had.' *Plus ça change...*

Of course chartists try never to be caught out, even if this means being wise after the event. They are shown in their true colours after they have made a market forecast based on a study of the charts, and it turns out to be wrong. In such instances, they are not apologetic as might be expected. Instead, they will offer an alternative, retrospective reading of the chart.

What then ensures the survival of these self-styled gurus with ideas as grandiose as their forecasting records are shabby? Like astrologers, tea-leaf readers, and other sorts of soothsayers, technical analysts have an indefatigable audience. This is because the one dream of everybody involved in the stock market – brokers and clients alike – is to foresee future price movements and market trends.

Some will try any method of prediction that is claimed to work. Anybody who wants to believe predictions badly enough does believe and, if enough fall into this trap, this can eventually make them true. Here is the real secret of technical analysis's occasional success, namely that it can become a self-fulfilling prophecy. Despite the many times that technical analysis does not work, chartists can be always relied on to pull in a certain type of client.

For this reason, if for no other, chartism cannot be ignored. Technical analysts are duly employed by major investment banks in London, and they soberly add their own computer-generated charts to the wealth of fundamental analysis provided by the firm. Some of the larger private client stockbrokers use technical analysis as part of their overall research process, although they know better than to rely on it exclusively.

Undeniably, technical analysts provide a wealth of colour. I recently attended a meeting by the Society of Technical Analysts, at which a lecture was given by a prominent technical analyst from a leading investment bank. He waxed lyrical about the 'Japanese candlesticks' charting techniques, and drew on his board slapdash little caricatures of a 'hanging man' and similar.

All this was great fun but did not seem convincing, and his case was clearly at odds with what some of his fellow chartists argued. In fact, 'Japanese candlesticks' are disliked by many technical analysts on the basis that this is an Eastern technique not easily applied to the stock markets of the Western world. As this speaker admitted at the time, technical analysts have to put up with criticism from each other as well as from a great many other investment professionals.

Even if they use the same techniques, two technical analysts will not normally agree on their findings. They will justify their differences by announcing to the world that technical analysis is an art, not a science.

There are only a few medium-term investors who have made substantial money on the stock market who set much store by technical analysis, although there is a larger number of short-term traders – particularly in commodities. One of the most fervent advocates of technical analysis is investment guru David Fuller.

How a successful technical analyst operates

David Fuller, who is chairman of London-based Chart Analysis Ltd, uses technical analysis backed by fundamental analysis to make his own investment decisions, so he puts his money where his mouth is. He uses charts that show simple price movements rather than, for instance, moving averages.

When I interviewed Fuller, a former Wall Street broker, for *The Sunday Times*, he told me that he offers private investors three initial guidelines for interpreting the charts. First, he advised against buying a share unless it shows relative strength against the FTSE 100 index, ideally after a prolonged period of under-performance.

Second, consistent trend-lines up or down – either for a share or a market index – will usually end by accelerating into a parabolic curve, Fuller said. From this point, price movement will become less consistent and it may be profitable to buy or sell. Third, Fuller said that private clients should watch the gilt market, as the stock market will usually follow in the same direction, although not necessarily to the same extent.

If much of this seems common sense, it was meant to be. David Fuller argued that private investors should see a chart not as a crystal ball but as the pictorial representation of price movements attributable to 'mob' psychology. The mob reacts predictably to repeated market situations, Fuller added. For instance, it buys heavily at the top of a bull market but digs in its heels while a bear market is at its lowest, he explained. However, the mob can spring a surprise and a chartist's forecasts are necessarily speculative, Fuller noted.

In his younger years, Fuller was once asked to teach a class on technical analysis. He was advised that all he had to do was to base his lectures on *Technical Analysis of Stock Trends*, the classic textbook of chartism written by Robert Edwards and John Magee first published in 1948.

Fuller felt that he could not base his classes on this text as he found its approach too mechanized. He suggested that the approach of most chartists is similarly too mechanized and their price targets are a stab in the dark. 'They create patterns like head and shoulders in their charts and see what they want to see', he said. 'These patterns are hokum. They are too inconsistent.'

David Fuller publishes his market views regularly in a newsletter (tel: 020 7439 4961). If you want access to the views of a professional chartist, you could do worse than read this. Here is a chartist who is at least prepared to discuss the pros and cons of his approach, and has a sense of humour.

Again in my capacity as a journalist, I managed to track down a chartist who, unlike Fuller, saw a limited significance in patterns that show up on the charts. This was Robert Newgrosh, who runs the Manchester-based technical analysis training operation New Skills (tel: 0161 428 1069), whose training courses are frequently advertised in *Investors Chronicle*.

Newgrosh believes that familiar chartists' reversal patterns such as head and shoulders and double tops, and continuation patterns such as triangles, rectangles and flags, have a valid message to convey. He considers, however, that the so-called mathematical indicators used by chartists are more reliable. He recommends the RSI or relative strength indicator, which, if it goes above 80, indicates that the market is overbought and, if it goes below 20, that it is oversold.

Like Fuller, Newgrosh favours point-and-figure charts, which filter out small random price movements, over line or bar charts. 'They present the clearest message', he argued. Even so, he admitted that technical analysis would sometimes get it wrong.

While chartists such as David Fuller and Robert Newgrosh are cautious in their claims, others will promise an almost infallible system. Dow theory is widely accepted by most as the basis for modern technical analysis, but beyond that there is disagreement. Some peddle complicated fringe theories, including Elliot Wave theory.

Fringe theories

Elliot Wave

There are not many who understand the Elliot Wave theory, which is based on the supposition that cycles in nature have the capacity for repeating themselves indefinitely. The cycles were found to have incorporated a numerical series discovered by Fibonacci, a 13th-century mathematician.

One of the Elliot Wave theory's staunchest supporters is stock market guru Robert Beckman, significantly in this instance an outspoken critic of Wall Street and the City whom the establishment has sometimes loved to hate. In one of his lectures delivered in London, Beckman said that the Elliot Wave principle 'certainly does have an outstanding track record'.

For every enthusiast of the Elliot Wave theory, there are a great many more critics. Leading technical analyst Martin Pring, president of The International Institute for Economic Research in Washington Depot, Connecticut, argues in his classic book *Technical Analysis Explained* that the Elliot Wave is a very subjective tool.

Pring writes that every wave theorist has at some stage become concerned with the issue of where one wave finished and another started. He argues that the maxim 'a little knowledge is a dangerous thing' applies probably more to Elliot than to other market theories.

Gann

Another fringe theory of technical analysis peddled by a small band of staunch supporters is that of Gann. Under Gann's quantum theory, 25 per cent, 50 per cent and 100 per cent moves in the share price are said to be frequent, while moves of one-third and two-thirds less so. How far a share price moves is said to be proportionately related to the time taken to achieve the movement.

Investors who are attracted by a potentially simple solution may find Gann appealing, until, as often happens, it does not work for them. In this book there is not the scope to discuss such fringe theories in any more detail, and nor are they of any great relevance to the Bargain Hunters' Investment FlexiSystem.

In not relying on technical analysis, we are in good company. Many of the world's leading investors such as Warren Buffett will not touch it, relying instead on fundamental analysis. The sheer variety of chartist methods – usually without revealing track records – makes it hard to assess the results.

The cynical view

John Train, president of New York-based fund manager Train, Smith Investment Counsel and best-selling investment author, once told me in a press interview that, in his view, technical analysis is based on fallacious logic. 'It doesn't work and distracts investors from what does', he argued.

In his seminal book *The Craft of Investing*, Train wrote that 'in human affairs, the effects of feedback cannot be expressed mathematically by a formula, at least not yet. Judging human reactions is a matter of intuition, based on flair and experience.'

In Train's opinion, technical analysis is used to 'bemuse customers of broking firms'. This works because it is easier to understand charts than company accounts, he said. Train has known dozens of investment management companies that have spent millions of dollars on technical analysis systems. 'They have almost always failed in due course', he concluded.

Others do not agree with such a cynical view. Bernice Cohen, the self-taught investor who has written books about her proven investment techniques and presented a series of lightweight television programmes about investing, believes technical analysis, although not to be relied on alone, is an important weapon in the armoury of a private investor.

Some sceptics about technical analysis, including Jim Slater, have recently come to give it a little more credence. Slater regards the relative strength of a share price against the market for both the previous month and the previous year as a significant indicator of possible future out-performance. He argues that technical analysts follow the important principle of cutting losses and running profits.

How to explore technical analysis further

If you want to explore technical analysis further – which as Chapter 13 makes clear, is worth doing at least to a limited extent if you will ever wish to branch out into short-term trading – you could attend one of the various advertised courses on the subject.

On the Internet, you will find that various Web sites offer some kind of education in chartism. The best and most entertaining Web site on the Internet for this purpose is, in my view, Db's Burrow (home.talkcity.com/moneyst/dbphoenix/DbsBurrow2.htm). An excellent free site with educational material and articles on chartism is StockCharts.com (www.stockcharts.com).

Try also DecisionPoint.com (www.decisionpoint.com), where subscribers ($10.00 a month at the time of writing) have access to a short course in technical analysis, as well as daily and historical charts. Some features of the Web site, including a chart spotlight that provides technical analysis of selected stocks and indices on a weekly basis, are available free. For market commentary with a chartist slant, one of the best sites is murphymorris.com (www.murphymorris.com), where market technician John Murphy will offer his insights to subscribers ($79.95 a year).

Alternatively, read an introductory book. In my view, by far and away the most readable, despite being rather basic, is *Charters on Charting* by David Charters (Batsford Business Books). Charters runs Investment Research of Cambridge, which publishes ready-plotted charts of companies and various chartist publications. If you are seriously interested in technical analysis, and you do not want the bother of plotting your own charts, it would be worth your while getting in touch with the firm (tel: 0112 335 6251) and asking for its catalogue.

If you would rather plot your own charts, you can do so on your computer, using Windows software. At the time of writing, Market Eye Chartist offers an easy-to-use charting product integrated with its familiar stock market information service. On the Internet, you will find a free and simple-to-operate charting facility at interactive investor international (www.iii.co.uk/quotes/research).

Alternatively, if you intend to follow only a few shares, you may plot your charts manually on graph paper – which forces you to scrutinize them more closely. If the chartism bug really bites, you could join the Society of Technical Analysts as an associate member.

Judging, however, from the disappointment experienced by my colleagues in the City when using the charts to predict share price movements for medium- to long-term investment, you would be well advised to use fundamental analysis – based on the scrutiny of a company's accounts – to accompany your technical analysis, if not to replace it altogether.

Golden rules covered in this chapter

Rule 66   Be sceptical of technical analysts, who take it for granted that patterns of past share price or index movements will be repeated.

Rule 67   Technical analysts are not well paid compared with their peers in the securities industry, but believe in the value of their charts.

Rule 68   Few major stock market investors set much store by technical analysis, but it pulls in a certain type of client and can become a self-fulfilling prophecy.

Rule 69   The sheer variety of technical analysts' methods and lack of records of their success rate makes it hard to prove that chartism is ineffectual.

Rule 70   Use fundamental analysis to accompany your technical analysis for medium- to long-term investment, if not to replace it altogether.

10
Your guide through the minefield of personal finance

We have looked elsewhere in the book at how to buy undervalued shares in difficult market conditions. In this chapter, we will look at how to select from a wide range of other investments. The first rule of thumb is to keep some emergency cash in reserve.

Get the highest available interest rate for your cash on deposit

Your cash reserve should be a sum with which you feel comfortable for possible emergency expenditure – perhaps £5,000. Deposit this money with a building society, making sure that you are receiving one of the highest interest rates available, subject to a convenient notice period.

The best rates are for accounts run by post, telephone or e-mail. You might tolerate a lower interest account if it is in one of the building societies that are large enough to demutualize as, if it did so, you would stand to gain a windfall. If you are interested in opening an account with a building society for this purpose, you may find it interesting to look at the Web site The Carpetbagger's Accomplice (www.carpetbagger.co.uk), which keeps you informed about relevant news for a subscription fee of £10 a month.

In the meantime, make sure that you have a current account with the highest interest rate possible, and that the penalties are not too great if you were to overdraw by mistake. At the time of writing, some of the online banking services are offering exceptionally high interest rates on current accounts for a limited period. For a list of some online banks with their Web addresses, turn to Appendix 9.

Non-equity investments

Except for fun, avoid premium bonds where the computer ERNIE selects random numbers for prizes ranging from £1 million to £50 to be awarded to bondholders. The odds against a substantial win are very steep, and the cash sitting in your premium bond could be invested elsewhere for, on balance, a probable higher return.

In deflationary times, it may be worth switching some of your money into fixed-interest National Savings Certificates, which earn interest tax free and guarantee a fixed rate for five years. For further information on National Savings products and related services, visit the Moneyworld Web site (www.moneyworld.co.uk).

In addition, it can make sense to have, say, 15 per cent of your entire investment portfolio in bonds when inflation is not perceived as an immediate threat, as they can flourish in deflationary times. Bonds are normally issued at a fixed percentage interest rate and for a fixed term, at the end of which the loan is repaid.

Investors usually pile into government bonds – also known as gilts – since these are a sound risk. They are loans to the government, which will not renege on its debt. If you are interested in gilts, you should consult the excellent Web site of Kauders Portfolio Management (www.gilt.co.uk/), which provides some exceptionally clear explanations about how gilts work, and free access to its newsletters. The site shows, for instance, how gilts outperform many other investments in a deflationary environment.

The safe haven of bonds

If you buy a gilt, you will receive a coupon representing a fixed income until the redemption date when the government pays back your loan. Gilts with less than five years until redemption are known as shorts, while 5–15-year gilts are mediums and those with 15 years or more are longs.

The capital value of the loan will fluctuate, rising when interest rates fall and vice versa. As the loan nears its redemption date, the gilt's value will become increasingly close to par value, ie the value of the original loan. Index-linked gilts, for which both the interest rate and the capital repayment on redemption are inflation-adjusted, are most popular in times of high inflation.

The cheapest way to buy gilts is through the post office, but if you want advice on selection, you will need to pay slightly more and use a stockbroker. Do not rush to buy gilts in unit trusts as these vehicles usually have an upfront 5 per cent fee and a 1.5 per cent annual management fee. For private investors, there is no capital gains tax on gilts although tax is payable at the highest rate on income.

In the short term, government bonds can do outstandingly well as they did in the UK after the Asian crisis hit the economy in 1997 and after the Brazilian Real was devalued in early 1999. In the long term, you will do better in equities.

To illustrate the polarity, in 1998, gilts produced a high real return of 21.7 per cent against 10.6 per cent from equities, and between 1990 and early 1999 also produced a higher return than equities, according to the Barclays Capital equity-gilt survey. However, over 80 years, gilts have produced a real annual return of only 2.4 per cent against 8 per cent from equities, the survey found.

In the US, by contrast, returns on the Dow Jones Industrial Average have beaten returns on Treasury bonds – the equivalent to gilts – over the past few years, which has been attributable in part to an unusually strong equities market.

Corporate bonds are similar to gilts but are issued by companies and so usually carry the risk that the issuer will go bust and be unable to pay its debts[1]. For this reason they may offer a much higher yield than gilts, and are consequently preferred by users of the Bargain Hunters' Investment FlexiSystem.

You can spread your risk by investing in a corporate bond fund, which offers an indefinite yield, compared with the individual corporate bond's yield, which lasts only until redemption. You can put your corporate bond or corporate bond fund (as you can gilts) in an individual savings account (ISA), enabling income to be taken from it tax free. We will look at the ISA in more detail in Chapter 11.

---

1 Exceptionally for corporate bonds, The London & Continental Railways Bond is guaranteed by the UK government and so as safe as gilts.

If you have a lump sum to invest, as opposed to wanting a savings scheme, consider a with-profits bond – a lump sum placed in a life company's with-profits fund that is invested in shares, property and fixed-income securities.

With-profits bonds

For these bonds, the underlying funds are less risky than most equity-based investments, owing to their regular, firm annual bonuses, which help smooth out the fluctuations of equity investment. Some profit will be retained by the company in good years to pay the annual – also known as reversionary – bonuses when times are harder.

When your policy matures, a terminal bonus should be paid. With-profits bonds are medium- to long-term investments, and early surrender charges penalize short-term investors.

For tax purposes, with-profits bonds are non-qualifying. Basic rate tax is charged to the fund. Basic-rate taxpayers have no further tax liability but higher-rate taxpayers may be taxed further. Up to 5 per cent per annum of your capital invested can be withdrawn free of higher rate tax.

Under the Bargain Hunters' Investment FlexiSystem, you will first look for a strong investment performance from your bond. Compare its annual bonuses in the past with those of other bonds, making sure that the figures are uniformly net (or gross) of charges, and with medium-term deposit rates.

Also check out the financial strength of the life company that issues the bond you favour. The higher the life assurer's free asset ratio, ie assets divided by liabilities, the stronger is the company. But if the figure is too high, the life company may have strengthened its own resources by giving too low bonuses to investors.

Meanwhile, do not pay too high charges for your with-profits bond. Look for low entry charges, in the form of the initial charge (typically 5 per cent), and the allocation rate, which shows the percentage of your capital invested from the start before the initial charge.

Be wary too of exit charges. There may be a reducing early encashment charge within the first five years of inception. Another concept to watch for is Market Value Adjustment (MVA), which gives the product producer the right not to pay out the full value of your investment. The MVA is applied only under severe market conditions to very short-term investors.

To assess the overall level of charges quickly, use the reduction in yield (RIY) figure. This shows you how much your investment will be reduced each year by the initial and annual charges combined.

Second-hand with-profits endowment policies

If you want a *regular savings scheme* with a higher return than your building society offers, but without the risk of direct equity investment, think about buying a with-profits endowment policy on the second-hand market, which can be a profitable hunting ground for bargain hunters. If you get your used policy at the right price, you will have a low-risk, high-yield investment that will probably give you a fairly good, but not spectacular return.

You will find it is simple to buy your second-hand policy as you will not be hampered by age or health restrictions. And if you find you cannot keep up the premiums, you can resell your policy. You can surrender the policy, make it paid up, or borrow against it.

The closer the policy is to maturity, the more easily its final value is estimated. And you can choose a guaranteed maturity date. For these reasons, the second-hand policy fits neatly into a financial plan. Policies can be clustered to pay school fees or supply you with a regular income or top up a pension. A policy may pay for a wedding, or enable you to make a future payment to a grandchild.

The problem is to find a policy at the right price. Sellers of used endowments are increasing in number and the prices are being set proportionately lower. It pays to shop around the market makers and to haggle the price, or, in this instance, to allow an IFA to do so on your behalf.

Market makers take mainly with-profits endowment policies on to their books from sellers. They make their turn reselling the policies. One advantage in buying from market makers is that their policies on offer are mainly from well-established insurance companies.

Alternatively, you may buy from auctions, which are not so selective over which policies they offer, but sometimes offer you a bigger bargain. At auctions, you will be bidding against professionals so you must know what you are doing.

On the second-hand market, you can sometimes buy your policy for as little as 10 per cent of the surrender value quoted by the seller's insurance company. What matters to you as a buyer is what the policy is worth when it matures.

Try to pay less than the policy's 'locked-in value', which is the guaranteed sum assured as well as bonuses already given. If so, and you keep up premium payments, you will make an almost certain capital gain. The policy's start-up costs will have been met by the first owner.

If you want to find out more information about second-hand endowments, browse through the Web site of the Association of Policy Market Makers (APPM), which you will find at www.moneyworld. co.uk/apmm/what.htm. You can also contact some of the market makers directly (a list is provided in Appendix 5). You might like to take a quick look at the Web site of market maker Neville James (www.neville-james.co.uk/), which answers some general questions.

Collective investments

Meanwhile, if you want to invest in equities but prefer to have your money managed on your behalf, with a broad spread of risk, you must consider collective investments. These may be unit trusts, on which you will find plenty of information at the Web site of the Association of Unit Trusts and Investment Funds (www.investmentfunds.org.uk).

Alternatively, consider open-ended investment companies (OEICs), which issue shares at a single price rather than a spread – more familiar to continental European investors than their UK counterparts – and allow comparatively cheap switching between sub-funds. In addition, there are investment trusts, on which you will find plenty of information at the Web site of The Association of Investment Trust Companies (www.aitc.co.uk).

If you invest small sums regularly in a collective vehicle – perhaps on a monthly direct debit – you will not be over-exposed to sudden massive stock market declines. In addition, you will reap the benefits from buying, amongst other times, when shares are at rock bottom.

Unit trusts

Against this, the vast majority of unit trusts do not even keep up with the market as defined by the main indices, despite the fund managers often visiting many companies in the year, and at vast expense. Clearly, your choice of fund will affect your wealth.

Consult *Money Management*, or the Web site of Micropal (www. micropal.com) for past performance statistics and only consider investing in a unit trust that has consistently been in the top quartile of performers over the past few years, and where there is no indication of a sudden change in management that could adversely affect performance. Alternatively, use the powersearch facility at Money World (www.moneyworld.co.uk/powersearch) to track down the top-performing unit trusts over a period of your choice (also applicable to other investments, including tax-free funds). If you lack the time or energy to take any of these measures, you would be better off investing in an index tracker fund.

An index tracker fund simply tracks the market – either the FTSE 100 index or the All-Share index, which has in the past been the better performer. Occasionally, the fund is presented with a new twist, as, for instance, Bristol-based discount broker Hargreaves Lansdown's Active Tracker Fund, which attempts to add value to the tracker concept by excluding or reducing exposure to stocks that are considered likely to under-perform the FTSE 100 index.

In general, index tracker funds offer a slightly lower return than the market after all charges have been deducted. These charges vary, with, for instance, Legal & General making available an index tracker fund for an annual charge of much less than that of Virgin. But in the case of all index trackers, the charges are low compared with those of actively managed funds.

In absolute terms, as opposed to when measured against the index they follow, tracker funds do not go so far as they might towards risk reduction as represented by diversification across industries. For instance, the FTSE 100 index, which some tracker funds follow, has limited diversification, partly because it is underweight in construction and property, which account for a substantial percentage of UK industry, and overweight in financials and pharmaceuticals, which represent a more limited proportion of UK activity.

In addition, index trackers, by definition, would follow any declining market downwards. They cannot transfer money into cash when the market is down. On a more positive front, promoters of index trackers have claimed with justification that their product has outperformed around 90 per cent of other funds in recent years after all charges have been taken into account.

If you are interested in tracker funds, you should consult the Motley Fool UK Website (www.motleyfool.co.uk), which is a particular fan of index tracking funds. In addition, consult *Tracker Magazine*, which is an online publication providing some commentary relevant to tracker funds (tracker.netpep.co.uk). Despite the case for the tracker funds, if you buy an actively managed unit trust from a discount broker, you will pay significantly lower upfront charges and so stand more chance of beating the index-trackers on a charges-inclusive basis, particularly if you have selected a high performer. Meanwhile, should markets be particularly volatile, consider investing in a protected unit trust.

Protected unit trusts

Protected unit trusts set a floor price. Theoretically, they let you have a share in any gains, while providing a safety net. Some are known as *cash and call* funds, where most of your money (95 per cent +) is kept in cash deposits, so guaranteeing your capital. The rest of your money is invested in call options. If the stock market rises, your options are worth more and your units become more valuable. If the market declines, your options lose all their value and you are left only with the cash value of your capital.

Other protected unit trusts, known as *stock and put* funds, invest mainly in large companies, with a small amount in put options. If the stock market falls, the options enable you to sell the shares at a pre-agreed price, so limiting the risk. If the stock market rises, the put options lose all their value but the fund gains from shares.

In the short term, protected unit trusts have sometimes outper-formed a volatile market but, in the long run, they do not offer such good returns as their unprotected equivalents. To maximize your potential return, it is often worth opting for a lower percentage level of your capital to be guaranteed, leaving more cash available for the purchase of options. Obviously this also increases your potential risk.

In volatile markets, investment trusts are often better value than unit trusts, although less information on them is available. This is understandable as, until recently, salespeople received no commission for selling investment trusts.

Why investment trusts can be excellent value

Investment trusts, unlike unit trusts, are geared, and can be extremely profitable. They can be a very good buy when the stock market is depressed and the share price has declined to a substantial discount to net asset value (NAV).

But such a discount (at the time of writing averaging 15 per cent) is not an unequivocal buying signal. The likelihood that the discount will narrow in the future must also be assessed. In the past, the discount has often narrowed, making investment trusts in general a better performing investment than unit trusts.

In your case, to increase the chances of this continuing to happen, make sure that the investment trust in which you are considering investing has proven management, and that the price had been at a smaller discount to NAV before any recent market correction. After you buy, the discount must narrow by at least 5 per cent simply to cover your dealing costs.

As a rule of thumb, investment trusts that mirror unit trusts run by the same manager tend to be among the least risky. If a fund is planning a share buyback, this is another point in its favour.

Some users of the Bargain Hunters' Investment FlexiSystem have found that investment trust savings plans are a flexible way to repay the capital on a mortgage, enabling you to stop or start contributions without penalty.

Your mortgage

You may need to buy or keep on a mortgage, or perhaps you are considering a buy-to-let mortgage. If so, visit the mortgage pages of the Money World Web site (www.moneyworld.co.uk/homebuying). The site will give you access to tools for selecting the best mortgage for your circumstances from more than 110 available. You will also find here guides to flexible mortgages, tracker mortgages, and others. In addition, there are online tools enabling you to evaluate your mortgage repayments, and how much insurance cover you need for your home contents.

If, as happened in late 1998, interest rates are falling and the prospect of deflation looms, consider locking into a fixed-rate mortgage while you can do so cheaply, but ideally avoid a product with stiff redemption penalties. If you have a variable-rate mortgage and threaten to leave the mortgage provider for a better deal, it may offer you a reduction in interest rates.

Alternatively, you may want to pay off chunks of your mortgage to avoid falling into a potential negative equity trap. If you are in a position to pay your mortgage off completely, consider keeping at least a few hundred pounds outstanding on the loan, as this would enable you to re-mortgage in the years to come.

If you prefer to pay off the entire debt, consider doing so at the *end* of the month if your lender as a matter of policy would charge interest for the full month in which you would make the final payment. Should you have an endowment policy with your mortgage, you are probably best off keeping it on as a savings vehicle.

Should you prefer to sell your policy, you will often get a better price on the second-hand market than from your insurer. Alternatively, you could make it paid up, which would mean you would get a residual sum at the end of the policy's term based on your premiums paid to date.

Alternative investments

Last, and in a sense least, in this chapter, we will take a quick look at alternative investments, which include pictures, antiques, memorabilia, racehorses, etc. A major reason for this area of investment being so often unprofitable is that investors tend to be enthusiastic collectors who overpay for items and then cannot bear to part with them. In a similar spirit, investors in fine wines like to drink away their profits.

There are, however, buyers of alternative investments who simultaneously work our system. If you want to follow suit, place your priority on investing for profit, not pleasure. To achieve this, you will need to have the same specialist knowledge as those who invest simply for the love of it. Subscribe to specialist journals, join relevant groups, and bone up on your field.

Such acquired expertise can pay off. Some users of our system who astutely bought top Bordeaux wines in the mid-1990s saw a more than 100 per cent capital gain on the investment within four years. Any realized proceeds on wine sales are free of capital gains tax provided that the bottles have been stored 'in bond' in a public cellar.

Similarly, classic cars can be hugely profitable, with the advantage that you can make use of your investment while you own it. But some classic cars on the market have turned out on purchase to have been fraudulently constructed. If you are to reduce the odds of unwittingly buying a dud, you must develop some expertise in classic cars (or draw on a friend's) *before* you commit your cash.

Finally, some alternative investments are high risk, even if you understand them fully. Many so-called 'angels' who invest in new theatre productions lose substantial sums. Investing in racehorses can also be highly speculative.

You should invest in such areas only with 'fun' money – a small sum in proportion to your assets, which you can afford to lose. In addition, use other ways to cut down the risk. For example, instead of joining a syndicate of up to 12 members that owns a racehorse jointly, consider joining a racing club that gives you a share in several horses for a far smaller outlay. The wisdom of spreading your risk applies as much to alternative as to more conventional investments.

Golden rules covered in this chapter

Rule 71   Corporate bonds are often better value than gilts.

Rule 72   Investment trusts have often proved a better investment than unit trusts.

Rule 73   Consider buying second-hand endowments as part of your financial planning.

Rule 74   Buy alternative investments for profit, not pleasure.

11

Give the taxman a run for his money

Invest first because an investment is worth having, and only then for tax efficiency. It is no good buying a tax-efficient investment if it then proceeds to plummet. If, however, you are happy with your investments, what are the tax issues you must take into account? We will run through some of these in this chapter, but you may also wish to consult the various useful tax advisory resources available on the Web site of interactive investment international (www.iii.co.uk/tax), and of the Inland Revenue (www.inlandrevenue.gov.uk/home.htm).

First, let us take a look at capital gains tax, for which recent investors in Internet companies may find themselves liable if they realize some of their stratospheric gains.

Capital gains tax

Capital gains tax (CGT) is payable on realized profits on investments that overreach a set limit – currently £7,100 – in any given tax year. Some users of our system will not realize enough profits when they start investing to overreach this allowance, but may do so later.

If you are a long-term investor who is likely to be stung by capital gains tax, you will benefit from the introduction that took place in March 1998 of a sliding scale for CGT, replacing the earlier flat rate. Under the current scale, the longer you have held the investments on which you are realizing profits, the less CGT you will pay.

On the punitive side, indexation, as a result of which any rise in your investments attributable to inflation had usefully been discounted for CGT purposes, was abolished in March 1998. A last-in, first-out rule was introduced under which, if you should sell part of an investment for a profit, you would pay the CGT tax rate applicable to your *most recent* contributing purchase.

Also in March 1998, bed and breakfasting was abolished. This was the practice of selling your investments on the last day of the tax year and buying back a day later at probably a similar price, simply to establish a gain or a loss for CGT purposes. The gap between selling and rebuying now has to be 30 days, although some have beaten the system by selling and then arranging for a friend to buy shares in the same quantity immediately, with the transactions reversed after 30 days.

How to shelter your capital from tax by use of TESSAs, PEPs and ISAs

Since 5 April 1999, it has no longer been possible to buy the familiar PEP, which shelters investments from income and capital gains tax, or the TESSA, through which cash kept on deposit for five years is similarly sheltered from tax.

However, you can retain any PEPs that you have already acquired, and should consider doing so, subject to the investments in it being suitable, or being appropriately replaced, and subject to the charges being minimal in comparison with those of other PEPs. Make sure that you have not divided your General PEP investment between different plan managers, so illicitly establishing more than one PEP in the same tax year.

In addition, you can retain your TESSA until its five-year term is up, following which you have the option of transferring it into an individual savings account (ISA). The amount transferred would not be included in the ISA's overall annual limit of £5,000 (£7,000 in 1999–2000).

If you instead give up a TESSA before its term is up, you will have to be prepared to lose all the tax benefits. This will not matter if future interest rates turn out to be low, so adversely affecting the return provided by your TESSA, and you have reinvested the money more wisely.

To replace the PEP and the TESSA, the ISA was introduced in April 1999 and is guaranteed to run for 10 years. It shelters your investments from all income and capital gains tax. Meanwhile, UK dividends within ISAs will have a 10 per cent tax credit until 5 April 2004.

If you are a taxpayer who will be liable for CGT in the foreseeable future, it *may* be worth investing what you can afford in an ISA every year subject to the overall annual limit, provided that, as for your PEP, you are happy with your underlying investments. Just as you should never invest in shares only for the shareholder perks, so you should never invest only for the tax concessions.

If you do not realize enough capital gains to use up your annual CGT exemption and foresee no prospect of this, the ISA would save you only income tax. In that case, do not go for an ISA unless the income tax saving is more than the charges on the vehicle. While you are a non-taxpayer, there is no benefit to you in having an ISA at all.

For taxpayers, an ISA consists of three components: cash, insurance and shares. Cash has an annual investment limit of £1,000 (£3,000 in 1999–2000), while insurance – for which little demand is expected – has a similar £1,000 limit.

You can invest up to the ISA's full overall limit in shares, provided you have used one provider for your entire ISA (maxi subscription), which is recommended for those users of the Bargain Hunters' Investment FlexiSystem who are active buyers of equities and expect to be hit by CGT, whether this year or in the foreseeable future. The ISA is quite flexible and does not have the geographic limits prescribed for the PEP, which countenance only EU shares or collective investments that have at least half their holdings in EU shares.

If you have used different providers for components of your ISA (mini subscriptions), your limit for investing in shares is £3,000. Be wary of being enticed by a building society into investing perhaps a small sum in a high-interest account that is actually a mini-ISA, as the move would prevent you from taking out a maxi-ISA.

Generally in an attempt to reassure you, the ISA has the option of meeting the government CAT benchmark, which stands for Charges, Access and Terms. For cash ISAs, the CAT benchmark ensures that interest paid will not be more than 2 per cent below the prevailing base rate. For insurance, the CAT guarantees that minimum premiums will be no more than £25 a month, while annual charges will be no higher than 3 per cent of a fund's value. Equities and bonds that qualify for the ISA CAT standard must have annual charges that do not exceed 1 per cent of net asset value.

At the time of writing, the CAT has been criticized by the investment industry, on the grounds that investment management groups –

with the exception of index tracker funds – cannot operate on margins of 1 per cent per annum or less and so will not be able to use the CAT benchmark. In addition, it has been felt that the public will demand the CAT benchmark, believing erroneously that it in some way guarantees investment performance.

This pressure on the industry is good news for you, as it will focus attention on levels of charges for unit trusts and other collective investments. At the same time, the few funds that have historically outperformed the index trackers on a charges-inclusive basis – a larger number if you buy from a discount broker where charges are lower – may not carry the CAT benchmark and, in such cases, you should not insist on this as a prerequisite for investing. However, the majority of funds that fail to meet the CAT benchmark will be poor performers with high charges, so do your homework before committing your cash.

As another string to your tax-efficiency bow, you could hold money in offshore bank deposit accounts, which give you a cash flow advantage in that it is not taxed at source. You must, however, declare offshore investments on your tax return.

Pensions and annuities

While a pension is, as always, a good idea, the full tax relief that is available on all your contributions to your pension pot is not so compelling a reason to invest in one as it was. This is partly due to declining interest rates forced by falling gilt yields on the annuity that is traditionally bought by some of the proceeds from your pension fund upon retirement. In addition, the present government has ended the tax relief that pension funds received on dividends, meaning, in many cases, less of an ultimate pay-out for you.

But the pension is undeniably effective as a long-term savings vehicle, if only because any money that you pay in is inaccessible throughout its term. Of course for this very reason, some prefer to forego the tax relief arising from buying a pension and invest in more liquid savings vehicles.

Unless you have specific alternative plans, you are recommended to take out a pension. For more information on how pensions work, consult the very useful DSS Web site, which contains the text of a DSS leaflet about pensions (www.dss.gov.uk/pen/index.htm). Start contributing to your pension as early as possible and pay into it as much as you can afford so that you benefit from the full tax relief on contributions.

In choosing your pension, look for strong past performance in your selected fund (comparative tables are in *Money Management*). A with-profits fund offers the security of adding annual bonuses to your pension, which cannot be removed provided that you maintain your payments. But in a rising equity market, a managed fund should do better than a with-profits fund. To put at least part of your pension money into an index tracker fund will on past form be no bad move. The merits of index trackers, and their drawbacks, are explained in Chapter 10.

Look also for a pension with little or no front-end loading. If this is high, it means that commissions to the salesperson are paid more out of your early contributions. The arrangement would prove costly for you, should you stop your pension early.

To get the best deal, it is a good idea to buy your pension from a discount broker, where the rebate can be extremely substantial. Otherwise, telephone sales operations offer a pension deal that is often cheap relative to that on offer in a face-to-face sales situation. Meanwhile, you will save money in charges levied on your pension during the initial years if you say that you will retire at 50. Despite this, once you reach the age of 50, you can continue paying into your pension if you wish.

Make sure too before you buy that your pension will enable you to stop or restart your payments without penalization, although watch how far such flexibility is paid for by higher charges. Meanwhile, if you are a higher-rate taxpayer, you should consider offshore bonds to supplement your pension, enabling you to defer British tax liability until the bond is cashed in.

Should you have an occupational pension – which is usually a better deal than a personal pension because the employer contributes – think twice before being cajoled by an IFA into taking out free-standing additional voluntary contributions (FSAVCs) to supplement your regular payments. They are more expensive than occupational additional voluntary contributions (AVCs) as provided through your employer, despite being more portable and offering a wider range of investment options.

Should you be planning to retire over the next few years and already have a pension, you will not want to take risks with your pension fund, which is likely to be heavily invested in equities. Ask your pension provider about the practicalities of shifting money invested away from equities into government bonds and cash, if this strategy is not already automatically in place. Do not put off doing this until the day that you buy your annuity using the fund built up in your pension.

When you buy your annuity, exercise the open market option, which enables you to look for the best annuity rate rather than the one offered by your pension company. Also, check if your pension has a guaranteed annuity rate. If you are a smoker or a person in bad health, you may be eligible for an impaired life annuity (at a higher rate). If you are willing to take a risk, consider a unit linked or with-profit annuity. If you need more information about how annuities work, consult the page about annuities on the Money World Web site (www.moneyworld.co.uk).

As an alternative to an annuity if your pension fund is worth at least £100,000, you may find it worthwhile to take an income draw. Under this arrangement, you would leave your pension fund invested and draw an income straight from it. But once you have chosen a draw-down provider and started to take your income, you cannot switch to another provider.

Meanwhile, as I started writing this book, the government was planning to introduce a new pension investment vehicle that would compete with the traditional pension. The vehicle, which will be called the lifelong individual savings account (Lisa), is not in itself a pension. It is a tax-efficient wrapper that allows pension savings to be retained in open-ended investment companies, unit trusts and investment trusts.

As with the traditional pension, the fund in your Lisa will not be available before retirement. In this respect, the Lisa does not have the same flexibility as the American 401K pension plan on which it is loosely based.

The advantages of the Lisa will include low charges relative to those of a traditional pension, and ease of transfer. While the product is expected to have wide appeal, it will be particularly suitable if you have an irregular income, or change jobs frequently.

Other tax-efficient investing

If you have invested in small unquoted companies, be sure to take advantage of any tax incentives open to you as a result. Meanwhile, some users of our system with the gambling temperament have bet on individual shares or on the direction of stock market indices through a financial bookmaker, meaning that if they make gains, they are not hit with a CGT bill.

One veteran user of the Bargain Hunters' Investment FlexiSystem of my acquaintance has made a fortune through such spread-betting. He takes huge positions and wins or loses up to £30,000 in a day or so. On balance, he finishes up much better off. Partly on the proceeds of his winnings, he is a half-millionaire who lives in a large luxurious house that he bought outright for cash.

My former colleague has revealed his secrets in a fascinating manual he sells through press advertisements for about £100 and which, it has to be said, makes him far more regular profits than spread-betting itself. This man is still only in his 20s.

From your point of view, bear in mind that the profits that my former colleague – who comes from an extremely entrepreneurial family – has been able to make out of spread-betting are not within the bounds of reasonable possibility for everybody.

Spread-betting is only for those who can afford to lose substantially, and who will still then bounce back to place another bet. Even then, you are working against the odds. In the words of Dirty Harry, the cop immortalized by actor Clint Eastwood in the eponymous movie, *'do you feel lucky, punk?'* If so, you can find out more by visiting the spread-betting page of the Web site Resources (www.updata.co.uk/resources/spreadbetting/). This page has links with leading financial bookmakers IG Index and City Index, and, at the time of writing, to a Motley Fool article on spread-betting.

Separately, in your own interests, be sure to claim a repayment from the Inland Revenue of any surplus tax you have paid. If you do not, the Revenue will offset the money against your next bill, paying only a very limited rate of interest on it.

Inheritance tax planning

Once you have assessed the potential value of your estate, including investments, you should take steps to reduce any inheritance tax (IHT) liability. Following your death, the tax starts at 40 per cent with no sliding scale, after an exemption of £231,000 in assets transfers.

However, assets left to your spouse are not subject to IHT, and you can avoid IHT by making lifetime gifts, although they are still a disposal for CGT purposes. If you live for more than seven years after the gift is made, there is no IHT liability. If you die within seven years, there is tapering IHT relief.

The catch is that should you give away an asset, it has to be with beneficial as well as legal ownership in order to benefit from IHT exemption. If, for instance, an elderly person gives away her house to her children but continues to live in it, IHT would still be levied on her death as she would have retained beneficial ownership. Most elderly people need their assets to live in or to produce income on which to live and so cannot take full advantage of the IHT exemption for life-time gifts.

More accessible are the IHT exemptions available for an annual figure of £3,000, for unlimited gifts of up to £250 each per annum, for all gifts to charities and, within limitations, for wedding gifts. Business and agricultural asses are not subject to IHT, with some exceptions.

For further advice on IHT planning, it may be worthwhile tapping an IFA for free advice. Alternatively, visit the inheritance tax page of the Money World Web site (www.moneyworld.co.uk).

Avoid the pirate tax haven consultants

Avoid using the pirate tax consultants who set up shop in the US and the UK, as well as in continental Europe, often hiding behind PO boxes and using false names. These consultants promise techniques for avoiding tax altogether and stress that they are legal. They and their publishers promote expensive reports and still more expensive consultancies.

Clients are advised never to stay in any country long enough to be liable to pay local taxes. The trick is to spend their lives as a hedonistic 'Perpetual Traveller' around the world. Nationality, residence and domicile are selected individually for fiscal convenience. Well-known tax havens are recommended for residence purposes.

To support your new roving lifestyle, portable business activities are required if you are not rich enough to stop working, while a second passport is recommended (and sometimes offered for sale) in case your usual one should be seized. A series of 'recommended' mail drops around the world will sever the trail of communication.

Such secrecy is seen as necessary because these activities can rouse the authorities in some countries to take retaliatory measures.

Unsurprisingly, many (not all) promoters of these tax avoidance schemes have criminal records. In their reports, they detail legal tax avoidance methods but, in their confidential consultancies, some reveal the 'real meat', which consists of illegal schemes.

As an investment professional and financial journalist, I have unavoidably crossed paths with consultants in this field, and would urge you to be wary. Some are *bona fide* but others are not. Some are rich but they have not always made their money by the proverbial sweat of their brows.

The worst of these consultants are out-and-out hucksters without a penny to their name. Some have spent years in US prisons for tax fraud. I know of one such consultant who was recently jailed for running a Ponzi-style pyramid scheme. Others have fled various countries pursued by the authorities. These are in a very real sense Perpetual Travellers – permanently on the run.

Undeniably, these less than conventional advisers cater for a demand, and their customers – often eccentrics and dreamers – will pay highly for their advice. Be careful about using such an adviser yourself. The second passport offloaded on you may turn out to be a dud. The expensive mail drop recommended to you may pay the consultant a hefty commission on every introduction.

Some of the less salubrious offerings are exposed on the scams page of a fascinating Web site, the offshore secrets network (www.offshoresecrets.com/scams.htm), which will tell you much about the world of unconventional offshore investing, second passports, alternative identities, citizenship, and information that is billed as what the IRS (the US tax authorities) 'doesn't want you to know'. The network is claimed to be owned by 'an independent group of entrepreneurs based in many different locations on the Globe'.

Golden rules covered in this chapter

Rule 75   Retain any PEPs you may have, and invest in ISAs, subject to satisfaction with the underlying investments, and low charges.

Rule 76   Select the best value pension and shop around for your annuity.

Rule 77   Be wary of unqualified tax consultants who promote the 'Perpetual Traveller' lifestyle as a way of avoiding all taxes.

12

Pick up properties and timeshares for a song

In this chapter, you will be introduced to the art of buying property exceptionally cheaply at auction, and furnishing it for next to nothing. You will also learn how to buy timeshare for a fraction of its full retail price. The issues involved in obtaining finance to fund your purchases will be aired with a frankness you are unlikely to see elsewhere in print.

The fact that the Bargain Hunters' Investment FlexiSystem is applicable in such areas as property and timeshare demonstrates how far-reaching are its principles. Truth is, investing for value makes sense as much outside the stock market as in it.

Become a property wheeler dealer

The easiest way to pick up a bargain property – particularly in times of an actual or pending recession – is at auction. But be wary. Properties sold this way are often in need of serious renovation, and may have various encumbrances. You will of course be bound to honour any purchase you make at auction.

To get started on this route, keep an eye out for property auctions advertised in *The Estates Gazette*, or in your local and the national press. Alternatively, telephone auction houses directly, and they will send you their regular catalogues. A list of property auctions is available online at various Web sites, including PropertyCity (www.propertycity.co.uk).

Before you think of bidding for a property at auction, inspect it carefully in advance – either independently, or on an organized viewing. You cannot afford to buy blind like professional dealers because you are not operating on so large a scale as they are. If you make a mistake, it may be your only deal.

So tread carefully. If you are keen on buying a property, it may be worthwhile taking advance legal advice on aspects relating to its lease. In any case, avoid bidding for properties with very short remaining leases, or with restrictions on the use of the property.

In addition, you could consider hiring a surveyor to carry out a survey on any property in which you are particularly interested, but you should fast develop a nose for detecting significant structural defects yourself.

To find the best bargain at auction, it is often best to go for a property that has been repossessed by a building society and is being auctioned for a quiet sale. Very likely it will have nothing fundamentally wrong with it.

If it is at the lower end of the price spectrum, the property may not be of great interest to property dealers. Should it be cosmetically unattractive, this may conveniently put off other bidders.

Sometimes you can buy an auction property in advance of the sale, provided that not many other parties are interested and you offer a fair price. This way, you will avoid price mark-ups at auctions initiated by cartels of dealers or the seller bidding up his or her own property. Alternatively, you can often buy cheaply those properties that have recently been auctioned but where the reserve price has not been reached.

Once you have bought a property at auction and put down your deposit, you will need to pay the balance within 28 days. This means you must have either cash or finance in place.

If you should fail to complete, the property would probably be resold, and you could be sued for the shortfall. You would also lose your deposit paid in the auction room, and would be obliged to pay the seller's expenses.

How to furnish your property for almost nothing

The cheapest way to furnish your property is by buying items very cheaply at auction. The auctions are advertised in the various newspapers. They are flagged more comprehensively in various subscription-only newsletters.

At these sales, you can often buy little-used dishwashers, chairs, computers, phones, microwave ovens, etc for a fraction of their true value. The stock may have been repossessed by finance companies, or taken by dealers in part exchange. Alternatively, the sale may be private.

The sale is typically organized at an auction house, or on the premises of the bankrupt company to which all the sale items belonged. You should visit the premises in advance and examine the goods, although you may not always be allowed to try them out. Look out carefully for defects.

Before buying at auction, check the conditions of sale, which the auctioneer will supply to you on request. The goods may be sold cheaply 'as seen'. Alternatively, they may be sold at a higher price but with a warranty, which means you would be able to have your money back if something were wrong.

If you bid for an item at less than its reserve price, the auctioneer will refuse to sell it, or will do so provisionally – subject to negotiation with the seller. If your bid is accepted, you may need to pay a deposit immediately.

As you leave the auction's premises, you will often be approached by street vendors who offer you apparent bargains. These are pirates and you should avoid any dealings with them. Their goods are likely to be duds, or to have been stolen and, if so, you will not find this out until you have handed over your cash and the vendor has vanished for good.

Avoid the pirate auctions

In a similar spirit, there are pirates who set up auctions of their own in huge showrooms all around the country but particularly in London's West End. They tempt large crowds into huge showrooms where they stage apparent sales.

The pirates appear to be auctioning TVs, hi-fis and other electrical goods, and letting them go at knock-down prices. In practice, no real sales are completed, with bargains being distributed only to stooges. Driven by greed, members of the public are coaxed into making an advance payment for a 'mystery gift' that they all assume will be a bundle of electrical goods.

Typically, in return for £5 paid, the mark is given a small packet wrapped in red opaque cellophane, with instructions not to open it until he or she has left the showroom. Ushered back into the street, the mark discovers it contains a worthless tin necklace or similar.

When some return to the auction hall to protest, bouncers at the door prevent them from re-entering. Once the fuss has died down, another auction is staged. Do not fall for this recurring scam.

How to bid at online auctions

As an alternative to furnishing your home at conventional auctions, you can use the online auctions. Should you decide to make an electronic bid, you will have to register with your chosen site (see Appendix 6 for a list of online auction houses). Consult the online catalogue to find the item you want, then enter the fray.

Your bid should start low and rise in stages against competing bids up to the highest amount you have committed yourself to paying, which you can increase if you wish. You may follow the auction online, and the result will be e-mailed to you. If your bid is successful, you must contact the seller within three days. For security, you can arrange for your money to be held in escrow until you have been sent the goods but it will cost you 5 per cent of the purchase price.

Save thousands buying and selling timeshare

Timeshare is an industry that attracts more than its fair share of get-rich-quick merchants and scam artists. But the concept of timeshare – giving you the right to use a unit of accommodation for a specified period every year, over a designated period, paid for in advance – is seen as legitimate by some. It is claimed to have the advantage of offering inflation-proof holidays and exceptionally high-standard accommodation at a reasonable price.

In your case as a potential buyer making use of the Bargain Hunters' Investment FlexiSystem, you can soon weed out the bargains from the wide variety of timeshares on offer. Under the system, you can buy timeshare for a fraction of its usual retail price, but, even then, you should only buy if you intend to use your timeshare every year for holidays. There is no guarantee that you will be ever able to rent or resell it for a realistic price.

Indeed, the difficulties in reselling timeshare are the very reason you can buy it cheaply on the second-hand market, taking it off the hands of desperate sellers. These owners were often hard-sold their time-share in the first place, and may not really use it.

Your easiest way to buy bargain timeshares

To buy your timeshare through a resale agency is usually the easiest and cheapest way. But *caveat emptor* prevails. At worst, the agencies are shady organizations that may go bust, particularly if they are newish and have spent too much on advertising, or were set up as a hit-and-run operation in the first place. Send such an agency your money and you may never see it again.

The better agencies in the US are licensed in the states where they are based, while, in Europe, they are members of a trade body, The Organization for Timeshare in Europe (OTE), of which the UK 'Chapter' is The Timeshare Council (www.timesharecouncil.com). The OTE-member agencies have been vetted for ethics and efficiency.

If you have a complaint about an OTE member agency, the OTE will take it up on your behalf. Although the OTE has no statutory powers, most resale members will fall in line as they will be reluctant to risk forfeiting their membership, which is a prerequisite for advertising in certain national newspapers and carries sway with the public. For a list of OTE/Timeshare Council member agencies, turn to Appendix 6.

In almost all cases, timeshare resale agencies do not act as principals, ie buying weeks themselves to sell on, but are instead agents acting as middlemen between the seller and buyer. They will often take money from vendors up-front in the form of registration fees and/or other deposits.

In the UK, Primeshare has become the market leader, and, on past experience, anybody who buys from this agency will get a reasonable service. Of the other agencies, some offer a fair deal, while others do not and you may have to find out which is which by trial and error.

Whichever agency you use, you should bargain hard as prices are negotiable at the vendor's discretion. You should look to buying 'second-hand' timeshare for no more than half the new price and, ideally, for 10–30 per cent of it. To achieve this, make a ridiculously low offer for your targeted resale timeshare – hundreds instead of thousands of pounds for each week for sale. If your offer is declined by the vendor, you can always raise it, or instead make a similarly low offer for an alternative timeshare on the agency's list.

As a committed bargain hunter, you are best off finding timeshares being offloaded by 'distressed' sellers who face for instance death in the family, inability to take more holidays for medical reasons or, in particular, financial problems. Owners resent paying compulsory maintenance fees – which cover such essentials as gas and electricity on the resort – and possibly loan repayments for a timeshare they do not want. A good time for you to buy from such a vendor is in January when maintenance fees for the forthcoming year are invoiced. Before buying, make sure that the fees have been paid to date.

Here is a further tip. The biggest reductions in percentage terms for resale timeshares are often to be found in resorts that have been notoriously hard-sold, since the practice has left a plethora of resentful owners desperate to offload their timeshares at almost any price.

After you have made your purchase, the more conscientious agencies will conveniently handle the legal transfer from the vendor to yourself as buyer. They will typically hold your purchase deposit in an independently controlled account while they check the seller's title on your behalf. In contrast, the type of resale agency that puts you in direct contact with the seller from the start of the negotiating process may not help you with the title transfer.

While resale agencies are usually the richest picking ground for reliable timeshares at a cut price, there are alternative sources, including timeshare auctions.

Timeshare auctions

Timeshare auctions not infrequently get cancelled for lack of attendance. But if they proceed, they may offer you a chance to buy timeshares at giveaway prices – particularly if no reserve price has been set.

Be wary, however. Current timeshare regulations do not affect purchases at auction, and so disclosure requirements are fairly limited while the cooling off periods required as part of the contract if you buy directly from the developer in most of Europe are usually non-applicable (as when you buy from resale agencies that are not OTE members).

In practice, auctions are sometimes used to offload timeshares not affiliated to the main exchange organizations. Such timeshares may be of a lower standard than is required for such affiliation, and may leave you stuck with going back to the same inferior holiday resort year after year. The timeshares continue to attract interest because they are so modestly priced.

Private purchase

It is possible to buy a bargain second-hand timeshares privately, but this will require a great deal of spadework. The kinds of people who advertise their timeshare for sale privately have an inflated idea of its value. They are often unrealistically trying to get back what they paid for their timeshares or more.

If you want to buy from this source, you must regularly scour magazines and newspapers for promising advertisements. Always look to paying no more than half the developer's current price.

The conventional sales presentation

Sometimes, you can buy a timeshare cheap from the original promoter at a sales presentation, to which you will typically have been lured by the promise of a free gift. But, if you are to talk down the asking price, you will need sharp negotiating skills – particularly abroad where some of the sales methods used are particularly unprincipled.

Upon attending a sales presentation, be prepared for around three hours of hard sell, including a video showing of the resort, to be followed by a salesperson's high-pressure close. Only once you appear hooked will the salesperson discuss the price.

At the average sales presentation, there is no standardization of prices, and the promoter asks the price it reckons you as an individual (or couple) will pay. For instance, at first asking, the price quoted for two high-season weeks at a penthouse suite in a desirable resort may be £30,000, perhaps twice the cost quoted for the equivalent in a lower-floor apartment in the same block. Likewise, a unit with a sea view will typically be priced at a premium.

As a rule of thumb, aim to pay no more than 50 per cent of the asking price. You will very likely be offered a 20 per cent discount initially, so it is up to you to bargain this down. Except in the case of a few up-market resorts, the promoter will very likely drop the price further on the basis having a few units going at a special price – perhaps resale weeks – if it is clear you will not otherwise buy.

Astute users of the Bargain Hunters' Investment FlexiSystem attend such sales presentations purely for research purposes, to learn about timeshare and what is available on the market. They then actually buy their timeshares elsewhere, more cheaply. This practice is akin to discussing your financial needs with several IFAs, and then buying products from a discount broker, as recommended in Chapter 2.

Direct press advertising.

A few developers market 'new' timeshare mainly through press advertisements. The marketing cost of selling timeshare this way is typically as little as 12.5 per cent of the retail price, as opposed to 35–60 per cent at standard sales presentations where prospective buyers are lured in by expensive mailshots and promises of free gifts.

For this reason, you can buy timeshare from off-the-page press advertisements at bargain prices. Once you respond to an advertisement, no salesman will visit but you will very likely be subjected to the hard sell over the telephone.

In the past, some timeshares sold cheap in bulk through press advertisements have been of a very basic standard, which has meant that their exchangeability has also been limited. In contrast, a few timeshares sold this way – including the excellent Paradise Club in Tenerife – have been of outstanding quality.

A brief checklist before you commit yourself to buying timeshare

Buy high-season weeks if possible because, although they are the most expensive, they are the easiest to exchange or rent. You must also buy your timeshare weeks in the right size of units. Try, for instance, to avoid buying into a studio as this can be very cramped and will be less saleable than a larger unit.

Make sure that the resort in which you buy your timeshare is affiliated to one of the two main exchange organizations: Resort Condominiums International (RCI) or its rival Interval International (II), which ensures certain standards for the development. Through the exchange companies, timeshares can be swapped easily for others of similar (or lower) standard in a year when you do not wish to take your holiday at the home resort.

Check that the resort makes provisions for an owners' committee, which will enable you to be involved in such matters as setting the level of annual maintenance fees. Check that facilities for timeshare owners such as golf courses mentioned by the salesperson do actually belong to the resort.

For security reasons, check that the resort uses a third party to convey legal documents. The process typically involves the club/trustee system of ownership registration, under which, as a new owner, you would receive a membership certificate from a designated trustee. However, the escritura system – used a lot in Spain – which involves the freehold transfer of your purchased timeshare, is no less secure.

Try to buy 'in perpetuity' as in Scotland, where this means forever, or in the rest of UK where you must instead look for an 80-year period of ownership, renewable by vote from a majority of resort owners. Avoid 10–15 year leases, which can cause your timeshare to plummet in value.

If you are buying from the developer or promoter, or from a retail membership that has OTE membership, check the contract for a cooling-off period during which you can change your mind about buying (14 days required in the UK and Portugal, 10 days in the rest of Europe excluding Greece, Italy, Luxembourg and Belgium).

How to have cheap timeshare holidays for the rest of your life without locking yourself into the system

Simply rent timeshare weeks from distressed sellers on the registers of resale agencies. Some will offer you very cheap rentals in the hope that, after your holiday at the resort, you will be tempted to buy the timeshare outright.

Alternatively, ring up any resort and ask to rent a unit. In the winter months particularly, you will often be able to negotiate a very cheap rental price indeed, so bargain hard.

Avoid falling prey to the loan sharks

Under the Consumer Credit Act, if you borrow from a finance or credit card company to buy your timeshare, you will be able to claim against it separately in case of misrepresentation by the timeshare promoter.

For this reason, finance companies vet the timeshare resorts for which they regularly provide purchase loans, a routine that can only benefit you as purchaser. However, the rates of interest on offer can be extortionate, particularly for unsecured loans. Secured finance is cheaper but it puts your home at risk if you start defaulting on repayments.

Generally for property or timeshare purchases, it is freelance credit brokers who may offer you the worst deal. They are not bound by the Financial Services Act and so have no obligation to give you best advice.

To attract inquiries from their press advertisements offering a loan facility, such brokers may claim to specialize in 'unsecured' loans. In reality, they prefer to offer you a loan 'secured' against your property as this pays them a much higher commission.

For the same reason, brokers will usually try to arrange credit for you at the highest total cost to yourself even if this is not in your interest. They will recommend long-term plans, stressing the low monthly payments and glossing over the overall high cost of the loan. They will try to steer you from the cheaper, short-term loans on the basis that the slightly higher monthly payments involved are 'less comfortable'.

Brokers will also try to persuade you to take on a bigger loan than you need. The application forms they send you are sometimes illustrated with sports cars, wedding scenes or dream holidays to fill your head with lofty dreams. A larger loan can pay off credit card and HP commitments, saving you money overall, the brokers advise.

Credit brokers may advise you to put on the form that you want to borrow for home improvements, even if it is not true. They know that this reason is accepted by lending institutions. They may recommend that you exaggerate your income on the application form, as proof is not always required.

If you must deal with such brokers, be sure to ask for several written quotes to which you are entitled by law. Compare the annual percentage rate (APR), which reflects all charges associated with the credit. The lower the APR, the lower the cost of the plan.

In addition to dubious credit brokers, there are rogue credit 'consultants' who may advise you to gain finance using less than straightforward methods. While writing for *The Sunday Times*, I exposed one of these gurus, who was operating out of a PO box in Leeds. He was selling a high-priced 'special report' that claimed to help credit seekers to borrow up to £300,000.

To build up to this happy position, buyers of the report were instructed that they could send in applications for 10, 20 or more credit cards, all on the same day, to maximize the overall acceptance rate. Borrowers should use cards for normal purchases for six months, repay the balances on time, and then ask for an increased credit limit, it was stated.

According to the report, borrowers should repay their debts on one card by borrowing on another. By using this technique on a multiple basis to establish themselves as creditworthy, borrowers could raise the limit on each credit card to around £12,000. Borrowers were told that they could enhance their credit rating by, for example, providing a telephone number to establish roots, and not appearing to have too many dependants on any credit application form.

Borrowers were recommended to adopt an impressive-sounding job title – for example, a buyer rather than shop assistant – and to avoid admitting to being in occupations for which it is hard to obtain credit such as taxi drivers, musicians, cooks, barbers, beauticians and actors.

Further advice was not to keep a business and personal account at the same bank, to minimize scrutiny, and not to discuss any matters whatsoever with their bank managers. Even if such techniques work in the short term, do not get sucked in.

Golden rules covered in this chapter

Rule 78   Buy property and its furnishings cheap at auction.

Rule 79   Develop a nose for structural defects in a property and consider taking legal advice on aspects relating to the lease.

Rule 80   Consider in particular buying auction properties that have been repossessed by building societies.

Rule 81   If you buy an auction property in advance of the sale, you will avoid false price mark-ups, which tend to occur in the bidding process.

Rule 82   To complete an auction purchase, have cash or finance in place, as you could otherwise lose the deal, and incur liabilities for any shortfall if the property is resold to another buyer.

Rule 83   The easiest and cheapest way to buy a second-hand timeshare is through a resale agency.

Rule 84   Ideally, find 'distressed' sellers who need to offload their timeshares for financial or other pressing reasons.

Rule 85   Buy your timeshare in January when timeshare owners are invoiced with the forthcoming year's maintenance fees.

Rule 86   The biggest price reductions are on timeshares that have been notoriously hard-sold by the developer.

Rule 87   Timeshare auctions are sometimes used to offload inferior-quality timeshares that are not affiliated to the main exchange organizations.

Rule 88   Take cheap timeshare holidays without locking yourself into the system by renting your weeks every year.

Rule 89   Freelance credit brokers are not bound to give you best advice and may try to sell you the loan that pays them the highest commission, regardless of the long-term cost to you. So before buying, compare the APRs on plans from several brokers.

13

Become a whizz share trader

In this chapter, we will look at what it takes to become a share trader from home. How to select the right broker, and basic trading techniques, will come under scrutiny. Trading will be set in the context of medium- to long-term investing.

This chapter is particularly important as, increasingly, users of the Bargain Hunters' Investment FlexiSystem and others operate as home-based share traders in the hope of making a quick buck. In the US, a few committed players rent desks at day-trading firms.

As this book goes to press, home-based traders have particularly profited from the rising value of Internet-related companies in the recent bull market. Of course, their success does not mean that trading is right for you.

To succeed in trading from home, you need more than just a computer with a powerful processor and trouble-free Internet access, and a reliable broker, although these are undoubted assets. You also need the right personal attributes, so that you are self-confident, logically minded and decisive in volatile markets.

Have you the intellectual grip to develop a trading system, and the self-discipline to stick to it? Can you seize a genuine trading opportunity, and not prevaricate? If you have answered yes to these questions, read on.

Choose a broker that will execute orders promptly and cheaply

As a home-based share trader who deals on your own initiative and often, it makes sense for you to use an execution-only broker that does not offer unwanted investment advice and so charges low commissions.

Amongst such brokers, the commission charged nonetheless varies widely, with the best deal usually offered by US online brokers – not necessarily suitable for your purposes. In any event, claimed low dealing costs can be deceptive. The US so-called 'deep discount' brokers – which attract custom on the grounds of cheapness – sometimes inflict hidden charges to make up the shortfall created by their extra-low commissions.

Every time a deep discount broker sends out a statement, or for every significant period over which you do not trade with the firm, you *may* end up being billed. When you compare prospective brokers for cost, check out the hidden charges. Base your comparison of charges on the size and number of deals that you expect to be doing, so taking into account any minimum commissions.

Avoid paying over the odds for real-time quotes or access to a broker's research bank, as similar facilities may be available free elsewhere. For instance, real-time quotes for US stock markets can be obtained free from the Web site of Wall Street City (www.wall-streetcity.com).

However low the commissions charged, you also need to know that your broker is reliable. Is he or she available to you without delay at peak trading times? How promptly does he or she execute trades? Should your Internet broker's Web site not be functioning, what backup method for placing trades is available? If there is none, have a reserve broker on tap.

Try some fantasy trading

Internet brokers may offer you an opportunity to test-drive their facilities, ie go through the motions of executing trades via the firm without actually committing your money. One of the best free test drives offered by brokers is from US-based online broker DLJ Direct. To try it out instantly, go to the broker's Web site (www. dljdirect.com).

Of course by mere paper trading you will not experience that feeling in the pit of your stomach that comes only when you are playing hardball with real money. More adventurous spirits may prefer to execute genuine trades – although in small amounts – until perhaps they feel confident enough to place big money on that all-important trade. Be cautious, however. Every time you lose, somebody else wins. Always ask yourself in advance what that other person may know.

Speak the right language

As a share trader, make sure that you speak the basic jargon. You will most often be placing a *market* order, ie buying stock at the prevailing market price. Alternatively it will be a *limit* order, which specifies the price you are willing to pay or accept. This could be valid on a *day-only* basis, or *until cancelled.*

You can start share trading from home without knowing still more specialist jargon but, if you want to impress your broker or fellow home traders, here is the lowdown. In the US, when a stock or index moves up and down within narrow bounds, this is called *chop-sop* by day traders. The Standard & Poor's 500 Futures Index is dubbed *Spoos,* while the 16ths that make up the spread between a given bid and ask price are shortened to *teents.* Of course, there is more to share trading from home than speaking the lingo.

Share trading differs from investment

The good trader – if not the genius in the field – is made, not born, according to many professional traders. In *trading,* market direction is more important than stock selection, and fast profits in rapid-fire succession rather than compounded investment gains are the name of the game.

Potentially, the world's stock markets offer you as a trader unlimited rewards – or losses. Because no physical effort is involved in share trading, and the money earned is unrelated to time put in, novice traders may fall into the trap of thinking the work is easy.

You may have to learn the hard way that share trading can be a bumpy ride. While it has been the making of some, it has bankrupted others. But if you *seriously* see trading as your route to riches, there are ways to improve the odds of it working for *you.*

Your first task is to dispense with those rules of the Bargain Hunters' Investment FlexiSystem that benefit a medium- to long-term value investing strategy. This chapter turns much of the investment advice in previous chapters on its head.

You cannot, for instance, afford the FlexiSystem's recommended technique of buying shares in high-dividend large-cap blue chip companies and waiting until they return to favour. Similarly, your grasp of ratio analysis may prove of sadly limited assistance when you are watching price fluctuations minute by minute with a view to seizing a fast profit.

Day traders sell out their positions every day

The focus on short-term profits becomes paramount if you are a *bona fide* day trader as you will then close out your position at the end of every day. That way, you can start afresh daily without being emotionally influenced by a position – held overnight – in which you have made or lost heavily.

For you as a day trader, investment for even two hours will be long term as you stalk companies sizeable enough to have liquidity that attract high-volume buying and selling on the day. All that counts is the day's share price movement.

In fact, many who are loosely termed day traders operate over several days or weeks, which can become more like ordinary investing. As a trader, do not be too frightened or too proud to cut your losses early, if necessary with the help of a stop loss system. If you do not, they will compound with potentially severe consequences.

Trade only with money that you can afford to lose

Although trading – properly executed – capitalizes on your reading of stock, sector and market trends, it is a high-risk activity at the mercy of setbacks beyond your control. For this reason, invest only with funds that you can afford to lose, which millionaire trader Robert Beckman has described in his public lectures as 'cool money'.

Some traders, following the precedent of the legendary trader Gann, put only 10 per cent of their trading capital on any single trade, or another measured proportion. Others take a more weighted position when they spot the unmissable opportunity, for which they have learned to wait.

Be careful not to overuse a margin account, which enables you to obtain a line of credit with your broker for trading purposes. The margin interest payable by yourself for such credit can be significant and, should the market turn against you, you stand to lose far more than the mere cash you put up.

Avoid averaging out – buying more of a stock held when the price falls on the basis that you are lowering the overall average price of your shares held – as you may not see the share price rise again so quickly as you would hope.

Timing is everything

In share trading, unlike in medium- to long-term investing, timing is everything. You will muscle in early on a rising stock and sell before its price plummets. The stock may rise in isolation from its peers, acknowledging perhaps a confirmed new product launch or rumoured merger activity. More likely, the stock will move in line with its sector.

For instance, a UK utilities regulator may declare a new pricing regime that benefits the entire sector and its stocks may subsequently soar all at once. In a cross-border scenario, a confirmed merger between two European banks may spark speculation about further such activity, causing most European banking stocks to rise.

The movement of stocks is influenced, particularly in the short term, by that of the broader market. For instance, rising stocks in a bear market are bucking the trend, and so may not rise as much as they would have done in a bull market. Conversely, in a bull market, stocks rising for an industry- or company-specific reason may lead the entire market's surge. How can you gain an instant fix on these recent index and stock fluctuations, complete with trading volume? For many traders, the answer is technical analysis or chartism.

Technical analysis comes into its own

In Chapter 9, I put the case that technical analysis does not work as a technique for predicting share price movements. In this capacity, it is barred from the Bargain Hunters' Investment FlexiSystem.

In trading circles, technical analysis is considered far more acceptable. Although controversy lingers about its forecasting value, it undeniably provides a graphic record of past trends. The picture – in this case a chart – can be worth its proverbial thousand words.

Technical analysis also records changes in trading volume for individual stocks – a valuable indicator of institutional buying or selling. When assessing the direction of the market as a whole, some technicians look at moving averages of the major indices, ie the average closing figure over a given period of days calculated regularly on a rolling basis. Some scrutinize overbought/oversold indicators for the stock market.

Despite the value of technical analysis in these areas, many world-class equities traders, including US-based Michael Steinhardt, have no use for charts in their work. Others beg to differ. For instance, the outstanding US trader Marty Schwartz had failed in his vocation for 10 years while using fundamental analysis. He became successful only when he started using technical analysis.

Traders who value technical analysis may controversially use it to time their trades as well as to keep records. If so, they are best off using it only as a guideline, and looking at several technical indicators at once. The simpler the technical rules, the more they are favoured owing to their correspondingly greater ease of use under rushed trading conditions. In a bear market, for instance, some traders use the Dow theory for making an instant assessment as to how far a rally may retrace the market's original decline.

In a bull market, technically minded traders prefer to buy shares that show relative strength – a strong share price performance over the last month or two and the last year, compared with that of other companies. While various sources, including *REFS* in the UK, offer a relative strength figure for quoted companies, you can work out a ratio for yourself.

Divide the price of your chosen share by the figure of the FT Actuaries All-Share index at close of business and the result is the relative strength ratio. Recalculate this ratio every few days over some months and plot the trend as a line on a graph. If the line is moving up, so is the share's relative strength, and vice versa.

More controversial in the field of technical analysis, even amongst its devotees, is the use of pretty patterns as buying signals. Some disciples of William O'Neil buy into a company on the US investment guru's advice at the point where the share price is breaking out of the classic *double bottom* pattern (shaped like a rounded w) or similarly out of the *teacup* (as described, complete with handle).

Buy stocks that are already at a high

Whether they are using charts to spot breakouts, or high-low share price statistics, some traders follow O'Neil's advice in buying stocks at an all-time high (or almost so). Their case is that companies are highly rated for a reason and are likely to reach further new highs – one after another. In this context, high PE ratios – shunned by most professional investors – are alluring.

To find out more about some of these theories, consult O'Neil's excellent free investment course, which does *not* recommend day trading. Gain access to this by tapping into the Web site of his newspaper *Investor's Business Daily* (www.investors.com), and follow the course critically.

In the long run, you should develop your *own* trading techniques based on personal experience. The best traders are independently minded, although many followers in the business have made substantial money. Certainly, copycat buying by home-based share traders chases popular stocks higher on the day.

Spice advice

As a share trader, follow the principle that *the trend is your friend*. In a similar spirit, you should *go with the flow* – advice that the now slightly faded pop star Emma Bunton (Baby Spice), as guest agony aunt on TV with her group the Spice Girls, offered a boy who confided his shyness about having sex.

Such principles were used by the perhaps more relevant authority Jesse Livermore, who has been dubbed by some in the know as the greatest share trader in history. If you want to read about how this wizard of the ticker tape operated early in the 20th century, obtain the classic, thinly disguised biography of his professional life *Reminscences of a Stock Operator* by Edward Lefevre (John Wiley, 1994). Some young City and Wall Street traders still read this book carefully in the hope that the maestro's techniques – laid bare in its pages – will in part rub off on them.

To become a home-based share trader borrowing in part from Livermore's or any other expert's methods (think seriously about O'Neil's), do not waste time trying to predict the direction of the market. Instead, make your trading decisions on the balance of probability. If, for instance, a major player in the market acquires a block of shares in a company, so setting its share price racing, you must buy the shares *early* and ride with the flow.

The Domino Effect

As a share trader, you must watch the major indices worldwide – particularly in the US, Hong Kong and Tokyo, and in major European countries. For instance, the performance of the US-based Dow Jones at the end of any given day will typically impact on how the UK's FTSE 100 and other major European indices open the following morning.

Similarly, the overnight performance of Hong Kong's Hang Seng index will very likely influence the day's share price performance of major UK quoted stocks that have a strong Asian presence such as HSBC and Standard Chartered. Other banks – ultimately throughout continental Europe as well as in the UK – may be influenced by the share price movements of this pair, and the insurance sector may be impacted. This is what some professional traders have termed the 'Domino Effect'.

While market movements often lead the way, you only need to take timely positions in one or two stocks to make money as a share trader, so do not get involved with more stocks than you can handle.

Do not ignore economics

As a short-term trader, your profits will be affected by market swings arising from economic forecasts and statistics. For instance, if an interest rate cut is expected, the market is likely to be buoyant as it stands to benefit, but if the cut does not transpire, the market may go into freefall.

In the US particularly, economic forecasts and statistics may sway markets worldwide. If the employment rate is too high, it signals infla-tion. Other US inflationary indicators when they are high include the Consumer Price Index, housing starts, and retail sales. Similar indica-tors in any country in Europe may sway markets throughout the conti-nent.

Professional share traders who work in investment banks adjust their positions ahead of expected economic statistics. They have heard the market gossip, and read the forecasts on their Bloomberg and Reuters screens. Their firm's strategists will have commented, and this alone can move markets.

As a share trader from home, how can you compete with such resources? It is no bad thing if you lack an excess of news sources as this could be distracting, but you must have at least one such source. Consult the Web site of Cyberinvest (www.cyberinvest.com), which offers a substantial collection of information and links for home-based traders.

Selling short – the trader's lifeline in a bear market

As a short seller,[1] you sell shares that you do not own hoping later to buy the same shares back at a lower price and make a profit. Although your profits may be spectacular, your potential losses are unlimited if stock should prove unavailable when you seek to buy it back.

In practice, you can usually close a loss-making position early, perhaps using a stop loss. But selling short is a tricky business, even for professional traders. Investor Robert Beckman has argued that only one in a thousand people can handle it. Many who try short selling go broke, so following in the footsteps of infamous New York-based short seller 'Sell 'em Ben' Smith early in the 20th century.

Many traders are undoubtedly put off by the tainted image of short selling before they even get started on it. For instance, short selling was made a scapegoat by some for the 1929 Wall Street crash. It has at various times been banned in the UK, the US and elsewhere.

The other side of the coin is that short selling and put options are the only two ways to make money in a bear market. Find a broker who will take the risk of dealing with you as a short seller. He or she will open for you a bear account in which your position is recalculated frequently. At all times expect to put up at least 30 per cent collateral for your outstanding position at any given time, which could be in the form of shares (valued at up to 80 per cent of the bid price) or cash.

Play cautious and sell short only in a declining market. For your stock then to rise, it would have to buck the trend – unlikely without a

---

1 In the UK, short sales must now be closed within a maximum 48 days (T+25 settlement and 23 days' one-time 'rollover' by the broker of a client's position).

good reason. Set aside only a small part of your trading capital for short selling, at least until you are used to it. Commit yourself to only one or two short sells at a time so that you can focus your attention on them.

Generally, avoid thinly capitalized stocks as you sometimes cannot buy these easily to cover your position. FTSE 100 shares are the best bet in terms of liquidity, although they do not always decline enough in value to benefit those who have sold the stock short.

Self-evidently in short selling, as in other forms of share trading, timing is crucial. You are looking to go short on overbought stocks *ideally* just *before* they decline in value, and never long *after* that point. What are the signals for you to make a move?

Short selling signal 1: when bad news hits a company

Sell short as soon as bad news about a company hits the press, or – better still – in advance. If you are fast enough, as well as lucky, you will make money from a subsequent decline in the share price. Be prepared to get it wrong, be wiped out, and to start again, hopefully learning from any mistakes you may have made.

How can you get wind of suitably cataclysmic news early enough? As a dedicated short seller, you may build up sources amongst journalists, brokers and industry contacts, including the targeted company itself. To retain these sources, you must be discreet. Careless talk can give rise to suspicion, albeit unjustified, that insider information is being exchanged. At all costs, avoid dealing in securities while in possession of insider information, which is a criminal offence.

In fact, insider information is harder to come by than is often supposed. It relates to particular securities or a particular issuer of securities, rather than to securities in general. The information must be specific or precise, not made public, and likely to have a significant effect on the share price if it were made public.

Again, to stay on the right side of the law, be wary as a short teller about getting involved in a bear raid. This involves traders in issuing statements about a company whose shares they have sold short as a way of scaring other shareholders into selling. If the statements are misleading, they may be in breach of S47 of the Financial Services Act.

Some argue that a share price may fall even in the short term on the back not just of adverse news but also of poor fundamentals. How far this is relevant is the subject of the next section.

Short selling signal 2: poor fundamentals

Some traders seek out overpriced stocks with deteriorating earnings for selling short. The US Motley Fool argues that shares that are candidates for selling short should have a PE ratio at least 30 per cent higher than their average growth rate, amounting to a PEG ratio of 1.30 or more.

Against this, many traders who succeed in selling short consider that fundamentals are of secondary importance, or even irrelevant. Some instead look closely at technical factors related to the stock.

Short selling signal 3: technical indicators

If you favour technical analysis, look to sell short stocks that have, amongst other things, declined in relative strength. In addition, you may go so far as to be guided by reversal patterns.

In the example of the infamous *head and shoulders* as traced on a graph, the recent share price will originally have risen to a plateau and dropped back, forming the first shoulder. It will then have risen to a peak representing the head, and dropped back again, then risen to another plateau that was perhaps the size of the first one, and retreated to complete that second shoulder's formation.

Some chartists claim that the base of the two shoulders, known as the neckline, marks a support level that, if breached by a line representing a declining share price, signals an entry point for short sellers. Be warned, however, that the *head and shoulders*, like plenty of other chart patterns, has let down many a devotee in the past.

Put options – a less risky alternative to short selling

If you want to bet on a falling share price without that risk of limitless losses that you incur when selling short, buy a put option, which gives you the right to sell the underlying share within a given time period at a fixed price.

As the holder of a put option on a stock, any losses that you incur are limited to the non-refundable premium you have paid. But if the underlying share price should decline as desired, a put option will not make you money so quickly as if you had sold short.

Should you buy a put option, make sure that it has at least six months to expiration as this will give the underlying stock enough time to move down. In practice, the premiums of long-term puts are typically expensive, and you should weigh up the cost *before* you commit your cash.

For free factual information about options, check out the *Chicago Board of Trade Options Exchange* Web site (www.cboe.com). Before you invest, bear in mind that four out of five buyers of options lose money, according to anecdotal evidence in the City.

A final word

Weighing up the risks and rewards of share trading

Becoming a home-based share trader is no easy option. Certainly, if you opt for day trading, you will be glued to your screen during working hours and will probably become addicted to your business, particularly when it is profitable.

Anecdotal evidence suggests that moderately successful home-based traders are making £100,000 plus a year from the work, based on a cautious approach snatching many small profits from many small ticket deals and keeping out of volatile markets whether they go up or down. It is while you are on a learning curve that you make the most mistakes and stand the biggest risk of being wiped out.

For some who got past that stage and traded boldly in the recent roaring bull market the rewards have proved amazing. The best US day traders made enough within months to buy a house or to retire from work for a good many years.

Most of these were gutsy or foolhardy enough – depending on which way you look at it – to give up their jobs for day trading in the first place. A few felt that they had no choice in the matter. It has certainly proved no hindrance that most knew little or nothing about the stock market.

Clearly day – and other short-term – share trading from home has been slower to catch on in the UK than in the US, partly because we are less savvy about investing and less entrepreneurial than our transatlantic counterparts. But it now looks set to boom in line with Internet usage, including online broking.

It may be that share trading is right for you and you can stomach the risks as well as reap some of the rewards. If you make this your business – full or part time – you will be following perhaps the most important tenet of the Bargain Hunters' Investment FlexiSystem – unspoken as it is – which is to take responsibility for your own financial wellbeing.

Golden rules covered in this chapter

Rule 90   Choose a cheap but efficient broker for share trading and make sure that a backup service is available.

Rule 91   Try fantasy trading in shares before you commit your capital.

Rule 92   For share traders, timing is everything.

Rule 93   Technical analysis can provide a useful picture of past trends for traders.

Rule 94   Follow the principles *the trend is your friend*, and *go with the flow*.

Rule 95   Trade only with money that you can afford to lose.

Rule 96   Sell short only in a declining market.

Rule 97   Put options are less risky than selling short but, if you get it right, will make you money less quickly.

14

How to make a complaint that bites

There are times when you may have been treated badly by a firm and need to make a complaint. In any area of financial services in the UK, the firm will usually attend to your gripe as, if it does not, it risks breaching FSA regulations.

If, however, your gripe is with a firm in an unregulated area such as timeshare or money-lending, there is often not much you can do about it. Timeshare, for instance, has a useful but ultimately toothless trade body – The Timeshare Council/OTE – to provide consumer protection. Some credit brokers retain licences issued by The Office of Fair Trading although they have ripped off the public for years.

Dealing with a UK stockbroker

Some SFA-regulated brokers have hopelessly incompetent settlement systems and some, far worse, do not recommend investments with the care that they should. For these reasons, it is just as well that every SFA-regulated broker is obliged to have a written complaints procedure in place. If your complaint is unresolved, it can be referred to an industry complaints bureau. The next step would be arbitration, which is strictly at the option of yourself as client, or court action – rarely both.

If an SFA-authorized broker with whom you are dealing defaults, there is a cross-industry compensation scheme that is available to meet claims. Under the scheme, the first £30,000 of any proven claim will be met in full, and 90 per cent of the next £20,000 will be met –

with £48,000 being the maximum compensation paid per claimant. Overall, the fund will not pay out more than £100 million in any single year.

Despite the availability of these procedures, act quickly if an offending firm fails to investigate and rectify its errors. You should always make your formal complaints in writing. Be factually accurate. Do not be rude as this could be used against you. Query whether the firm has been acting in a 'fit and proper' way or has been executing its duty 'honestly, fairly and competently'. This is the type of jargon used by regulators, and will put the fear of God into the firm.

At all times, keep a detailed record of all your dealings with the firm. As you repeatedly voice your complaints, you may find that you are passed from one person to another, so make a written note of names, times and dates of telephone conversations, and of what was actually said.

If all else fails, threatening any financial services firm, including brokers, with exposure to the national press can work wonders. Adverse publicity of this kind is very damaging for firms. It hits their reputation and reduces their custom, and it may force regulators to start a probe.

How to approach the press

If you have had serious problems with a broker or any other financial institution, to get your story run in the press is not difficult and may get the matter seen to immediately by the offending firm, but you have to go about the job the right way.

First, identify the journalist whom you think it best to approach. My advice is that, in most cases, you should avoid the local and trade press. It is nationals that carry the most impact. The posh Sunday papers are ideal as their journalists are desperate for potential good new stories and, unlike their counterparts on the dailies, have enough time to follow them up in depth.

Send the journalist a letter outlining your complaint about settlement procedures, administrative muddles, reckless investment advice, or whatever. Write clearly without rambling, setting out the key points. It may be worth enclosing copies of any evidence. Follow this up by telephoning the journalist, and offer to talk him or her through what has happened.

Alternatively, he or she may telephone you. The journalist almost always takes the side of the ordinary person against financial institutions, provided that you have a justified complaint. Before or after publication, to lessen the adverse publicity arising, the offending firm may make you a compensation offer for problems caused.

Here is a crucial word of warning. Do not under any circumstances deal with the more down-market tabloid national newspapers. Do not talk to their journalists, no matter how much money they offer you. Do not give them your evidence, tell them where you live, or, above all, allow their newspapers to photograph you.

I have, as a journalist, been offered huge sums for providing or writing stories for the down-market tabloids. I have refused the undeniably tempting offers and instead dealt with more respectable papers, sometimes for a tenth of the sum on offer.

In days when I did not have the experience I do now, I made the mistake of allowing the single most notorious of the Sunday national rags to interview me about a financial book I was writing. In his published feature, the journalist put words into my mouth, and tried to hold me up to ridicule.

This is a sadly familiar story for those who have dealt with the tabloid press. Any persons with whom I have spoken who talked to tabloid journalists at length to assist with an article that was later published regard the event in retrospect, without exception, as the worst mistake of their lives. The mass-market tabloids do not place truth high on their list of priorities. Their main consideration is how likely they are to be sued if they run a given story.

A true-life example of how problems can be cleared up like magic once you threaten press exposure

From early August through November 1998, I had been having appalling problems with the grossly incompetent dealing services of one major telephone-based dealing operation. The firm was compounding its errors as it ignored my complaints. It was only after I threatened press exposure that my complaints were properly investigated.

In my naivety, the company had initially seemed a good bet to me. Dealing costs were very low – 0.75 per cent commission on every deal up to £4,000 and 0.1 per cent on the excess, with all deals subject to a minimum £50 commission. As a perk, the firm would provide me with brokers' forecasts and views free. It was only after I had committed my money that the nightmare began.

To spend my maximum entitlement on a general PEP (£6,000) and a single-company PEP (£3,000), both on a self-select basis, I initially deposited the requisite £9,000 in a high-interest account provided by the dealing operation, as requested. Once the funds were cleared, I bought shares for my PEPs and was duly issued with contract notes.

My shares were being held on my behalf in a nominee account. I asked whether I could instead hold them directly and be issued with share certificates. The firm's representative did not know but he referred me to a colleague. She too had no clear answer.

After phone conversations over some days complete with what seemed interminable waiting, I stumbled upon a better-informed clerk. As I had PEPs, she said, I held a nominee account and could not be issued with share certificates. If only the confusion had ended there.

A few days later, the dealing operation sent me new versions of the previous contract notes for shares in my general PEP, as if for the first time. I rang up and queried this move. The company could throw no light on it but promised to 'look into' the matter. I heard nothing.

In a letter dated 21 September 1998, the firm demanded almost £6,000 in respect of 'your recent purchase'. It required payment 'by return, in the envelope provided', and stressed it would not allow further purchases while an account remained overdue.

I contacted the operation on the phone to complain that I had already paid for the shares in my general PEP to which the demands seemed to refer, and I was again passed from one person to another. Finally an administrator suggested that my PEP purchases 'may have been' mistakenly transferred to another computer – triggered, she suggested, by my earlier request for share certificates. This 'may have' resulted in duplicate records, she said. At my request for written clarification, she sent a letter dated 30 September offering 'sincere apologies' for the erroneous charge. She said that 'the matter has now been resolved and your account is in order'.

Imagine my consternation when, on 16 October, I received a letter from the 'recoveries manager' who demanded settlement for the claimed £6,000 outstanding 'without further delay'. He threatened to sell any assets under the firm's control to close the position, charging a fee of £25 and 'interest on the overdue amount, in addition to our normal dealing charges'. He added that 'in the event the above action does not fully discharge the amount owing, you will be liable for the amount remaining outstanding'.

I wrote a letter of complaint to the company, threatening that I would write about the company in the national press if there was not immediate resolution. Suddenly, the dealing operation tried to rectify its errors although, even then, it could not get it right. The firm sent me share certificates apparently for some of the shares that I owned, then demanded these back, on the basis that they had been sent out mistakenly. It asked me to sign transfer forms for the purpose, but the forms were blank and did not name the securities that were being transferred.

Further contradictory information provided by the company in a series of illiterate letters from various of its representatives did not clarify the matter. However, the company eventually admitted failure to operate effectively, and offered a paltry £50 compensation. I took the matter to the extremely helpful Complaints Bureau, operated by the SFA, as a result of whose intervention the company raised its compensation offer to £150. In addition, it said it would waive PEP charges and transfer my account to another PEP-provider free.

Learn from my mistakes. Consider, as I did, threatening to complain to the press if your own broker has failed to respond satisfactorily to your complaints. Better still, make sure *before* you sign up with a broker that it has an adequate administrative structure in place, and that the firm is run by competent people. Of course such fundamental necessities do not always come cheap. Never choose your execution-only broker simply on the basis of its low commission charges.

Avoid ineffectual broker complaints committees

If you are dealing with a broker that provides a less than satisfactory service to a number of clients, you will sometimes find that a complaints committee is formed.

You may be invited to contribute information, time and, above all, funding to such a committee. At this point, I would urge caution. In the past, I have known such committees to be almost completely inef-fectual. While a few organizers of these committees are competent, some are cranks with a chip on their shoulder about the City.

Like attracts like, and many clients who pledge their support to the broker's self-styled complaints committee have no valid case but simply seek a scapegoat for losses arising from ill-conceived share purchases. Sometimes, the firm in question has done little or nothing wrong.

Alternatively, the firm may be inherently corrupt but covering its tracks well. In either case, the combined action of small clients would probably fail to construct a viable case against the firm. I stress this because I have seen private clients waste a great deal of time, effort and money travelling down this route.

At best, the complaints committee, helped by its members, will manage to make its complaints public. Contacts may be established, albeit unskilfully, with investigative journalists on the national press, and with MPs. But these targeted professionals have their own agendas and, when approached together, may succeed in closing the firm down without gaining satisfactory resolution of client complaints. At this point, the complaints committee sometimes continues to fight its lost cause.

I have known members of such committees telephone brokers at home, and, while recording the conversation, desperately try to trick them into admitting fraud. The mistake these disgruntled clients have made is to think that any broker could be stupid enough to fall for such a trap.

Even more stupid is when disgruntled clients sanction dubious 'consultants' or self-styled debt collectors to chase brokers for cash invested. This way, they risk being linked with any criminal activity initiated by the consultant.

To warn you as to how such a case can unfold, let me tell you a true story, with names changed to avoid embarrassing some of the individuals who were involved.

Sara, 32, a department store manager, and Sean, 52, a builder, were both clients of a London-based share-dealing operation that had ceased trading. They were holding shares in an unquoted Internet services provider, Technocraft, in which there appeared to be no ready market. Sara had paid £5,000 for her shares while Sean had paid £10,000.

The pair were founder members of a client complaints committee for the defunct broker. The committee hoped to 'recover' the funds that it argued had been fraudulently acquired from investors in Technocraft. In reality, fraud was unproven and no claim could be made for compensation under the Financial Services Act.

But a self-styled debt collector, Magnus Teddington, had appeared on the scene and was claiming that there were 'other ways' to get money out of the defunct firm. Addressing some of the firm's former clients at a client complaints committee meeting, Teddington offered to 'retrieve' money paid by investors for the shares on the assumed basis that it had not been genuinely invested.

With his bruiser's face, reddened by drink, Teddington did not inspire confidence, but some of the committee members were desperate enough to use him. Sara and Sean – the two most aggrieved of the committee members – gave Teddington a letter that stated that they authorized him to 'retrieve' from brokers any money that they had invested in Technocraft and to take a 20 per cent cut of all sums so gained.

At Sara's and Sean's request, the complaints committee released to Teddington the personal phone numbers of the 30 brokers who had worked for the now defunct firm. Teddington duly started telephoning these brokers in their homes and demanded that they should repay, out of their own resources, all the £15,000 invested by Sara and Sean.

Only two of the brokers had dealt with Sara and Sean, but they were as uncooperative as the rest. Almost to a man, the brokers fobbed off Teddington, in some cases changing their telephone numbers. Some of the brokers referred him to colleagues simply to get him off their backs. Teddington eventually focused his attentions on the point of least resistance – a young broker called Tim, who lived with his parents in a London suburb.

Teddington started pestering Tim on the telephone, demanding the full £15,000 on behalf of unnamed clients, who were not, in fact, his own. He demanded a meeting during which he would show what he claimed was a dossier proving 'fraudulent' dealing practices on the part of Tim and his fellow dealers. In exchange for the cash, Teddington said he would hand over the dossier. If there was no deal, he said that he would give the dossier to the Director of Public Prosecutions.

Tim prevaricated, and Teddington continued pestering him *without keeping Sara and Sean appraised of his strong-arm tactics.* Every few evenings, Teddington visited Tim's parents' house and rang the doorbell. When he was not let in, he rang again and banged the doorknocker hard. He then took photographs of the house, using a flash gun whose glare penetrated between the curtains in several of its windows.

As a last resort, Tim contacted the police and complained of Teddington's approaches. The local CID diagnosed blackmail, reckoning Teddington was out to get the cash for himself. The police fixed a tele-recorder to Tim's parents' phone. Making a taped call under police supervision, Tim arranged to meet Teddington in the local pub, where he said he would hand over money in exchange for the dossier.

When Teddington's day of reckoning arrived, the police 'wired up' Tim with a recorder taped to his chest, and gave him a briefcase that contained £10,000 in genuine bank notes. In advance of the meeting, six plain-clothes policemen were ensconced in the pub, posing as casual drinkers.

Teddington, in a dark suit, arrived as arranged and ordered a beer. He nodded to Tim who was sipping a vodka and tonic at the other side of the bar. The pub was crowded, with the police blending indistinguishably with other drinkers in the background, and 'Yesterday' was blaring reassuringly from the juke box.

After waiting 10 minutes, Teddington sauntered over. He eyed Tim suspiciously. 'Let's do our business somewhere else', he said. 'Anywhere you like. I get an uneasy feeling here. There might be people you know in this pub. There might be people I know.'

Tim swallowed hard. If he agreed to leave the pub, it would put the kibosh on the sting. 'Let me see the dossier first', he said. Teddington nodded and handed over the precious file. Tim skimmed it as he sipped his drink. It contained letters from members of the complaints committee, alleging that the broker for which Tim had worked had operated fraudulently in selling shares in Technocraft.

'This dossier could be very damaging to me', said Tim theatrically. Teddington nodded. 'You can say that again. But we will discuss it somewhere else...' His words tapered off as Tim started opening the briefcase. Like a snake hypnotized by a flute-player, Teddington gazed lovingly at the bank notes stashed inside, his eyes swaying in unison with the slight movement of the case.

Tim shoved the briefcase into his hands. 'Take this for now, and follow me. We will go elsewhere to do the business.' Teddington hesitated only briefly before his grip closed on the case.

It was the cue for the police to come forward, and Teddington backed away like a cornered animal. He put up a struggle as they wrenched the briefcase and dossier from him. 'You leave these alone, they are private property', he roared. Drinkers and bar staff alike were gawping, and the music stopped.

Teddington was arrested and he spent the night in a police cell. He was eventually tried in the Crown Court where he was found guilty of blackmail and given a stiff jail sentence. In this true case, Sara and Sean were not implicated in Teddington's criminal activities. However, they could easily have been drawn in – and to no avail as no monies were 'retrieved'.

The moral of this true story, dear reader, is that, if you want to make complaints, do so through legitimate channels or via the press. Do not play the vigilante or get anybody else to do so on your behalf.

Golden rules covered in this chapter

Rule 98   If you have a complaint about any financial services firm, keep written records of your dealings with it.

Rule 99   If necessary, threaten the firm with press exposure and be prepared to initiate this.

Rule 100   Do not play the vigilante in dealing with brokers whom you consider dubious.

15

How to detect and avoid dubious insurance promoters

In recent years, dubious insurance companies have been raking in premiums, but failing to meet valid claims. In this chapter, I will give you an inside view on how they conduct their business and what happens to your premium payments. But first let us identify a less dangerous breed – the life insurer that is *bona fide* but deploys hard-selling tactics.

Come into my parlour, said the spider to the fly

Hard-sell insurance salespeople – usually bed agents rather than IFAs – may still entice you into their office, perhaps with loud music blaring in the background, while they sit on a raised chair and lecture you about taking responsibility for your financial future. Alternatively, they visit you at home, and try not to leave until they have closed the sale. They aim to get you committed *before* you compare their products with the competition.

Such salespeople try to make you feel guilty about having neglected financial planning. One executive of a hard-sell firm whom I have known points an imaginary gun at his potential clients, and says: 'Bang. You're dead. Now how is your spouse going to manage?' These manipulators may try to sell you more health insurance, life cover and redundancy insurance than you need, and an unsuitable pension.

Hire 'em and fire 'em

Their employees operate a hire 'em and fire 'em strategy. New recruits are told to make a list of everybody they know, including relatives and the bank manager, and to make appointments to sell them financial services products – typically savings plans that pay a hefty commission. In addition, these salespeople cold-call employees of companies listed in the *Yellow Pages.* They will have obtained their names and positions from the relevant switchboard on some pretext.

Get on or get out

These opportunists keep their jobs only as long as they make sales, and perhaps only one in 20 recruits lasts longer than a year. The old hands are typically given 'managerial' status within a pyramid sales structure, which means they take a cut of commissions earned by more junior salespeople under their wing and so have an incentive to pass on their know-how. In the worst firms, this know-how consists only of sales techniques, and detailed product knowledge is discouraged, despite the industry's recent introduction of compulsory professional exams. A persuasive sales pitch has been found to achieve much more in the short term than expertise.

The sales quota must be reached

Users of the Bargain Hunters' Investment FlexiSystem have found that there is a distinct correlation between a hard-sell approach and under-performing products. Of course the salespeople from such a firm, usually novices, rarely know or care about the quality of their product. But they do know that if you buy the right products, they are well rewarded. In addition, they are further towards fulfilling their monthly sales quota and winning that luxury holiday for two in the Seychelles or diamond brooch. They will then stay in touch to cater for your future 'needs'.

Discover the worst offenders

I will tell you a secret way to identify the worst of these tied agents. Look in the sales vacancies section of your local or national newspaper. The life insurance firms that advertise for new salespeople several times a week, every week, clearly have a ridiculously high turnover. This probably means that they don't care about their sales staff, but are simply using them to sell (maybe unsuitable) insurance policies and other products to their personal contacts for as long as it lasts. Cannily, these firms do not usually put their names in the advertisements, so you will have to ring the switchboards to find out who they are, if necessary by subterfuge.

What is less blatant than the hard-sell operation, and far more damaging, is the sophisticated insurance scam, which will have you paying your premiums for nothing. This way, many people in the UK and continental Europe as well as the US have been caught, and you need to be careful not to join their ranks.

The tell-tale signs

The kings of the rogue insurance industry may be insurers underwriting their own book of business, or fly-by-night agents operating on their behalf. Owing to their ease of initial access and apparent cheap offers, the insurers do not need to use hard-sell tactics to attract business. For this reason, the uninitiated may find it hard to detect the fraud.

Some of the clearest indicators have been provided by Edward Pankau, chief investigator at Intertect, a private investigation firm in Houston, Texas. When I met Mr Pankau in my capacity as an editor of *the Re report*, a leading reinsurance newsletter, at a conference on insurance fraud in Chicago a few years ago, he argued that the key to insurance fraud prevention was to investigate people, not companies.

The Pankau techniques

Mr Pankau claimed that dubious insurance promoters commit small frauds and then, if undetected, move on to large ones. They move around, using international boundaries to create layers of skin like an onion. Amongst favoured bases from which to operate were the Isle of Man and the Channel Islands.

According to Mr Pankau, any insurance executive who travels outside his or her jurisdiction more than 10 times a year could be a sharp operator. Other tell-tale signs are if the executive owns a particularly expensive car, or a yacht, or a top-of-the-range Rolex watch. Being an officer or director of 10 or more companies is in his view a giveaway sign, as is any insurance company that claims to own £1 million worth of property without a mortgage, or fails to file financial reports. What is the insurance fraudsters' *modus operandi*?

The grand cover-up

Earlier in the 1990s, the US Federal Bureau of Investigation addressed this question in its classic report *Insurance Company Insolvency Study*. The Bureau noted that the most prevalent form of insurance fraud in the US was when the promoter diverts premiums for private use, often by money laundering. To achieve this, an insurance agent or broker fails to remit premiums to the underwriter, or the insurer rakes in as much premium income as quickly as possible 'without any intention of ever paying the majority of claims'.

For obvious reasons, linked dubious insurers often sound like each other. For instance, in recent years, Greater Indemnity & Casualty of the Turks and Caicos Islands, which had been banned in California, was associated with Greater Indemnity & Casualty Insurance Co, Greater Indemnity Insurance Company, Greater Indemnity Casualty Co, Greater American & Casualty Insurance, and Greater American and Casualty Insurance Company. The California state insurance department could not discover whether the operations were predecessors to Greater Indemnity or separate entities.

Ducking and diving

The dubious insurers may be fronted by *bona fide* insurance executives who have worked for good companies but since fallen on hard times. The ringleaders may operate behind the scenes as 'consultants'. The insurance companies that they run are typically backed by assets that have been valued by an obscure and inaccessible bank or other entity. The firm may claim that its auditor is one of the Big Six firms.

In reality, it will have merely *approached* a Big Six firm, or used it for some minor purpose unrelated to auditing. The real auditor is likely to be some offshore accountant that operates out of a PO box and serves many dubious companies. As a result of such misunderstandings, Big Six accountant Cooper's & Lybrand spends 'stupid amounts of time chasing the facts and putting people right', according to its partner Peter Mynors. Some of the other Big Six accountants tell a similar story. If you want to query the dubious insurer's assets, you may find that its representatives and real auditor are conveniently unavailable. A few of the insurers are based at locations that do not exist.

Games without frontiers

The use of a fictitious domicile is still seen as an option. In the past, Professional Indemnity Corp was ordered to cease operating in the US state of Oregon because its claimed domicile – the Federal Republic of Corterra – was found not to exist. The insurer had already sold professional liability insurance to about 1,000 chiropractors in the US, through the Chiropractic Association for Research and Education.

In a more notorious case in the early 1990s, Texas-based insurer California Pacific – domiciled in the non-existent Melchizedek – had pushed dubious insurance policies for several years on either side of the Atlantic, and was subsequently wound up by the UK's Department of Trade & Industry in the public interest. Melchizidek was represented as a 'floating' Pacific island with a highly religious government and an 'embassy' in Washington DC.

No ordinary bunch of Holy Joes

Melchizedek has listed holy-sounding characters alongside recognized dubious insurance promoters in its organizational structure. For instance, the nation's president is claimed to be Eliajah Arazi, and its secretary of state Mr Ben David. To enforce standards, Melchizedek has vested substantial regulatory powers with Mr Frank Merovingi, its minister of finance. This dignitary 'may seize or take possession of any licensed company if it violates the statutes as promulgated hereunder flagrantly or violated minimum capital requirements', it has been stated. There has been no record of any action on his part to date.

Melchizedek has claimed that 2,500 financial companies have used it as a base, and it is not afraid to defend itself by unconventional methods. When for instance a California newspaper voiced criticisms, Melchizedek retaliated with an indignant letter signed by the 'hand of the holy ghost'. According to its representatives, Melchizedek was founded by one David Pedley, an intensively religious man who later died in a Mexican jail. In reality, Melchizedek is a fraud and is highly illegal, according to Douglas McLellan, chief bank examiner of the District of Columbia office of banking and financial institutions.

Melchizedek offers its services

This has not stopped Melchizedek from offering its services. As a journalist, I phoned the Melchizedek 'embassy' posing as the boss of a start-up insurance company, and was put through via a telephone link to California to speak with the entity's self-styled Ambassador Korem, aka Branch Vinedresser, a convicted fraudster who had been promoting Melchizedek. Vinedresser was ready to sell me a licence to set up an insurance company domiciled on the island for US $5,000. To keep paperwork to a minimum, I was invited to fax to the embassy a copy of articles of association in, for instance, the Isle of Man or the Bahamas – with all reference to the location deleted. Melchizedek's name would be substituted and the documentation used to incorporate.

Do not do business with insurance companies that may be domiciled in such non-existent nations, however badly you need the policy, and however low the premiums. If you are suspicious, find out where the insurer is supposed to be based, and ring up local regulators to see if they can comment. A useful source of information is the International Association of Insurance fraud agencies (www.iaifa.org), which is a network of regulators, insurance professionals and others dedicated to combating insurance fraud. The key point about insurers that hide behind dubious domiciles is that they are often operating without proper asset backing. As a variation on the theme of citing a fictitious domicile, some sharp insurers use an unreal entity specifically to verify their assets.

Heap big insurance fraud

A notorious example of such a fraud was Sovereign Cherokee Nation

Tejas, which in the early 1990s backed insurance companies master-minded by the late British insurance fraudster Alan Teale. Tejas represented itself as a *bona fide* Indian tribe with an ancient culture, which had been created by an 'act of God' following the separation of its 154-acre territory in the channel of the Rio Grande from Texas by hurricane Beulah. Upon investigating Tejas, a US congressional subcommittee suggested that the concept had been invented by Herbert 'Little Bird on the Shoulder' Williams, a retired US Air Force colonel who conspicuously lacked Indian pedigree. While the colonel claimed that he had bought the land for $20,000, it belonged to Mexico, the subcommittee alleged.

Tejas said that it was associated with two federally recognized Indian tribes, the Cherokee Nation, Oklahoma, and the Eastern Cherokee Indians, North Carolina. But the two tribes denied a link. Tejas further claimed that its role was to 'help the indigenous Indian people' but was unable to substantiate this. The subcommittee found that it was created for 'monetary rather than social or political reasons'.

Tejas housed and valued supposed assets for a number of insurance companies. They included treasury bills for $25 million that were claimed to be 'backed by the full faith and credit of the sovereign Cherokee Nation Tejas'. It transpired that there was no other backing. Other worthless assets backed by Tejas included a 'life mask' of the actor Marlon Brando, valued at $1.5 million, and 'processed minerals' that had been reburied in the ground, under the parking lot of a mine in Central City, Colorado.

When you are in Rome...

For a long time, Tejas staved off investigation by the US authorities on the basis of its 'sovereign' status. For instance, when a subcommittee representative had tried to subpoena documents that would provide evidence of Tejas's dubious insurance activities, the tribe banned him from the premises on the grounds that he had not been fingerprinted and photographed first, in accordance with its laws. When a second subpoena had been served, the Tejas tribal chief William Fry, aka 'Chief Bear Who Walks Softly', wrote and complained to President Bush. The cowboys often complain to well-known figures in a front to lend plausibility to their operations.

Insurers with assets backed by the Tejas nation were found to be fraudulent only *after* many members of the public and companies

alike had been fleeced. Such insurers, when under official investigation, typically hide behind a panoply of lawyers – often good ones – as
they keep raking in money on borrowed time. If one company closes
down, another may set up in a separate jurisdiction, under a new
name, to carry on its predecessor's good work. Assets are sometimes
substituted with others, in response to regulators' demands, but even
then, the substituted assets may turn out to be of no higher value. The
same assets are sometimes rented by two insurers simultaneously, or
else similar-sounding assets are used to confuse often naive insurance
regulators.

Insurance regulators can be ignorant about the industry

Colin Holder, insurance administrator of the Turks and Caicos Islands,
has argued that insurance regulators do not understand the insurance
business because they have not worked in it. He said that they show
their ignorance when they continually fail to adequately assess the
business plans submitted by get-rich-quick insurers that do not know
their business.

Similarly, a report some years ago on insolvency regulation by John
Dingell's Congressional subcommittee in Washington DC accused US
state regulators of erecting a 'supervisory Babel where blind faith
often substitutes for real knowledge and tough enforcement'. More
disturbingly, some US state insurance commissioners have since
proved open to bribery and corruption.

Poachers turned gamekeeper

Insurance regulators have found that professionals who work in
dubious firms are the best source of information. They are often
prepared to leak information and documents that testify against their
colleagues, so that they can represent themselves in a holier-than-thou
light or simply save their own skin.

The ringleaders when caught may squeal, hoping to reduce or to
stave off a long prison sentence for insurance fraud. For instance, in
1994, Alan Teale was jailed for 17 years in Alabama after he had
pleaded guilty to multiple charges of insurance fraud. In jail he

repented and turned to Christianity. He piously revealed all that he knew about his former colleagues to the US federal authorities in the hope of negotiating a plea bargain. Although he died after serving only months of his sentence, he had said enough to enable the authorities to indict some of his former colleagues.

Steer clear of the swamps

With luck you will not come across the dubious insurers unless you use bucket-shop agents, and seek hard-to-get insurance, or very low-cost premiums. But at all times be vigilant, using the advice in this chapter to detect and avoid the sharp operators.

Golden rules covered in this chapter

Rule 101   Do not buy from pushy financial services salespeople before you have compared their product with the competition.

Rule 102   The dubious insurer diverts premiums for private use – often by money laundering.

Rule 103   The dubious insurer may use a fictitious domicile, operate from a PO box, pretend to have been audited by a Big Six accountant, and hide behind a panoply of lawyers.

16

Cash is king

Cash flow is seen by professional investment analysts as more reliable than earnings per share (eps) for valuing a company. The reason is that cash flow, unlike eps, cannot be manipulated. Despite this, analysts often give earnings more priority than cash flow, as it is more widely recognized.

But given the importance of cash flow, how is it used to value a company? In this chapter, I will explain the discounted cash flow techniques used by market professionals. When you have read the next few pages, you will understand how the investment professionals operate.

Intrinsic value

A stock is sometimes given an *intrinsic value*, which may be defined as the present value of its stream of future dividends. The formula used to find the intrinsic value is the so-called dividend discount model, which is the intrinsic value (P) = next year's cash dividend (D1), divided by the shareholders' required rate of return (k) less expected growth of dividends (g). This reads as follows:

$$P = D1/k - g$$

For example, let us assume that a given company has a dividend of £1, a required rate of return of 10 per cent, and a dividend growth rate of 5 per cent. Applying the formula, we reach the following equation:

$$P = 1/0.10 - 0.05 = 20$$

On this basis, the company has an intrinsic value of £20. But, if you believe that the growth rate, or rate of return, will be slightly different, and include your figures in the formula, this can greatly affect the intrinsic value. If, for instance, the growth rate was set at 4 per cent, rather than at 5 per cent as in the above example, the intrinsic value ends up at only 16.6. Similarly, a small change in the shareholders' required rate of return (k) will dramatically change the intrinsic value. If, for example, k should be increased from 10 per cent to 12 per cent, the intrinsic value would be reduced to 14.3 per cent.

How relevant is the dividend discount model?

But it is hard to decide on exact figures for k and g, owing to differing views on the required rate of return (discount rate) for individual stocks – an issue we will address later in this chapter. In addition, it is usually difficult to predict dividend growth rates. For such reasons, the dividend discount model is of limited relevance. Nonetheless, companies are still often valued usefully on the basis of discounted cash flows.

How to calculate a company's discounted cash flows

To start the ball rolling, you need to find a company's *present* cash flow, which, for the purposes of this book, we shall define as net operating cash flow (NOCF). You may calculate NOCF by taking the company's earnings before interest and tax (EBIT), less corporation tax paid, and capital expenditure. Add back depreciation and amortization, as they do not represent a movement of cash outside the company. Next, add or subtract the overall change in working capital.

Do not worry if you find all this hard to remember. The important point is that you understand the principles discussed, so that, when you come across analysts' research, you can understand the processes they will have gone through in discounted cash flow analysis.

The net operating cash flow needs to be estimated not just for this year but also for future years, to build up a reliable picture of future cash flows. Cash available in future years is worth less in today's value than if it were available this year, owing to inflation. The trend in interest rates will have an effect on inflation levels.

On this basis, cash flows of every future year must be discounted by a given percentage to reach a present value. It must be acknowledged that the cash flows will continue into the future, beyond the period of years over which the discounted cash flows are spread. The period beyond is known as the terminal value and, unless there is evidence to the contrary, it is assumed to cover cash flows that extend into infinity.

All future net operating cash flows reduced to their present value, combined with the terminal value, make up a company's overall value. How accurately the company is valued this way depends on the reliability both of forecasts for net operating cash flow, and of the discount rate used. It also depends on how many years are included in the discounting. There is room for disagreement about all these matters.

An important calculation

The formula for discounting future cash flows is as follows:

FV = PV (1+r) to the power of n

Or, by implication:

PV = FV/(1+r) to the power of n

where:

the future value of the NOCF is FV;
the present value of the NOCF is PV;
the discount rate is r;
the period over which the future value is discounted is n years.

Using this formula, you can easily calculate the future value of a present cash flow, or the present value of a future cash flow. For example, if in three years' time the cash flow of a company will be £140.49 million, and the discount rate to be applied is 12 per cent, we may find the present value by applying the formula as follows:

PV = 140.49/1.12 to the power of 3 = 100

The numerator here is the future value, ie 140.49, while the denominator is 1 + the discount rate expressed as a decimal, to the power of the number of years to be discounted (three). Applying the formula, the present value is 100.

How do you work out a company's terminal value?

The easiest way to work out a company's terminal value, ie the value that extends beyond the allocated period of discounted cash flows, is to divide the expected net operating cash flow (undiscounted) for the final year under consideration by the discount rate. For example, if you have a net operating profit of £6 million and a discount rate of 20 per cent, you must divide 6 by 0.20, and you will find the answer is 30, ie £30 million. The terminal value must then be discounted back to its present value.

All future cash flows, discounted at the appropriate rate, together with the similarly discounted terminal value, are said to represent the value of the company. Obviously crucial to the value is the discount rate used. The larger the discount rate, the smaller is the net present value of future cash flows.

How do you select an appropriate discount rate to use on future cash flows?

How do you select an appropriate discount rate (also known as required rate of return) to use on future cash flows? One technique is to use the same rate of return as enjoyed by comparable companies. But it has proved difficult to make accurate comparisons. It has proved more reliable to use a given company's weighted average cost of capital (WAAC) as its discount rate. So what is the WAAC?

Generally, companies raise their capital through equity or debt. The WAAC represents the cost of capital to the company, weighted in terms of debt and equity. The cost of debt is the current yield to maturity on the company's bonds. The cost of equity is measured by the Capital Asset Pricing Model (CAPM), which is used to determine the required rate of return on equity by comparing the underlying share's performance with that of the market as a whole.

The Capital Asset Pricing Model

The Capital Asset Pricing Model (CAPM) aims to find the required rate of return on equity by comparing a stock's performance with that of the market. The model was invented by Nobel prize laureate Bill Sharpe who was developing work by Harry Markowitz and Jamez Tobin.

According to the CAPM (pronounced Capem), investors should be rewarded for acquiring investments that carry more *market* risk – which cannot be diversified away – rather than *specific* risk.

In the CAPM formula, the market risk of a stock is measured by its so-called beta, which measures its volatility against the market. If a share fluctuates in line with the market, it will have a beta of 1. If the share has a beta of 0.50 or 2.0, it will fluctuate proportionately less or more than the market.

The stock with a high beta outperforms in a bull market but under-performs in a bear market, and its counterpart with a low beta does the opposite. A stock's beta can be estimated from its past performance against a major index, a service undertaken through regression analysis by Datastream and the London Business School. Beta is an estimated figure, and it is historical; a share's volatility may change, affecting its beta.

Another measure used in the CAPM formula is the risk-free rate of return (Rf). This is the interest rate on long-term government bonds, as listed on the currency and money pages of the *Financial Times*. Also used is the average return for the market as a whole (Rm), which is higher than the risk-free rate of return. The difference between Rf and Rm is known as the equity market risk premium; it averages around 8 per cent and does not change much in the short term.

The CAPM formula is as follows:

Rate of return R = Rf + (Rm–Rf) beta

Let us look at the formula in action. If the interest rate on long-term government bonds is 6.5 per cent, and the dividend yield from the FTSE All-Share index is 10 per cent, and an appropriate beta for a company is 1, the CAPM is applied as follows:

R = 6.5 + (10–6.5)1
R = 6.5 + 3.5
R = 10

The CAPM is widely accepted in the investment community. It is not, however, foolproof, and a portfolio of high-beta stocks does not always outperform one of low-beta stocks. In practice, beta works better over a period (decades rather than years) or at times when the stock market is fluctuating more than usual.

The Arbitrage Pricing Theory

A more flexible alternative to the CAPM is the Arbitrage Pricing Theory (APT). The APT introduces a number of factors, instead of the single beta used in the CAPM, to measure a share's performance against the market. The APT model does not specify what these factors are, but they may include exchange rate, inflation, production, etc. However, the APT is less widely credited than the CAPM.

Economic value added

City analysts try to find companies that try to create the maximum shareholder value. Companies with this in mind are constantly cutting extraneous costs and making their operation both leaner and fitter. For example, Lloyd's TSB, the UK bank, increased shareholder value with outstanding success in the late 1990s.

The principal measure of how far a company creates shareholder value is economic value added (EVA). Experts agree that EVA is not a valuation measure; it is rather a measure of management performance. The definition of EVA is net operating profit after tax (NOPAT) – (WAAC × invested capital).

EVA arises only in projects where all cash flows, discounted back to the present value, are positive. The present value of EVAs are equal to a company's market value added (MVA), which is the difference between its market value and the book value of its assets.

If you have followed this chapter so far, you have developed a broad-brush understanding of discounted cash flow analysis. This is perhaps the most important skill applied by investment analysts and, if you want to explore it further, there are plenty of books and courses on the subject. In my view the most readable of the bunch is *Streetsmart Guide to Valuing A Stock*, by Gary Gray, Patrick J Cusatis and J Randall Woolridge (McGraw-Hill), which explains the principles of discounted cash flow analysis clearly, with practical examples, and in non-technical language. You may also be interested to read *Buffettology* by Mary Buffett (Simon & Schuster, UK), which covers, in a highly readable style, Warren Buffett's methods for valuing a business on the basis of the annual compounding rate of return.

Amongst more advanced treatments of cash flow valuation methods, a highly respected work is *Valuation: Measuring and Managing the Value of Companies*, by Tom Copeland, Tim Killer and Jack Murrin of McKinsey & Company (John Wiley & Sons). You could also consult the classic textbook *Principles of Corporate Finance*, by Richard A Brealey and Steward C Myers (McGraw-Hill).

These are *not* books for beginners on the stock market, and you may find some of them hard going. For this reason, I have omitted them from Chapter 17, where we look at further reading. But if you become fascinated by the ways that professionals analyse stocks, these books will take you much further forward.

Golden rules covered in this chapter

Rule 104   Cash flow is seen as more reliable than earnings in valuing a company.

Rule 105   A company's value consists of all its future net operating cash flows, combined with the terminal value, discounted to their present value.

17

Further reading

The better your knowledge of how the stock market works, the more critically you will be able to assess what your broker recommends. Getting to grips with this book will take you some way. But, particularly if you are a beginner in investment, there is a lot more you can do in the way of reading and research.

To get hold of the specialist business books recommended in this chapter is not always easy. You will find some of them in the business sections of good bookshops, particularly in the City of London. Out of these bookshops I favour Books Etc – recently acquired by American book chain Borders – which, at the time of writing, has a policy of returning your money on any book purchased in its stores if you have not enjoyed reading it.

In many bookshops, you can have a good peek at the goods before you commit your money, and this is their advantage. If, however, you find it hard to get to a good bookshop, you can buy by mail order. The most comprehensive range of business books I have ever seen in the UK is available by post from Hampshire-based Harriman House (tel: 01730 233870). Call and ask to be sent the firm's catalogue.

Alternatively, you may buy your books online, from market-leading online book-store Amazon (www.amazonco.uk), or another financial bookshop (sometimes via links with an online dealing or other financial Web site). If you buy this way, you can often obtain your book at a substantial discount. If you want to find the cheapest online bookshop, go the Web site of Booksco.uk (www.booksco.uk), which provides useful price surveys and other comparisons.

Beginners' guides to the stock market

Before investing on the stock market, you need to understand the basics. When I started out developing my interest in the stock market from scratch in the early 1980s, I had no use for the many beginners' guides – written usually by journalists – which were factually informative but dull.

What I needed was a simple but reliable introduction that would make gripping reading. I found this in *Fair Shares* by Simon Rose. This gem of a book, popular over a decade ago, has been recently revised and republished by Management Books 2000. The author, an independent financial writer, writes about the investment world as he sees it, with a cynical eye and penetrating wit. It makes for a juicy little primer on the nuts and bolts of investment.

In addition, I would strongly recommend *The Motley Fool UK Investment Guide* (Boxtree), by David Berger, who is – of all people – a young medical doctor, and his US-based mentors David and Tom Gardner. The book and a related Web site (www.fool.co.uk) provide a cynical dissection of the financial services industry, rendered palatable by the satirical writing style.

The Motley Fool UK Web site at the time of writing is run by four people, including Berger. They are self-confessed Fools (with a large F) in the Shakespearean sense, ie who tell the king the truth when others merely flatter him. Like-minded Fools who have tapped into the Web site are urged to register with it free, enabling them to communicate 'Foolish' thoughts via an electronic message board.

All Fools are particularly critical of the Wise, an umbrella term for commission-hungry financial services professionals. The feeling is that the Wise exploit the mystique associated with finance to manipulate the public into acting on dubious investment advice.

This is not to say that the Motley Fool is anti-business. On the contrary, it aims to encourage share buying but from an independent perspective that largely dispenses with the need for (and cost of) professional advisers. The UK Web site runs several mock share portfolios on an ongoing basis, some of which work better than others. It provides daily market updates as well as in-depth features.

The men who run the UK Web site are not finance professionals but they have an astute understanding of financial services. While not journalists, they have a talent for writing. This overall lack of professionalism is the Web site's charm and also its weakness. The writing is not as rigorous as professional journalism. It sometimes gilds the lily and it has a homely ring to it. But the insight and humour in the material presented makes this Web site unmissable.

At the time of writing, the Motley Fool UK has just moved out of makeshift headquarters in a poky basement flat in Kilburn into West London offices, and has recruited extra staff. A new Motley Fool office is planned for Germany, and a major publishing deal for several investment books and courses is under way.

Tap into the Motley Fool UK Web site and you will either love it or hate it. Personally speaking, I have never found such accessible and entertaining writing about personal finance anywhere else at any time (except at the US site). I know of many so-called Fools who are hooked on this heady cocktail. If you want to receive an investment education in a relatively painless way, try it.

In fact, the Motley Fool Web site is a subsidiary and an as yet experimental version of the far more sophisticated US model run by the Gardner brothers. If you want to really understand the Motley Fool approach, buy The Motley' Fool's *Rule Breakers, Rule Makers, the Foolish Guide to Picking Stocks*, by David and Tom Gardner (Simon & Schuster). In this fascinating book, you will discover, amongst other things, the mainly qualitative criteria used to select young technology companies for the Motley Fool US online portfolios.

As another valuable guide to investment, the output of private client stock market guru Jim Slater should be on your reading list. For complete beginners, Slater has written *Investment Made Easy* (Orion Business), which is far more lively and individual than most equivalent-level books. Next, read Slater's first book *The Zulu Principle*, which concentrates on stock market investment and is not really for beginners. View these books critically, as some of Slater's arguments are controversial. He has since refined and changed some of his ideas, and to keep up with his train of thought you really need to subscribe to his newsletter (referred to later in this chapter and in Appendix 6).

Amongst other basic books on investment, I have found *How to Read the Financial Pages* by Michael Brett (Century Business) particularly useful. The book is written a bit like a course, but it is clearly set out and an invaluable source of reference. An alternative that I have found more wordy but still useful is Bernard Gray's *Beginners' Guide to Investment*, an *Investors Chronicle* book (Century Business).

If you like a chatty style, go for *The Armchair Investor* (Orion Business), the first book of self-taught investor, *Daily Mail* columnist and TV presenter Bernice Cohen. Although the book, in my view, is too enthusiastic about technical analysis, it is quite readable.

If you want to read something on the economics of markets, I have made great use of *Market Movers*, by Nancy Dunnan and Jay J Pack (Warner Books), which has a US emphasis and is the only readable introduction to the subject I have come across to date. For reference, I have found *The Economist Guide to Economic Indicators* useful.

Perhaps you would enjoy being scared out of investing in the stock market. If so, read *The Bear Book. Survive and Profit in Ferocious Markets*, by journalist John Rothschild (Wiley). In this controversial book, Rothschild argues the case for selling your shares to avoid the ravages of a bear market. He suggests that if you suspect deflation, you are better off buying bonds. In inflationary times, you should, in his view, be in cash or commodities. I found it amusing to see the book heavily criticized in the October 1998 edition of *Analyst*, a tipsheet that makes its stock recommendations on the basis that serious investment is for the long term.

More enjoyable than any of these books are some of the lighter studies of the securities industry. These give you more of an insight than some would admit on what is happening in stockbrokers' offices. I would recommend *The Buck Stops Here* by Jim Parton (Simon & Schuster). This offers a hilarious description of the inner workings of an investment bank from a junior salesman's perspective.

Still more entertaining, and an absolute must for your reading list, is *Where Are the Customers' Yachts?* by Fred Schwed Jr, first published in 1940 (John Wiley & Sons). Let me tell you a secret: this is the one book on the stock market that many in the City have enjoyed above all others. I have heard it argued that there is more wisdom about the stock market in this little book than in a dozen weightier tomes. I will anyway vouch for its readability.

Most of these books are not specifically geared to helping you with share trading from home. There have been some books on the subject published in the US that mostly focus heavily on technical analysis, despite the fact that not all successful traders use this technique much, if at all. The Motley Fool UK Web site goes so far as to advise investors against day trading in most circumstances.

If you have not yet been put off becoming a share trader, you should read *Market Wizards* by Jack D Schwager (HarperCollins, 1993), in which master traders are interviewed. The book is not easy going, but it demonstrates the sheer variety of professional techniques in use.

As a lighter read, it is worth looking at the published transcripts of the *Beckman* lectures (Milestone Publications), in which investment guru Robert Beckman gives no-holds-barred advice on trading techniques – including technical analysis – and on selling short. Unfortunately, these transcripts are now out of print and, in my view, Beckman's books – including *Supertiming*, which covers his interpretation of the Elliot Wave theory – are wordy and do not make so useful reading.

For advice on psychological tactics for successful trading, consult *The Disciplined Trader* by Mark Douglas (New York Institute of Finance, 1990). You will probably find it an enlightening read, even if, in the final analysis, you do not want to be a trader. Modern technical analysis is covered from beginners' to advanced level in a probing style suitable for traders in *Technical Analysis Explained* by Martin J Pring (McGraw-Hill, 1991).

If you are particularly interested in short selling, you must read *Profit of the Plunge*, by Simon Cawkwell (to be reissued by Batsford). This is a rambling, opinionated and eccentric book but a true classic about selling short penned by a master of the trade. It is packed with specific advice and streetwise tips on how to sell short, mixed with Cawkwell's low opinions of the UK's worthy regulatory system and selective anecdotes from his own vast experience. Do not miss it.

On the still more specialist subject of Lloyd's of London, various books have been published in recent years. You may want to read one of the better books if you are thinking of investing in Lloyd's investment vehicles (see Chapter 3). The most entertaining book on Lloyd's, citing a large number of interviews, is *For Whom the Bell Tolls* by Jonathan Mantle (Sinclair-Stevenson). To say that the book does not show Lloyd's in a good light is the understatement of the year.

More informative but a much duller read is *Nightmare on Elm Street* by journalist Cathy Gunn (Smith Gryphon). Particularly authentic in conveying the atmosphere of Lloyd's is the novel *Blonde Ambition*, written by rebel ex-insurance broker Samantha Phillips (Century).

Less good, I regret to say, is *The Great Lloyd's Robbery* by Sir Francis Dashwood (Merlin Books). While it is sad that the author had to resort to vanity publishing to bring out this novelette, he did manage to stage a magnificent book-launch party at Lloyd's.

The problem with most books on investment and related matters, including Lloyd's and the insurance markets, is that they do not present a learning programme in a systematic way. If you are *serious* about getting educated about investment, while there is no substitute for practical experience, it may be a good idea to consider a course.

Take a general investment course

There are various investment courses on offer but tread carefully. Even on the best investment courses, many students give up when they discover that hard study is required, so make sure that you are committed before you part with any course fees.

Note too that investment courses are not regulated under the Financial Services Act as they give only general investment advice. Avoid those that claim they can make you a fortune overnight. As a journalist, I have come across many courses of this ilk. The giveaway signs are that they are very expensive, the course material is amateurishly written and presented, and the promoters hide behind answer phones except when actually doing business.

The glowing testimonials included with the sales literature on such courses may be false and the posh-sounding office may turn out to be an accommodation address. Any 'help line' on offer will not work once the course promoter has cleared your money.

Many investment courses cover specialist areas and this can be a minefield for the unwary. If a course costs little or nothing, investigate before committing your time. Such a course – whether conducted on site, by post or via the Internet – may be a thinly disguised front for selling a software system or advisory service.

In contrast, investment courses run by local adult education colleges can be good and cost very little. They can also be appalling. A good free alternative, which is not really a course, comes from London-based Proshare, an independent non-profit-making organization that promotes wider share ownership.

On receipt of an SAE, Proshare (tel: 020 7600 0984) will send inquirers free of charge eight investor 'updates' that address the questions most frequently asked by novice investors. They cover unit trusts, investment trusts, PEPs, gilts and every basic area of the stock market.

If you are prepared to spend around £300 to learn the basics, and will put in about 100 hours of study, consider studying the syllabus for *The Registered Persons Exam*. This covers the basics of stock market investment, including accounting.

The course is designed as an introduction for new securities industry professionals but it is taken by a wider range of people. It can be done on a distance-learning basis if required, and, despite its bias towards the needs of market practitioners, is arguably the quickest, easiest way to pick up the basics from scratch. There are a number of providers of tuition for this course. I would recommend Financial Training in London (tel: 020 8960 4421).

If you prefer a course more geared to the needs of the personal investor rather than the professional, you should consider *Successful Personal Investing (SPI)*, which is the market-leader in the consumer distance-learning sector.

Since it started in 1987, *SPI* (tel: 01235 553696) has attracted more than 100,000 paying students, although many have not completed the course. The typical *SPI* student is a male aged between 35 and 45 who is reasonably well off but wants to make proper retirement provisions.

The good news for those who have forgotten how to put a pen to paper is that there are no written exercises or exams. *SPI* is purely a reading course that takes an average 18 months to complete. It provides no formal tutor feedback or simulated trading. So what do you get for your money?

The course is a systematic learning programme – to be completed at home – that tries to include every area of investment from pensions and the stock market to racehorses and antiques. Although books cover similar ground, they are not usually so comprehensive.

The text is made extra user-friendly by a varied typeface and layout, and space is included for the student's private notes. *SPI* is written in the language of television and radio and so is conveniently jargon free.

Because the course aims to be accessible to any adult in the country, it places the most emphasis on basics. However, it still manages to include relatively sophisticated investment ideas, including up-to-date general advice on Lloyd's membership.

The 37 lessons do not come cheap, but they can be bought individually. They are regularly updated and the new versions are offered to existing students at half price.

Tipsheets and market letters

Once you know the basics of investment, tipsheets and market letters can be a useful addition to your reading list, provided that you are selective. These publications proliferate in bull markets, and try to retain subscribers when times are volatile. They vary in quality and you should not follow even the best of them blindly.

The best tipsheets (for contact details, see Appendix 7) are not written by journalists. *Analyst* – written and published by a team of analysts – is arguably the cream of the crop. It offers a system for investing based on value principles. Another excellent newsletter is *Jim Slater: Investing for Growth*.

Many of the other stock market newsletters are written by financial journalists, most of whom have no real ability to analyse companies, and no knack of picking winners. They can write a recommendation that seems plausible but the skill is in the writing, not in the analysis or insight.

This observation is not entirely to denigrate newsletters written by journalists. Undeniably, there are a few journalists – including renegade chartered accountants – who understand the financial statements of quoted companies. As a group, journalists are more independent than *bona fide* investment analysts, who cannot usually afford to offend corporate clients. An exception may be found in some of the financial columnists who double up as stockbrokers.

Meanwhile, be wary of the charismatic newsletter writers who are stronger on personality than on good stock tips. These are often canny operators who may use gimmicks to attract subscribers. Some, for instance, colour their publications a lurid shade or use a unique shorthand throughout the text.

To raise their personal profile, these self-styled gurus may collect titles, or letters after their name, or express outrageous political views. To boost their circulations, they strike up distribution deals with similarly maverick publishers in other countries around the world.

The more outrageous the newsletter, the more extravagant are its claims. Promotional material may focus too selectively on those tips that made good. Some newsletters are backed by false testimonials, a growth area of sharp practice that is almost never checked.

Once you are familiar with the basics of investment and are following the stock market on a regular basis, you will find it worthwhile investing some of your time in a level of reading that will take some of the ideas introduced in this book much further.

More advanced reading

Should you want to become better versed in the ideas of Benjamin Graham and Warren Buffett, I suggest you read the chapters on these two pioneering investors in John Train's best selling book *The Money*

Masters (Harper Business). Alternatively, read Janet Lowe's easy-to-read books summarizing their ideas. Her most useful, in my view, is *Value Investing Made Easy* (McGraw-Hill).

If you then wish to read Graham's own work, *The Intelligent Investor* (Harper & Row) is the least difficult of his tomes. *Security Analysis*, his claimed masterpiece, is for when you are feeling energetic.

For something on growth investing, *One Up On Wall Street* by Peter Lynch (Penguin Books) is highly readable and informative. The book stresses the greater freedom of choice that the private investor has over the professional fund manager.

To discover what stock market investment systems have worked better than others over a period of decades in the US, read *What Works On Wall Street* by James O'Shaughnessy (McGraw-Hill).

Getting to grips with company accounts

On a more specialized front, if you are to invest in the stock market using the principles of the Bargain Hunters' Investment System, it is worth learning to read company accounts. The book that you will find most useful in this initiative is *Interpreting Company Reports and Accounts* by Geoffrey Holmes and Alan Sugden. This classic text will guide you – not without a struggle – through the nuts and bolts of a set of accounts, and will explain to you how to calculate crucial ratios. It omits coverage of the more esoteric, cash flow-related ratios used by some City analysts.

You will find it helpful to supplement your scrutiny of a book like this with related reading. There is a wealth of books on interpreting financial statements, ranging from the oversimplified to the downright obscure. A personal favourite of mine is *How to Use Company Accounts for Successful Investment Decisions* by Michael Stead (Pitman).

It is also worthwhile reading one of the more authoritative books on creative accounting on the market. The most interesting, because it names companies, is *Accounting for Growth* (Century Business), by ex-UBS head of research Terry Smith. An alternative good read is *Creative Accounting* (Routledge) by Ian Griffiths, which has also been published in an updated version entitled *New Creative Accounting*.

When I was initially learning to read company accounts from scratch, I found personally that books did not give me the practical exercises and feedback I required to master the subject. I needed a course.

Although I was not working in the City at the time, I decided to do the Interpretation of Financial Statements course, which is one of the options for the Securities Institute Diploma taken by ambitious stockbrokers and investment bankers. The course was excellent, covering the basic areas treated in Holmes and Sugden in a systematic way. Most valuable of all, it involved looking at three sets of up-to-date company accounts.

If you want to do the same course, which requires no prior knowledge of accounting, there are a number of organizations providing specialized tuition. I would again recommend you use Financial Training in London, which for this course has on-site or distance-learning programmes with clearly presented manuals, above average pass rates and a friendly constructive approach.

If you want to learn basic book-keeping/accounting as a preliminary to interpreting accounts, which is what I did, I would recommend the distance-learning courses provided by Ideal Schools in Glasgow (tel: 0141 248 5200). I have done two of their courses and found them worthwhile. However, as I have stressed when writing on the subject in the *Daily Telegraph*, the value of the professional qualification that some such courses have provided is uncertain.

If you have mastered Chapter 4 of this book or already have some grasp of accounting, you will know how to calculate and compare ratios to evaluate companies. As I have indicated earlier in this book, for everybody, and not just the uninitiated or lazy, relevant reference books will provide ratios ready calculated.

How to find statistical information on quoted companies

To find such ratios, your most comprehensive source is the directory *REFS*, which stands for *Really Essential Financial Statistics*. The publication, which was started in 1994, provides investors with the company data used by the ubiquitous Jim Slater for his own investment decisions.

To get started, *REFS* provides free to subscribers a 174-page book *How to Use Company Refs* and an explanatory video that lasts an hour and 40 minutes. *REFS* presents a clear picture of how the company is doing on paper – a good starting point. Figures are calculated on the so-called rolling 12-month basis where relevant, enabling fair comparison between companies with different year-ends.

REFS gives you all the information that you need (and more) to invest in the stock market under the rules of the Bargain Hunters' Investment FlexiSystem, although you will not be able to grasp its layout in five minutes. The ratios supplied for each company include price to sales, price to research and development, price to cash flow, and Slater's ubiquitous PEG. Many subscribers are ex-senior management who retired in their early 50s and have some understanding of company finance, according to *REFS* publisher Peter Scott.

While *REFS* concentrates exclusively on UK companies, *The Estimate Directory (TED)* has separate editions that cover stock markets in every region of the world. While it has far less information on individual companies than *REFS*, it presents it very clearly. *TED* has comprehensive brokers' estimates, with a sprinkling of basic company information including profit, turnover, and earnings per share. For details of the publishers of *REFS* and *TED*, turn to Appendix 7. The publication comes monthly or quarterly, like *REFS*. However, it is also available electronically with weekly updates, if you can afford the high price tag.

Another electronic source you should use for company information is Hoover's Online, which provides details of more than 15,000 companies worldwide via the Internet (www.hoovers.com). The basic information is free, and for an annual subscription you can obtain more in-depth reports on a number of companies.

Tap into the resources of the World Wide Web

You can conduct a great deal of further research via the Internet simply for the price of a local phone call (free in the US) and you can now gain access to an increasing number of service providers free rather than paying a monthly charge. You can find useful Web addresses by typing the company's name or a word describing its service in the relevant space provided by a search engine such as Excite or Lycos. You can then 'bookmark' any important address, a procedure that enables you to go instantly to the Web site at any time.

What information could you be looking for on the Web? Share price information, archives of newspapers for past press reports about a company, and, of course, any up-to-date press. In Appendix 8, I have provided an up-to-date list of financial Web sites that users of the Bargain Hunters' Investment FlexiSystem have found useful, and you should visit these sites. You will enjoy browsing the Web this way, and will be amazed at the amount of news, data and analysis that you will come across to help you with your investments.

For access to a wide range of financial information from one starting point, it is worth going to the site of Interactive Investor (www.iii.co.uk). For general information on US stocks, try Financial Web (www.financialWeb.com), which provides news, research, Securities & Exchange Commission filings and company reports. The site scans US stocks for income, value and growth.

You will also need up-to-the-minute prices of the stocks that you are following. You can get real-time prices of UK shares from Freequotes on the Web (www.freequotes.co.uk). For US stocks, real-time quotes are available at Wall Street City (www.wallstreetcity.com). Prices obviously fluctuate according to relevant news flow, and you will need to keep abreast of this.

As far as past press stories for UK companies are concerned, the Electronic *Telegraph* (www.telegraph.co.uk) archive (as referred to in Chapter 3) is a free source of past *Daily Telegraph* news coverage, while the *Financial Times* Web site (www.ft.com) has an archive that can be accessed for the last six months free. In the US, the magazine *Forbes* has a good site for researchers (www.forbes.com). For up-to-date UK news stories, try *Bloomberg*'s site (www.bloomberg.co.uk), or (also suggested in Chapter 3) the London *Evening Standard* site (www.thisislondon.co.uk).

To access quoted companies' Web sites can be useful as, at best, they provide accounts, news releases and other valuable investor information. But the sites vary in their level of investor friendliness. For instance, the typical financial services company uses its Web site to sell products rather than to provide information for potential investors in the company itself.

Access to the Web is useful when it comes to understanding how the dubious share dealers work. To keep abreast of dud stock offerings in the US, I would refer you again to the best vigilante Web site (www.stockdetective.com), as mentioned in Chapter 8 of this book. The site is the best source of free information about pirate share pushers in the US and Canada that I have ever come across. At the time of writing, the pirates are capitalizing on the craze for Internet stocks. Stock Detective is run by Kevin Lichtman, who has inside knowledge of how the share scams work. He knows how to make his site entertaining as well. Do not miss this treat.

If this source is not enough, there are some good books published that throw light on the specialist (and exciting) area of dubious share offerings.

Books on dubious share dealers

The most accessible books that advise investors on how to handle the sharp operators in the share-dealing game are those written by City PR man Michael Walters. In his previous, more abrasive role as deputy City editor of the *Daily Mail*, Walters exposed many of the licensed dealers in securities that fleeced the naive investing public in the late 1980s and early to mid-1990s, and he has capitalized on this knowledge in his books.

In short, Walters understands fairly well how the dubious share dealers operate, and he has cultivated many contacts over the years from behind the closed doors of their plush offices. He is a man who has been given a begrudging respect in crooked City circles, obtaining much of his information from insiders who are quietly doing the dirty on their colleagues.

In his books, Walters explains, amongst other things, how the dubious share dealers operate, and he names some of the worst offenders. His first book, *How to Make a Killing in the Share Jungle* (Batsford Business Books), has gone through several impressions. Walters is now starting to publish his own books, and to plug his publications in his capacity as a columnist on the Internet. If you buy one of his titles, try to make sure it is a revised edition.

If you want a more erudite approach to the subject of sharp operators in the share-dealing business, you may find it worthwhile reading *Too Good to be True – How to Survive in the Casino Economy* (Bodley Head) by Rowan Bosworth Davies. This ex-policeman's rant is, in my view, dully written and pompous, but it is, in places, well informed.

Perhaps I should refer again here to my own modest contribution to the literature about sharp share dealers on the market (see Chapter 8). In the late 1980s, my book *The City Share Pushers* (Scope Books) achieved significant success, despite vicious attempts by the single least reputable specimen of the Sunday national tabloids to distort and trivialize its message.

I described the world of shady share dealers in still more detail in my first novel, *The Survivors*, which was published shortly afterwards. The sharp operators still work in the way I have described in my books, but nowadays they push high-tech stocks via the Internet, as well as still operating telesales boiler rooms in secret offices abroad.

While investigative journalists have crashed the barrier of silence put up by the securities industry and its regulators, they have not, for the most part, succeeded in penetrating the wealthy and deeply corrupt timeshare industry.

Books on timeshare

There is, and always has been, a *serious* shortage of independent books/reports about the timeshare industry on the market. The few books published over the years have mostly been written by industry practitioners, with all the emphasis that that entails.

For every genuinely independent report on timeshare, there are many that pose as such. However, early in the 1990s, the Office of Fair Trading produced an excellently informed and appropriately cynical report on the timeshare industry that even now, outdated as it now is, makes fascinating reading.

As you may have gathered from reading Chapter 12, I have a special interest in the timeshare industry. About a decade ago, I spent a couple of years researching the industry full time, and I visited many resorts the length and breadth of Europe in a quest to find some way of enjoying them without being ripped off.

The solutions, which have been referred to briefly in an updated form in Chapter 12, were at the time reported in full in my independent report *How to Save Thousands of Pounds Buying and Selling Your Timeshare* (Brompton Publications). This report is now out of print but, if you can ever get your hands on a copy, it will tell you a few things that you probably never knew about the timeshare industry.

Avoid getting sucked into the beam-end business opportunities market

Last but not least, do not delude yourself that you are investing wisely, if at all, should you put your money in unchecked home-based businesses. While some of these businesses are *bona fide*, many are not, and it takes experience to separate the wheat from the chaff. In recessionary times, the duds naturally flourish.

To illustrate the dangers, let me take you behind the scenes and show you how somebody who used to work with me in the City – I am afraid, not the most straightforward of characters – now regularly makes a pile in the dud business opportunities market.

Since he was made redundant, John (not his real name) has operated hit-and-run businesses by telephone from his living room. A London telephone line transfers calls anonymously to his flat in the provinces. John invariably targets the beam-end business opportunities market, which is the last resort of the unemployed and hard-up, the gullible and the housebound.

In one venture, John raked in £25,000 clear profit in two months. The 'punters' sent in a £60 cheque for an unspecified business opportunity. In return, they received an impressive 'money-making' manual and became John's agents.

The manual instructed agents to advertise at their own expense the very business opportunity they had bought, passing details of respondents to John for a small remuneration. A few agents tried it out and John offered their respondents the same unspecified opportunity. The only one who actually made money was John.

John operated through a swanky accommodation address, answering his calls in a false name. He only stopped trading after a High Street bank inquired why he had included with his sales literature photocopies of false cheques drawn on its name as claimed examples of agents' vast earnings.

Meanwhile, his agents were demanding their money back, since the prospect dangled by John of making vast capital gain or becoming 'area managers' with salaries and a company Golf GTI had proved pie-in-the-sky.

John disconnected his phone line and skipped to the Lake District for a relaxing holiday. He had taken care to filter all the profit out of his company, partly through creative invoicing by a like-minded company owner. He had paid no corporation tax and had ignored his last advertising bill.

John has since set up several other such operations, giving him maximum short-term money, in the form of cheques through the post, for minimum effort. In his long, leisurely days, John entertains girl-friends, treating them to weekend breaks, cream teas near stately homes, £50 bottles of champagne at top-class hotels and candle-lit restaurant meals.

John boasts that his businesses work because his punters think that they are 'buying a job'. His public-school accent, his convincing sales patter and his professionally presented manuals set him streets ahead of rival sharp operators.

Most business opportunity scams are not conducted so elegantly as John's. Stock market investment schemes for instance can be as full of holes as a colander. One of the most absurd recently offered investment advice based on astrological analysis. As a marketing ploy, the sales literature for the scheme required prospective buyers to sign a form undertaking that they would not reveal its details to anybody. This gimmick made the unworkable system seem important to the unpractised eye.

The books and reports that detail such dubious investment systems or similar are normally sold by mail order. This means that you do not inspect the goods before parting with your money. The books are often self-published and not up to the standards of professional publishing houses.

In particular, there are many crooked systems for winning the pools or winning on the horses for sale. Recently, a spate of systems claiming to make you a lottery winner have reared their ugly head.

While writing for *The Sunday Times*, I exposed a forerunner of these schemes. Anybody who sent £20 to Millennium Products, based at a PO box in Guernsey, would receive a 'hand-held selector' that was 'made to pick out, automatically, the winning lottery numbers for the week', according to promotional literature signed off by claimed manager Jean Saint-Clair.

The mathematical formula used to select the numbers was falsely claimed to have been 'checked and verified' by a named university. The formula was claimed to be the invention of Australian multi-millionaire 'Mr Lucky' who, by its use, had shown that he had 'the knack of winning on the lottery week after week'.

Millennium claimed that when the system was launched in the US, it was a 'runaway success' and 'made thousands of people rich in the first few weeks of becoming available'. Early attempts to ban the system proved fruitless because it was legal, the promoter said.

The system was claimed to make winning small amounts every week on the lottery a 'near certainty' while reducing the odds of 'the big one' from several million to only 450 to one. If you followed the system and did not win in 30 days, you were 'guaranteed' your money back.

Millennium described Mr Lucky as an 'easy-going' family man who decided to 'give his system to the world for the good of everyone involved'. His only proviso was that, should you win over £5 million, you would 'donate a percentage to your favourite charity in Mr Lucky's name'.

Refuting Millennium's claims, UK lottery organizer Camelot claimed that Mr Lucky's system could not work because the lottery's winning numbers were chosen at random.

There are many who are duped by such a scheme into suspending all common sense and sending their cheques. Do not invest in systems that five minutes' thought will show you could not work.

Once you buy what may be broadly defined as a business opportunity manual by mail order, your name will probably be rented out as part of a list of buyers of that manual, on a continuing basis. This means that you will be made all sorts of offers, similar or otherwise, by other promoters. This is *caveat emptor* territory. Do not say you have not been warned.

The most dangerous schemes of all involve parting with up to tens of thousands of pounds and never seeing it again. Avoid, for instance, any offer of a business deal sent to you personally from Nigeria that promises you a fortune for allowing your bank account to be used for lodging government funds.

This is one of many such scams organized by criminal syndicates posing as Nigerian government officials. The name of the game is to get you to pay advance fees for various purposes – taxes, licences, registration, etc. These fees are bogus, and once you have paid them you will neither hear from the crooks again nor be able to trace them.

An antiques dealer of my acquaintance was a prime candidate for fleecing in this way as he was in desperate need of cash. He was sent a letter written by a person purporting to be a Nigerian government official. The deal apparently offered was a handsome rake-off from several tens of millions to be deposited in his bank account from supposed government funds.

The broken English used in the letter obscured the clarity of the message. At the same time, its tone seemed to ooze sincerity. My acquaintance was blinded by greed, and exchanged several letters with his apparent benefactor. He was invited to Nigeria to meet the supposed government officials, to whom he would be paying an advance fee of £10,000 in cash.

To prepare for his trip, my acquaintance had injections recommended for African travel. He withdrew the requisite £10,000 (and a little extra in case of further opportunity) from his building society and booked his flight.

Only just in time, my acquaintance saw in the *Financial Times* a press statement made by the Central Bank of Nigeria warning that schemes involving advance fee payments to supposed Nigerian government officials were scams. He cancelled his flight and withdrew in the nick of time but, to this day, will not admit that he was nearly duped. Other usually smart businessmen have been caught by this one.

As this book goes to press, the Nigerian fraudsters, despite having been exposed on UK television, are fishing for further victims on the Internet. The trademark of these particular frauds is the stress on confidentiality and urgency.

Golden rules covered in this chapter

Rule 106   Read *Fair Shares* by Simon Rose and/or *The Motley Fool UK Investment Guide* to give you a basic grounding in investment.

Rule 107   Read Jim Slater's books on the stock market, but critically as they are controversial.

Rule 108   Some of the lighter studies of the securities industry offer insight as well as entertainment.

Rule 109   Consider taking a course on the basics of stock market investment. However, avoid courses that claim they will make you a fortune overnight, or those that are cheap or free but are a front for selling software.

Rule 110   Read tipsheets selectively.

Rule 111   Get to grips with company accounts with the help of selected books and/or courses.

Rule 112   Consult *REFS* or *TED* as a source of up-to-date statistical information about quoted companies.

Rule 113   Use the Internet to keep abreast of share prices, for news flow, and to research investments. A list of Web sites is available in Appendix 8.

Rule 114   To understand how dubious share dealers operate, tap into a vigilante Web site, and read the books of Michael Walters.

Rule 115   Avoid getting sucked into the beam-end business opportunities market.

A final word from the author

If you have read this little book carefully, you will by this stage have travelled a long way. You have learned how professionals evaluate shares, and of a secret investment system. You have discovered how to buy investments and other assets at discount houses and auctions, and how to get the better of your financial adviser.

You are equipped now to avoid the dubious share pushers and a whole range of financial sharp operators. You know how to buy property and timeshare for a fraction of its retail cost. You are properly informed about day trading, and about use of the Internet in your investment procedures.

There are many other areas of investment and asset buying that, for lack of space, I have not touched on in these pages, but this does not matter. The principles I have shown you for buying cheap during a volatile stock market can be applied to any purchase of assets. Of course, you won't make money just sitting down and reading. Your next step is to put some of these ideas into practice.

This should not be hard, for two reasons. First, the Bargain Hunters' Investment FlexiSystem is solidly based in principles that have stood the test of time and, second, it is flexible. You will make some mistakes initially, and to avoiding repeating these, it is important to keep and look back on records of your investments.

Keep your contract notes and share certificates carefully, with any notes that you have made from conversations with your broker, complete with time and date. You should record share price changes at regular intervals, and the level of the FTSE 100 or the Dow Jones at the time.

This way, you can later review your entire investment programme. The system requires commitment to make it work so, when it has its ups and downs, take a long view. In the wacky world of stock market investment, the grass is always greener until you start seeing a decent return on your *own* investments.

In the meantime, thank you so much for taking the time to read this little book – the *only* written record of a dynamic system used by City professionals for personal investing – and I am convinced it will (excuse the pun) pay dividends for you. Happy bargain hunting.

How is the Bargain Hunters' Investment FlexiSystem working for you? Write to me via the publisher or e-mail me at alexanderdavidson@lineone.net. Your feedback and comments will be invaluable for the rapidly growing numbers of investors who use our system, and may therefore assist subsequent editions of this book.

Appendix 1

Some useful names and addresses

Regulators

Securities and Futures Authority (SFA)
25 The North Colonnade
Canary Wharf
London E14 5HS
Tel: (020) 7676 1000

Investment Managers Regulatory Organization (IMRO)
Lloyds Chambers
1 Portsoken Street
London E1 8BT
Tel: (020) 7390 5000

Personal Investment Authority (PIA)
1 Canada Square
Canary Wharf
London E14 5AZ
Tel: (020) 7538 8860

Other organizations

Association of Policy Market Makers (for information on second-hand endowment policies)
Holywell Centre
1 Phipp Street
London EC2A 4PS
Tel: (020) 7739 3949

Association of Private Client Investment Managers & Stockbrokers
112 Middlesex Street
London E1 7HY
Tel: (020) 7247 7080

IFA Promotion (for financial services advice)
IFA Promotion
4th Floor
28 Greville Street
London EC1N 8SU
Tel: (0117) 971 1177

Timeshare organizations

American Resort Development Association (ARDA)
1220 L Street NW
Suite 500
Washington DC 20005
Tel: (+1) (202) 371 6700

The Timeshare Council/Organization for Timeshare in Europe
23 Buckingham Gate
London SW1E 6HB
Tel: (020) 7821 8845

Appendix 2

A selection of online brokers

Barclays Stockbrokers
www.barclays-stockbrokers.co.uk

Cave & Sons Limited
www.caves.co.uk

DLJ Direct
www.dljdirect.co.uk

e-cortal
www.e-cortal.com

www.etrade.co.uk

Fastrade
www.fastrade.co.uk

Goy Harris Cartwright
www.ghcl.co.uk

Halifax
ShareXpress
www.sharexpress.co.uk

Killik & Co
www.killik.co.uk

myBROKER
www.mybroker.co.uk

NatWest Stockbrokers
www.natweststockbrokers.co.uk

Redmayne Bentley (REDM – Online Trading)
www.redm.co.uk

Charles Schwab
www.schwab-worldwide.com

The Share Centre
www.share.co.uk

Stocktrade
www.stocktrade.co.uk

TD Waterhouse
www.tdwaterhouse.co.uk

Xest
www.xest.com

Appendix 3

Some brokers that offer execution-only telephone dealing

This is not a complete list. However, all firms included are members of The Association of Private Client Investment Managers and Stockbrokers.

James Brearley & Sons
56–60 Caunce Street
Blackpool FY1 3DQ
Tel: (01253) 21474

Brewin Dolphin Bell Lawrie Ltd
5 Giltspur Street
London EC1A 9BD
Tel: (020) 7248 4400

Cave & Sons Ltd
Lockgates House
Rushmills
Bedford Road
Northampton NN4 7YB
Tel: (01604) 21421

Charles Schwab Europe
Cannon House
24 The Priory Queensway
Birmingham B4 6LY
Tel: (0870) 601 7777

Charles Stanley & Co
25 Luke Street
London EC2A 4AR
Tel: (020) 7739 8200

City Deal Services Ltd
North House
9–11 St Edwards Way
Romford
Essex RM1 4PE
Tel: (01708) 742288

Fairmount Stockbrokers Ltd
Huntingdon House
Princess Street
Bolton BLI IEJ
Tel: (01204) 362233

Gall & Eke Limited
Charlotte House
10 Charlotte Street
Manchester M1 4FL
Tel: (0161) 228 2511

Henderson Crosthwaite
32 St Mary at Hill
London EC3P 3AJ
Tel: (020) 7283 8577

Hill Osborne & Co
Royal Insurance Building
12 Silver Street
Lincoln LN2 IDU
Tel: (01522) 513838

NatWest Stockbrokers Ltd
55 Mansell Street
London E1 8AN
Tel: (020) 7895 5955

Redmayne Bentley
Merton House
84 Albion Street
Leeds
LS1 6AG
Tel: (0113) 243 6941

The Share Centre
PO Box 1000
Tring
Herts HP23 5AN
Tel: (0800) 800008

Albert E Sharp
Temple Court
35 Bull Street
Birmingham B4 6ES
Tel: (0121) 200 2244

Torrie & Co
132 Rose Street
Edinburgh EH2 3JD
Tel: (0131) 225 1766

Vartan & Son
The Singing Men's Chambers
19 Minster Precincts
Peterborough PE1 IXX
Tel: (01733) 315155

Walker, Crips, Weddle Beck
Sophia House
76–80 City Road
London EC1Y 2BJ
Tel: (020) 7253 7502

Waters Lunnis & Co Ltd
2 Redwell Street
Norwich NR2 4SN
Tel: (01603) 622265

YorkShare Limited
Howard House
6 Bank Street
Bradford BD1 1EE
Tel: (01274) 736736

Appendix 4

Some discount brokers

Chelsea Financial Services
St James' Hall
Moore Park Road
London SW6 2JS
Tel: (020) 7384 7300

Financial Discounts Direct
PO Box 85
Alton
Hants GU34 IX5
Tel: (0500) 498477

Hargreaves Landsdown
Kendal House
4 Brighton Mews
Clifton
Bristol BS8 2NX
Tel: (0800) 850661

Maddison Monetary Management
44 High Street
Bagshot
Surrey GU19 5AP
Tel: (0800) 0742233

The PEP Shop
14 Gordon Road
West Bridgford
Nottingham NG2 5LN
Tel(0115) 9825105

TQ Direct
St Mark's Church
Chapel Ash
Wolverhampton
WV3 OTZ
Tel: (0800) 413186

Appendix 5

Some second-hand endowment policy dealers

All included here are members of The Association of Policy Market Makers.

Absolute Assigned Policies Ltd
Russell House
140 High Street
Edgware
Middlesex HA8 7LW
Tel: (020) 8951 1996

Beale Dobie & Company Ltd
Fullbridge Mill
Maldon
Essex CM9 7FN
Tel: (01621) 851133

H E Foster & Cranfield (auctioneers)
20 Britton Street
London EC1M 5NQ
Tel: (080) 072 0264

Neville James Ltd
Page's Court
St Peter's Road
Petersfield
Hants GU32 5HX
Tel: (01243) 520000

PolicyPlus International plc
2–4 Henry Street
Bath BA1 IJT
Tel: (0845) 202 0200

Policy Portfolio plc
Gadd House
Arcadia Avenue
London N3 2JU
Tel: (020) 8343 4567

Securitised Endowment Contracts plc
SEC House
49 Theobald Street
Boreham
Herts WD6 4RZ
Tel: (020) 8207 1666

Appendix 6

Online auction houses and timeshare resale agencies

Online auction houses (not a complete list)

UK

www.ebid.co.uk
www.icollector.co.uk
www.loot.com
www.qxi.com

US

www.amazon.com
www.ebay.com

Timeshare resale agencies that are members of The Timeshare Council/OTE

Primeshare
Primeshare House
Broomvale Business Centre
Little Blakenham
Ipswich
Suffolk IP8 4JU
Tel: (01473) 830083

BFW Time Share Marketing SL
CIF B-38507679
C/Enrique Taig, 10
E-38400 Puerto De La Cruz
Spain
Tel: (+34) 922 3892

ETOO
Trafalgar House
Grenville Place
Mill Hill
London NW7 3SA
Tel: (020) 8906 9999

European Deed Service Ltd
Kingfisher House
Station Road
Barnet EN5 INZ
Tel: (020) 8364 9711

Global Resale Services (UK) Ltd
Park House
18 Wells Street
London W1P 3FP
Tel: (0800) 783 9538/9 (buyers); (020) 7436 0080 (sellers)

Holiday Property International plc
(Trading as Timeshare Resales)
Unit 2
3–5 North Street
Leatherhead
Surrey KT22 7AX
Tel: (01372) 363163

New Dimensions Resales
Woodland Point
Wootton Mount
Bournmouth BH1 1PJ
Tel: (01202) 3619990

Primiservix SL
C/Cariota Alessandri, 232
Of.2
E-29620 Malaga
Spain
Tel: (+34) 952 375 647

PTR
Aachener Str 165
D-40223 Dusseldorf
Germany
Tel: (+49) 211 157560

Timeshare Computer Link
Cambridge House
5 Newbold Street
Royal Leamington Spa
Warwickshire CV32 4HN
Tel: (07000) 784778

Timeshare Direct
1 Windsor Place
Windsor Street
Stratford-upon-Avon CV37 6NL
Tel: (01789) 415671

Time-Share-Borse
Nogenter Platz 1
Postfach 1803
D-53721 Siegburg
Germany
Tel: (+49) 2241 55177

Travel & Leisure Advisory Services Ltd
Talas House
47–48 Ballingdon St
Sudbury
Suffolk CO10 6BX
Tel: (01787) 881111

Tourism Advisory Group
TAG House
1 Meadow Lane
Sudbury
Suffolk CO10 6TD
Tel: (01787) 880100

Vacanze Nel Mondo SPA
Via Del Gracchi, 35
I-20146 Milano
Italy
Tel: (+39) 02 467 5429

The World-Wide Timeshare Hypermarket
1st Floor Offices
Royal Bank of Scotland Chambers
55–56 Worcester Street
Kidderminister
Worcs DY10 1EL
Tel: (01562) 827070

Appendix 7

Tipsheets and sources of company statistics

Tipsheets

The AIM Newsletter
Newsletter Publishing Ltd
Osborne House
3–5 Portland Road
Hythe
Kent CT21 6EG
Tel: (01303) 230046

Analyst plc
PO Box 12496
London EC2Y 8LJ
Tel: (020) 8289 7966

Jim Slater Investing for Growth
Investors News Ltd
City Innovation Centre
26–31 Whiskin Street
London EC1R 0BP
Tel: (020) 7278 7769

Penny Share Focus
Chartsearch Ltd
28 Charles Square
London N1 6HT
Tel: (020) 7417 0700

The Penny Share Guide
Fleet Street Publications Ltd
271 Regent Street
London W1R 7PA
Tel: (020) 7447 4040

Techinvest
3 Harbour Place
International Financial Services Centre
Dublin 1
Ireland
Tel: (+353) (0) 1 670 1777

Sources of company statistics

REFS
Hemmington Scott Publishing Ltd
City Innovation Centre
26–31 Whiskin Street
London EC1R OBP
Tel: (020) 7278 7769

The Estimate Directory
Edinburgh Financial Publishing Limited
3rd Floor
124/125 Princes Street
Edinburgh EH2 4BD
Tel: (0131) 473 7070

Appendix 8

Useful financial Web sites

Below you will find listed a few of the financial Web sites that users of the Bargain Hunters' Investment FlexiSystem have found useful. It is a highly selective list. You will find that many of these sites link with other ones, so providing you with an infinite merry-go-round.

General stock market and personal finance information

mrscohen.com
www.mrscohen.co.uk
A lively but very basic Web site on the stock market and personal finance, run personally by Bernice Cohen, a well-known author and broadcaster. A question-and-answer column and regular news commentaries are included.

MoneyWorld
www.moneyworld.co.uk
An introduction to personal finance and the stock market, with plenty of updated articles, investment performance statistics, and facilities for setting up a share-tracking portfolio.

TrustNet Limited
www.trustnet.co.uk
Information on UK unit trusts, OEICs and investment trusts, and US equivalents. Facilities for checking past investment performance.

Lipper
www.lipperweb.com
Offshore funds.

John Charcol
www.johncharcol.co.uk
A leading IFA gives basic advice on financial services.

Find
www.find.co.uk
An Internet directory for UK financial services, and a site that will
help you find IFAs and discount dealers.

The Association of Investment Trust Companies
www.aitc.co.uk
Explanations about investment trusts.

Association of Unit Trusts and Investment Funds
www.auitif.co.uk
Explanations about unit trusts.

Sort
www.sort.co.uk
Independent financial advice for a fixed fee.

Micropal
www.micropal.com
Statistics on past performance of unit trusts and other investment
funds.

interactive investor international
www.iii.co.uk
Variety of financial information from one starting point.

Association of Policy Market Makers
www.moneyworld.co.uk/apmm/what.htm
Advice on buying and selling second-hand endowments.

Neville James
www.neville-james.co.uk
A second-hand market maker with a helpful Web site.

The Offshore Secrets Network
www.offshoresecrets.com
Information about the twilight side of offshore investing.

DSS (on pensions)
www.dss.gov.uk/pen/index.htm
Leaflet by DSS to help you make an informed decision about your
pension.

Kaunders Portfolio Management
www.gilt.co.uk
A Web site that gives excellent explanations about gilts.

Annuities page of Money World
www.moneyworld.co.uk/glossary/gl00051.htm
An explanation about how annuities work.

Mortgages page of Money World
www.moneyworld.co.uk/homebuying/
Comprehensive information about mortgages.

Inheritance tax page of Money World
www.moneyworld.co.uk/glossary/gl00149.htm

Money World Powersearch (to find top performing funds)
www.moneyworld.co.uk/powersearch/

Spread-betting page of Resources
www.updata.co.uk/resources/spreadbetting/

The Carpetbagger's Accomplice
www.carpetbagger.co.uk
Useful information for those who want to open an account in building
societies with a view to benefiting from any eventual demutualization.

Slater Investments Ltd
www.global-investor.com/slater/slater.htm
Details of Mark Slater's investment fund.

Stock market data and fundamental research

Datastream
www.datastreaminsite.com/insite.htm
Financial data on all UK quoted companies.

Hemmington Scott
www.hemscott.com
The Hemmington Scott Web site. Free brokers' consensus earnings forecasts. Details of international equities. Fifteen-minute delayed share prices on UK listed stocks.

citywire.co.uk
www.citywire.co.uk
Information on directors' own dealings.

DigitalLook
www.digitallook.com
Monitors newspaper tips.

Richard Holway Limited
www.holway.com
High-tech stocks.

corporate reports
www.corpreports.co.uk
Online annual reports provided.

Multex.com
www.multex.com
Brokerage reports.

Merrill Lynch
www.askmerrill.com
The Merrill Lynch site. Free trial to access research.

Salomon Smith Barney
www.smithbarneyresearch.com
The Salomon Smith Barney site. Free trial to access research.

J P Morgan
www.adr.com
Information on ADRs.

Wit Capital
www.witcapital.com
Free research.

Durlacher
www.durlacher.co.uk.research
Free research.

Wright Research Center
http://profiles.wisi.com
Free analysis of many UK shares.

trackerfunds.com
www.trackerfunds.com
Details of the techMARK index tracking fund managed by Close Fund
Management.

Jim Slater
www.global-invstor.com/slater/index.htm
Web page of private client stock market guru Jim Slater. His investment strategies are explained. Headlines of research reports you can
buy.

Investext Group
www.investext.com
Brokers' research.

Financial Times – Lex column
www.ft.com/hippocampus/lex.htm
Facility to access back copies of the *FT*'s influential Lex column.

msn microsoft
www.moneycentral.msn.com
Stock research (US site).

Hoover's
www.hoovers.com
Detailed market information at a price (US site).

Zacks.com
www.zacks.com
News and brokers' reports (US site).

Dr Ed Yardeni's Economics Network
www.yardeni.com
Free economics and stock market research from Dr Ed Yardeni, the
chief global economist of Deutsche Bank Securities in New York.

OFEX
www.ofex.co.uk

Stock Detective
www.stockdetective.com
Vigilante Web site.

FinancialWeb
www.financialweb.com
News, research, Securities & Exchange Commission filings, and
company reports as well as share prices.

London Stock Exchange
www.londonstockexchange.com
A highly informative and user-friendly Web site, containing useful
information about the London stock market, the AIM, TechMARK,
securities industry regulation, and so on.

NASDAQ
www.nasdaq.co.uk
The US's self-styled 'stock market for the next 100 years'.

Association of Private Client Investment Managers and Stockbrokers
www.apcims.org
Directory of member brokers, and other useful information for private
investors.

New issues

issues direct
www.issuesdirect.com
A members' club for those interested in new issues.

epo com
www.epo.com
News on new issues.

Share price quotes

Freequotes
www.freequotes.co.uk
Free real-time quotes on stock market companies. News on major companies.

Market-Eye
www.market-eye.co.UK
Various services for price quotes and data.

Wall Street City
www.wallstreetcity.com
Real-time quotes for US stocks.

Financial news

Bloomberg
www.bloomberg.co.uk
Excellent financial news site.

Financial News Digest
www.pigeon.co.uk
Coverage of quoted companies in quality Sunday press.

The Motley Fool UK
www.fool.co.uk
News and analysis for the UK stock market.

The Motley Fool Finance and Folly
www.fool.com
News and analysis for the US market.

The *Financial Times*
www.ft.com
Financial news and data.

FT Your Money
www.ftyourmoney.co.uk
Personal finance.

Electronic Telegraph
www.telegraph.co.uk
Access to news archives.

Guardian Unlimited
www.guardian.co.uk
Access to news archives.

Times-Money
www.times-money.co.uk
Access to personal finance news archives.

Evening Standard online
www.thisislondon.com

This Is Money
www.thisismoney.co.uk
News archives of the *Daily Mail, Mail on Sunday,* and *Evening Standard.*

Forbes
www.forbes.com
US magazine. Useful site for researching US market.

Yahoo
uk.news.yahoo.com/s
Business news.

Internet investor
www.internetinvestor.co.uk
Web site of a magazine that specializes in Internet investing.

Tracker Magazine
http://tracker.netpep.co.uk/
An online magazine about tracker funds.

Newsletter Publishing
www.newsletters.co.uk
Details of how to subscribe to *The AIM Newsletter* (and sister publications). Sample copy provided online.

Investors Chronicle
www.investorschronicle.co.uk
Incredibly useful Web site of shares magazine *Investors Chronicle*. Archives of back issues, and investment education material available.

Tipsheets.co.uk
www.tipsheets.co.uk
Details of leading tipsheets on the market, and how to subscribe.

Message boards

The Motley Fool (US)
www.fool.com

The Motley Fool UK
www.fool.co.uk

Yahoo
www.finance.yahoo.com

Raging Bull
www.ragingbull.com

Silicon Investor (subscription-based, but high quality)
www.techstocks.com
Web page providing links to message boards of Market Eye, Hemmington Scott, UK Shares and Interactive Investor.

www.freeyellow.com/members6/scottit/page7.html

Setting up an online portfolio

Interactive Investor
www.iii.co.uk/portfolio

Investment courses and education

Investor's Business Daily
www.investors.com
Online free investment course.

financial planning horizon
www.financialplanning.uk.com
Basic independent help with your financial planning as a preliminary
to seeing a financial adviser.

Access to brokers via links

Electronic Share Information
www.esi.co.uk

Datastream
www.datastream.com

Online trading

Hollywood Stock Exchange
www.hsx.com
Fantasy trading in film stars and musicians as practice for stock
market trading.

InvestIn.com
www.investin.com

Cyberinvest
www.cyberinvest.com
Information and links for home-based trading.

Options

Chicago Board of Traded Options Exchange
www.cboe.com

LIFFE
www.liffe.com
Web site of the London International Financial Futures & Options
Exchange.

Tax

Interactive investor international
www.iii.co.uk/tax
Personal and business taxes levied in the UK are explained. Help is
given with completing personal tax returns, and on tax-related issues.
There is news of tax-efficient investments. An online tax discussion
group is in operation.

Inland Revenue
www.inlandrevenue.co.uk
Information on taxes.

Insurance fraud

International Association of Insurance Fraud agencies
www.iaifa.or

Technical analysis

DecisionPoint.com
www.decisionpoint.com
Daily charts and reports, course in technical analysis, online charting.

chart-expert
www.chart-expert.com
Charts of complex data.

interactive investor international
www.iii.co.uk/quotes/research
A free and simple-to-operate charting facility.

Stock Point
www.stockpoint.com
Free charts for UK stocks and indices.

StockCharts.com
www.stockcharts.com
An excellent (US) free site on technical analysis.

Db's Burrow
http://home.talkcity.com/MoneySt/dbphoenix/DbBurrow2.htm
Excellent and entertaining beginner's guide to technical analysis.

murphymorris.com
www.murphymorris.com
Commentary on technical analysis by acclaimed technical analyst
John Murphy.

Property and timeshare

PropertyCity
www.propertycity.co.uk
A Web site about property sales that includes details of auctions.

Timeshare Council
www.timesharecouncil.com
Information about timeshare.

Online bookshops

Amazon
www.amazon.co.uk

Books.co.uk
www.booksco.uk
A site that compares online bookshops.

Paying bills

To reduce your phone bill, visit the following Oftel-endorsed Web site:

www.phonebills.org.uk

To get the best deal on water, gas, electricity and mobile phone bills, visit the Web site of Buy.co.uk at:

www.buy.co.uk

Appendix 9
Some online banks

Barclays Online Banking
www.ibank.barclays.co.uk

Citibank Direct Access
www.citibank.com/uk/intbank/index.html

Egg
www.egg.co.uk

First Direct
www.firstdirect.co.uk/PCBanking/html/index.html

First-e
www.first-e.co.uk

Bank of Scotland
www.bankofscotland.com/electronic/

Lloyds TSB Online
www.lloydstsb.com

NatWest On-Line
www.natwest.com/frontpage/dhtml/index.htm

Royal Bank of Scotland
www.rbos.com/dbpc/default.htm

Tesco Online Banking
www.tesco.co.uk/finance/index.htm

Co-operative Bank
www.co-operativebank.co.uk

Smile
www.smile.co.uk

Appendix 10

The share sharks' secret hymn book

Here are some secret and shameful songs that have done the rounds of the bucket-shop training floors over at least the past decade or so. They show what some dealers think of their clients, and how they treat them.

Ode to churning (ie excessive dealing for the purpose of generating commission)

> Put your clients in, take your clients out,
> Put your clients in, and then churn them all about,
> Then do the (name of dealing firm) shuffle, and you turn
>   yourself about,
> That's what it's all about.

Alternatively, to the tune of the theme song of *Rawhide*, a cult Western starring Clint Eastwood:

> Churn in, churn in, churn in,
> Keep them clients churning.

The buy/sell share rip-off

Buy at six and sell at four,
This is what we're looking for.
Buy at six and sell at four,
What a pity you didn't have more.
In at five and out at three,
Sorry, that's the way it'll be.
(Chorus) Sound off 1, 2.
Sound off 3, 4.
Bring it on down 1, 2, 3, 4.
1-2-3-4!!!

Alternatively, to the tune of 'Good King Wenceslas':

Old mug punter he was phoned,
With a view to dealing.
His dealer gave him a tip,
Made it sound appealing.
**** is its name, he said,
It is set to double,
So he bought ten grand's worth,
God, now he's in trouble.

One week later he phoned up,
To see how they were faring.
What's the stock?, his dealer said,
His voice sounded so caring.
**** was the stock I bought,
Yes, 10p bid at present,
I got in at 20p net,
This is not so pleasant.

Never mind, the dealer said,
Not everyone's a winner.
But, said the client, money's short,
My wedge is getting thinner.
Here's a churn, the dealer thought,
I'll stick him in a new one.
Buy these shares and sell ****
You never should have bought it.

A tribute to clients (to the tune of 'We Three Kings of Orient Are')

We three dealers of (name of firm) are,
Sell your house, get rid of your car,
Think it's funny,
Lost your money,
Oh what a fool you are!

Glossary

Acid test See quick ratio.

AIM The Alternative Investment Market. A market for small companies created and regulated by the London Stock Exchange.

American depositary receipts US domestic securities representing ownership of a foreign stock. These are available through brokers that deal in US shares.

Analyst A professional within a broking house who researches companies, and then makes profit forecasts and buy or sell recommendations.

APR Annual percentage rate. A figure that reflects *all* charges associated with credit.

Arbitrage pricing theory A more flexible alternative to the Capital Asset Pricing Model (qv), which uses a number of factors instead of just beta to measure a share's performance against the market.

Balance sheet The part of a company's financial statements that provides a snapshot of its financial position on a given day. It shows the company's assets less liabilities, balanced against shareholders' funds (qv).

Bargain Hunters' Investment FlexiSystem The set of investment guidelines described in this book, which has been used profitably in the past by some City professionals.

Bear market A declining stock market.

Beta A measure of a share's volatility against the market.

Blue chips Very large, relatively safe quoted companies such as ICI or British Telecom.

Bonds Securities issued by governments (gilts) or companies (corporate bonds) to finance debt.

Bottom-up analysis   Scrutinizing company specifics first, and the broader/macroeconomic perspective only later if at all (see Top-down analysis (qv) for contrast).
Bull market   A rising stock market.
Burn rate   The rate at which a company, typically in the high-tech industry, gets through cash.

Call option   See under option.
Capital Asset Pricing Model (CAPM)   The formula commonly used to determine return on equity by comparing the share's performance with that of the market as a whole.
CAPM   See under Capital Asset Pricing Model.
Cash flow statement   The part of the financial statements that shows cash movements within a company.
Chartism   Now used interchangeably with technical analysis (qv).
Corporate bonds   See bonds.
Creative accounting   The frowned on but legal manipulation of financial statements and ratios to present a company in a more flattering light.
Current ratio   A useful check on a company's liquidity. It is calculated by dividing current assets by current liabilities.

Day trading   Trading in shares on the day, closing your position before the end of play. As yet, day traders are mainly from the US where, at the time of writing, some have made small fortunes from speculating on Internet-related companies.
Discount broker   A financial services sales operation that will rebate some of the commission payable on products it offers but will not give you investment advice.
Discounted cash flow   The reduction of future cash flows to their present value.
Discounted rate of return   A company's annual return on equity – usually over a period of years – reduced to its present-day value using a discount rate.
Discretionary portfolio   When you pay a broker to make investment decisions on your behalf.
Dividend   Regular payment to shareholders from a company's profits. Growth companies sometimes pay no dividends, instead ploughing all profits into expansion.
Dividend cover   By how many times a company's dividend is covered by its net earnings. This should be at least 1× if the company is to pay the dividend out of current earnings.

Dividend yield   Gross annual dividend, expressed as a percentage of the share price.

Dow Theory   A theory originally researched by Charles Dow that, while not used much today, forms the basis of modern technical analysis.

Earnings per share (eps)   Profits after tax, divided by the number of shares in issue. This is a crucial measure in assessing the value in shares. Confusingly, it may be calculated in a number of slightly different ways. A company's eps should ideally be growing regularly, and, all things being equal, should compare well with those of other companies in the sector.

EBITDA   Earnings before interest, tax, depreciation and amortization.

Economic value added (EVA)   A measure of management performance, which is defined as net operating profit after tax, less weighted average cost of capital multiplied by invested capital.

Efficient market theory   A theory that in its strongest form stipulates that everything that is known or could be known about a company is reflected in the share price.

Elliot Wave Theory   A specialized form of technical analysis devised by Ralph Elliot. It interprets price swings as part of a universal movement that involves, amongst other things, timing and ratios.

Enterprise value   Market capitalization (qv) plus debt less cash.

Equity risk premium   The difference between the risk-free rate of return (qv) and the average return for the market as a whole.

Execution-only broker   A broker who will carry out your orders on the telephone or via the Internet, but will not give you tailored investment recommendations.

Eyeballs   The number of visitors to a Web site.

Fast stocks   Volatile, high-growth stocks, particularly in the high-tech sector, of which the price may fluctuate substantially within a very short period.

Fill-or-kill   When an order is executed immediately, or not at all.

Fundamental analysis   Analysing company accounts and investment ratios. The opposite to technical analysis (qv).

FTSE 100   The UK index that includes the 100 largest UK companies by market capitalization, representing more than 70 per cent of the total All-Share market capitalization. The index is amended quarterly.

Gearing   A company's level of borrowing. Broadly speaking, the lower the better. If it surpasses 50 per cent of shareholders' funds (qv), there may be cause for worry. Gearing is typically defined as interest-bearing loans and preference share capital, expressed as a percentage of ordinary shareholders' funds.

Gilts   See Bonds.

Growth investing   Buying shares of growing companies, which are sometimes overvalued in fundamental terms.

Independent financial adviser   A salesperson who can offer you financial services products (excluding individual shares) from a range of providers.

Index tracker fund   A fund that aims to keep up with the movement of the market as a whole rather than to outperform it. Stocks are selected by computer to track the market – hence the low management charges.

Internet company   A company that benefits, directly or indirectly, from the growth of the Internet.

Intrinsic value   The present value of a stock's future dividends.

Investment club   A group of like-minded investors who invest collectively, splitting profits.

Investment trust   A highly geared collective investment vehicle in the form of a quoted company which invests in shares and other assets on behalf of shareholders.

ISA   Individual savings account. A tax-efficient savings vehicle that was introduced in April 1999.

Japanese candlesticks   A novel Eastern method of technical analysis (qv).

Limit order   An order that you place with your broker for shares, in which you specify the highest price that you will pay for a stock, or the lowest price that you will accept for selling it.

LISA   Lifelong individual savings account. A tax-efficient wrapper that allows pension savings to be retained in open-ended investment companies (qv), unit trusts (qv) and investment trusts (qv).

Market capitalization   A company's stock market value. It is defined as the number of shares in issue, multiplied by the share price.

Market order   An order that you place with your broker to deal in shares at the prevailing market price.

Market value added (MVA)   The difference between a company's market value and the book value of its assets.

Message board   Space on a Web site that enables investors to communicate with each other.

Money Management   A magazine for independent financial advisers (qv) sold on the high street. It has useful performance league tables for funds of unit trusts and other investment vehicles.

Nasdaq   A US stock market that is powered by young, high-tech growth companies.

Net asset value (NAV)   A company's market capitalization (qv) divided by its net assets (assets less liabilities). This is a recognized measure of value for companies that have significant net assets, such as insurers.

New issue   Where shares are first issued to the public.

Nominal value   The face value of a security, as distinct from its share price. Also known as par value.

Ofex   An off-exchange trading facility for small companies. This facility is extremely risky and mainly for gamblers or those in the know.

O'Higgins system   An investment system pioneered by US fund manager Michael O'Higgins that involves investing regularly in out-of-favour blue chip companies that pay high dividends.

Online broker   A broker with whom you can deal via the Internet.

Open-ended investment companies (OEICs)   A form of collective investment vehicle that issues shares at a single price rather than via a spread.

Option   The right but not the obligation to buy a share at a fixed price within a given period (call option) or to sell it (put option) after payment of a set amount (premium).

Par value   See Nominal value.

PE ratio   The share price divided by earnings per share (qv). This is a key ratio in the City that is used to indicate how cheap a stock is. The ratio can be expressed in historic, present or prospective terms.

PEG   A company's PE ratio, divided by prospective average earnings growth. The lower it is, the better value the company's shares are perceived to be. The PEG should ideally be well under 1.

Penny share dealers   Share dealers who specialize in penny shares. They usually buy the shares cheap from bulk vendors and, as principals, sell them on to clients at a hefty mark-up.

Perpetual Traveller   A controversial tax avoidance technique that involves living in several countries on a revolving basis so that you are not a resident for tax purposes in any of them.

Price/sales ratio   A company's total market value divided by the previous year's sales. It can be a strong indicator of value, particularly for Internet and other high-tech companies.

Profit and loss account   The part of a company's financial statements that records its profits and how they were reached over the previous year.

Protected unit trusts   Unit trusts (qv) that limit the risk of losing money but, in the long run, do not offer such good returns as their unprotected equivalents.

Put option   See under Option.

Quick ratio   Current assets less stock and work in progress, divided by current liabilities. Also known as the acid test (qv).

REFS   A regularly updated reference book published by Hemmington Scott, which contains key ratios for quoted companies. The presentation was devised by UK investment guru Jim Slater.

Registered Persons exam   The basic qualification for brokers. To pass it requires about 100 hours' of study, and obtaining a high mark in a simple multiple-choice exam.

Relative strength   How well a share has performed against the market as a whole.

Resale agencies   Operations that sell second-hand timeshares, often acting as middlemen on behalf of owners.

Return on capital employed   A key measure of management performance. It consists of profits before interest and tax (ie removing elements beyond management control) divided by capital employed (assets less liabilities excluding long-term loans).

Rich media   Video and audio material, as delivered via the Internet.

Rights issue   This is a way of raising fresh capital from existing shareholders, typically for expansion purposes but sometimes from desperation. The company offers shareholders new shares in proportion to existing shares, at a slightly cheaper price.

Scrip dividends Where companies issue extra shares instead of paying a dividend.

Scrip issue Where free shares are issued to existing shareholders, reducing the price of individual shares but increasing their number. Taken as a whole, the new holding is theoretically of the same value as the old one.

Selling short Selling shares that you do not own with a view to buying back later at a lower price and pocketing the difference. The practice has been subject to bans in some countries at times of stock market turmoil, and was made the scapegoat for the 1929 Wall Street crash.

Share split Where the nominal (qv) value of a share is split. The shares are proportionately multiplied, and the share price is similarly diluted.

Spread betting Where you bet on the direction of individual shares, etc through a financial bookmaker. You open your bet at one level and close it at another, the difference constituting your profit or loss.

Stag To buy and sell shares within a very short time frame with a view to making an instant profit.

Stickiness A term that refers to for how long visitors stay at a Web site.

Stop loss A technique used by many professionals to limit losses that involves selling shares if they fall below a preset level. This level could be 20 per cent below either the price at which you bought them or – on a trailing basis – that to which they have risen.

Switching office An office that appears to be in use by share sales-people but that simply diverts calls to their real office. It is used by dubious firms to hide their whereabouts.

Technical analysis The controversial technique of analysing past trends in stocks, indices, etc in order to predict future movements. Also known as chartism, this is the opposite of Fundamental analysis (qv).

Tied agent A financial services salesman who can offer you only the products of a specific product provider, usually an insurance company. Compare with Independent financial adviser (qv).

Top-down analysis Scrutinizing the broader macroeconomic picture first, followed only then, if at all, by company specifics (see Bottom-up analysis (qv) for contrast).

Unit trusts A form of collective investment vehicle where a trust holds investments for holders of its units. The unit trust's value directly reflects that of the underlying investments.

Value investing   Buying undervalued shares on tested criteria and sitting on them with the idea of eventually reselling at a profit.

WAAC   See Weighted average cost of capital.

Warrants   Low-priced securities, tradable in their own right, that give the right to buy a new share at a fixed price on a specified date (unlike options that give the right to buy an existing share). If not taken up, warrants will expire worthless.

Weighted average cost of capital (WAAC)   The company's cost of borrowing, weighted in terms of equity and debt.

Index